新经济
新动能
新实践

New Economy
New Growth Drivers
New Practice

张宇 洪运 邓玲 编著

张梅 译

西南财经大学出版社
Southwestern University of Finance & Economics Press

图书在版编目(CIP)数据

新经济　新动能　新实践/张宇等编著 . —成都:西南财经大学出版社,
2021. 6
ISBN 978-7-5504-4877-3

Ⅰ.①新… Ⅱ.①张… Ⅲ.①区域经济发展—研究—成都
Ⅳ.①F127.711

中国版本图书馆 CIP 数据核字(2021)第 093752 号

新经济　新动能　新实践
XIN JINGJI　XIN DONGNENG　XIN SHIJIAN
张宇　洪运　邓玲　编著　张梅　译

策　　划:汪涌波
责任编辑:汪涌波
装帧设计:付瑜
责任印制:朱曼丽

出版发行	西南财经大学出版社(四川省成都市光华村街 55 号)
网　　址	http://cbs. swufe. edu. cn
电子邮件	bookcj@ swufe. edu. cn
邮政编码	610074
电　　话	028-87353785
照　　排	四川胜翔数码印务设计有限公司
印　　刷	成都金龙印务有限责任公司
成品尺寸	175mm×245mm
印　　张	15. 5
字　　数	262 千字
版　　次	2021 年 6 月第 1 版
印　　次	2021 年 6 月第 1 次印刷
书　　号	ISBN 978-7-5504-4877-3
定　　价	78. 00 元

新经济发展理论与实践系列丛书
New Economic Development Theory and Practice Series
本书系成都新经济发展研究院《新经济 新动能》英文刊发项目成果

CiNED

成都新经济发展研究院

　　成都新经济发展研究院是中国首个新经济领域的特色新型智库，致力于新经济发展的理论与政策研究，为政府和新经济市场主体提供决策咨询服务，并承担新经济交流、合作与宣传，新经济支撑服务平台建设和运维等工作。

　　作为成都市新经济委所属事业单位，成都新经济发展研究院自成立以来，始终紧密围绕市委市政府中心工作和市新经济委重点工作，为新经济发展提供态势感知、趋势预测、政策设计、决策判断、平台运营、对外合作、生态建设等方面的服务和支撑，逐步确立新经济智库建设、新经济数据支撑服务平台搭建、企业综合服务机制构建、新经济品牌打造四大工作方向。

Chengdu Institution of New Economic Development

Chengdu Institution of New Economic Development is China's first new-type think tank with characteristics in the field of new economy. It is committed to the theory and policy research of new economic development, provides decision-making consulting services for the government and new economic market entities and undertakes new economic exchanges, cooperation and publicity. The new economy supports the construction, operation and maintenance of the service platform. As an institution affiliated to Chengdu New Economy Development Committee, Chengdu Institution of New Economic Development, centering on the work of the Municipal Party Committee and Chengdu New Economic Commission, has focused on providing services and support for new economic development in aspects of situation awareness, trend prediction, policy design, decision-making and judgment, platform operation, foreign cooperation, ecological construction, etc, and gradually establishing four major work directions: construction of new economic think tank, new economic data support service platform, enterprise comprehensive service mechanism, and new economic brand.

本书编写组成员
Editorial Staff

张 宇 成都新经济发展研究院 副院长 经济学博士 高级经济师

Zhang Yu, Chengdu Institution of New Economic Development, Vice President, Doctor of Economics, Senior Economic Manger Senior Economist

洪 运 四川省社会科学院 经济学博士 副研究员

Hong Yun, Sichuan Academy of Social Sciences, Doctor of Economics, Assistant Professor

邓 玲 成都工业学院 教授

Deng Ling, Chengdu Technological University, Professor

张 梅（翻译） 四川农业大学 副教授

Zhang Mei (Translator), Sichuan Agricultural University, Assistant Professor

成都新经济发展研究院 于惠洋 邓跃东 贾伟 孙月梅 李艳春

Chengdu Institution of New Economic Development, Yu Huiyang, Deng Yuedong, Jia Wei, Sun Yuemei, Li Yanchun

张 宇

四川大学遗传学硕士、世界经济博士，国家信息中心宏观经济方向博士后，成都市青年联合会第十二届委员会委员，长期研究头部企业、跨国公司，新经济、新场景、新赛道及宏观经济等。曾在成都、北京、深圳、贵阳等政府科技创新部门工作，现任成都新经济发展研究院副院长兼法定代表人。

Zhang Yu

Master of Genetics from Sichuan University, Doctor of World Economics, Postdoctoral in Macroeconomics of the National Information Center, member of the 12th Committee of Chengdu Youth Federation. His research includes leading companies, multinational companies, new economy, new scenarios, new tracks and macro Economy etc. He has worked ingovernment departments for science and technology innovation in Chengdu, Beijing, Shenzhen and Guiyang. He is currently the vice president and legal representative of Chengdu Institution of New Economic Development.

CiNED

序言

Preface

2008 年国际金融危机以来，全球经济经历了严重衰退，增速放缓，未来不确定性增强。当前正值"十四五"开局、"两个一百年"奋斗目标的历史交汇期，我国经济面临着错综复杂的全球化新形势和国内经济下行压力，亟待创造新的增长极和挖潜新动能。2016 年中央政府工作报告首次提出"新经济"概念，将其作为打造经济新动能的重要推动力。中共中央十九届五中全会提出坚持创新在我国现代化建设全局中的核心地位，坚定不移建设"网络强国""数字强国"，到 2035 年实现进入创新型国家前列的目标。我国经济发展正处于新旧动能转换和经济结构破旧立新的关键时期，核心动力由投资驱动向技术驱动、商业模式驱动演变。发展新经济作为推动城市战略转型、经济变道超车的重大抉择，正在推动着我国经济发展"量"和"质"双重跃升。

Since the international financial crisis in 2008, the global economy has experienced a severe recession, with the low growth rate and increased uncertainty in the future. At present, at the beginning of the "14th Five Year Plan" and the historical intersection period of the "Two Centenary Goals", China's economy is facing the complicated new situation of globalization and the downward pressure of the domestic economy. It is urgent to create new growth poles and exploit the new potential development. In the 2016 work report of the central government, the concept of "new economy" was proposed for the first time as an important driving force to create new economic driver. The Fifth Plenary Session of the 19th Central Committee of the Communist Party of China proposed to adhere to the core position of innovation in the overall situation of China's modernization construction, unswervingly build "network power" and "digital power", and achieve the goal of entering the forefront of innovative countries by 2035. China's economic development is in a critical period of the transformation of new and old drivers and the establishment of the new economic structure. The core driving force has evolved from the investment-driven mode to technology-driven and business-driven mode. The development of new economy, as a major choice to promote urban strategic transformation and economic speeding-up, is promoting the "quantity" and "quality" of China's economic development.

创新是一种能力，更是一种精神和文化。成都作为最适宜新经济发展的城市、国际消费中心城市，在成渝地区双城经济圈建设背景下，秉持包容审慎的监管理念，推进从"政府配菜"向"企业点菜"转变，从"给优惠"向"给机会"转变，从"个别服务"向"生态营造"转变，激活市场内生需求，深耕新经济发展环境沃土，深入实施创新驱动发展战略，促进城市经济结构优化调整，推动经济增长动力接续转换，不断提升城市综合竞争力，为建设全面体现新发展理念的国家中心城市注入了强劲动能。

Innovation is not only a kind of ability, but also a kind of spirit and culture. Chengdu, as the most suitable city for new economic development and an international consumption center city, adheres to the concept of inclusive and prudent supervision under the background of the construction of Chengdu-Chongqing Twin Cities Economic Circle, and promotes the transformation from "government allocating dishes" to "enterprise ordering dishes", from "giving preferential treatment" to "providing opportunity", from "individual service" to "ecological construction", to activate the internal demand of the market, fertile the soil of the new economy development, implement the innovation-driven development strategy, promote the optimization and adjustment of urban economic structure, promote the continuous transformation of economic growth power, and continuously improve the comprehensive competitiveness of cities, thus injecting strong driver into the construction of a central city that fully embodies the new development concept.

2021年5月31日，习近平总书记在主持中共中央政治局关于加强我国国际传播能力建设的集体学习时强调，讲好中国故事，传播好中国声音，展示真实、立体、全面的中国，是加强我国国际传播能力建设的重要任务。本书作为中英文双语版本，向国内外读者展现了近年来我国新经济发展的主要经验及成就，为世界新经济发展与新动能培育提供了参考借鉴。第一章对新经济的内涵、定义、特征与发展规律以及新动能助力中国经济高质量发展的最新理论进行了阐释。第二章梳理介绍了国内外发展新经济培育新动能方面的探索实践。第三章从新经济发展带来的挑战与机遇方面，分析判断了新经济发展对传统经济模式及行业监管带来的主要挑战及机遇。第四章总结归纳了成都新经济发展的"一二三四五六七"理论架构，给出了新经济发展的成都理念与方案。第五章从要素支撑体系入手，分析了人才、技术、资本、数据要素对成都新经济发展及新动能培育的保障作用。第六章围绕成都新经济的"六大形态"，即数字经济、智能经济、绿色经济、创意经济、流量经济以及共享经济，归纳其内涵特征，并选取培育新动能的特色场景案例进行阐释。第七章聚焦以场景营城理念引领新旧动能转换，围绕成都场景营城概念及相关理论、场景营造与培育新动能的联系、场景营城理念指引新旧动能转换及成都机遇等方面展开论述。

Xi Jinping, General Secretary of the Communist Party of China (CPC) Central Committee, has stressed improving the country's capacity for engaging in international communication so as to tell China's stories well and present a true, multidimensional and panoramic view of China, when presiding over the group study session of the Political Bureau of the CPC Central Committee on May 31, 2021. As a bilingual edition, this book shows readers at home and abroad the primary experience and achievements of China's new economic development in recent years, providing reference for the world's new economic development and new growth drivers cultivation. The first chapter analyzes the connotation, definition, characteristics and development law of the new economy, as well as the mechanism of the new growth drivers to promote the high-quality development of China's economy. The second chapter introduces the exploration and practice in developing new economy and cultivating new growth drivers at home and abroad. The third chapter analyzes and judges the main challenges of the traditional economic model and industry supervision, as well as the new opportunities brought by the new economic development from the two aspects of challenges and opportunities. The fourth chapter summarizes the theoretical framework of new economic development in Chengdu, and shows Chengdu's new economic development plan. The fifth chapter analyzes the guarantee function of such factors as talents, technology, capital and data on the development of Chengdu's new economy and new growth drivers' cultivation from the supply of factors. The sixth chapter summarizes the connotation and characteristics of Chengdu's six new economic forms, namely, digital economy, intelligent economy, green economy, creative economy, flow economy and shared economy, and selects characteristic scenescape cases of cultivating new growth drivers. The seventh chapter focuses on the way to lead the transformation of old and new growth drivers with the concept of "City Growth by Scenescapes", centering on Chengdu's concept of scenescapes and related theories, the connection between scenescapes construction and cultivation of new growth drivers, the guidance of scenescapes towards the transformation from old to new growth drivers, and Chengdu's opportunities.

本书编写主要立足于成都市新经济发展委员会、成都新经济发展研究院的前期工作及研究基础,借鉴了邓玲教授、蒋永穆教授、黄寰教授等专家学者的部分研究成果,在此向他们致谢!同时,感谢四川农业大学张梅副教授为此书翻译付出的努力。

The book is compiled mainly on the basis of the preliminary work and research foundation of Chengdu New Economic Development Commission and Chengdu New Economic Development Research Institute, using research achievements of Professor Deng Ling, Professor Jiang Yongmu, Professor Huang Huan, etc. for reference. We express our deep and sincere gratitude to all of them here. Thanks are also given to Associate Professor Zhang Mei from Sichuan Agricultural University for her efforts in translating this book.

张宇　　**Zhang Yu**

2021 年 5 月　May, 2021

CiNED

目录
Contents

CiNED

第一章
新经济新动能的理论认识

Chapter One
Theory of New Economy
and New Growth Driver

　　传统经济的增长主要靠资本积累和扩大再生产，无论是内涵扩大再生产还是外延扩大再生产，都离不开资本劳动的投入和技术革新。在传统经济的增长过程中，资本和劳动的作用呈明显的下降趋势，技术进步的作用则明显上升。但总的来讲，传统经济的增长动力主要来源于资源、劳动和企业的规模效益，其增长速度属于算术级增长。新经济增长的主要动力是创新。在这种知识型的经济增长模式中，知识是经济增长的最主要的要素；知识化产业、高科技产业和智业是新经济增长的主要生长点和支柱产业，其增长速度呈几何级增长。新经济没有完全否定传统经济，如同工业经济没有完全否定农业经济一样，传统经济依然是整个社会经济的重要基础。传统经济的比重虽然在下降，但并不会消失，它仍然有存在的必要和空间。传统经济为新经济提供必要的物质基础。新经济只不过是用新的方式和新的产品代替传统经济以满足人类的需要，或者填补人类需要的空白。一旦用新经济方式生产或经营传统经济的产品，那么传统经济也就改造成了新经济[①]。

　　The growth of traditional economy mainly depends on capital accumulation and expanded reproduction. No matter it is expanded from connotation or extension, it is inseparable from capital labor input and technological innovation. In the traditional economic growth, the role of capital and labor shows an obvious downward trend, while the role of technological progress increases significantly. However, generally speaking, the growth power of traditional economy mainly comes from resources, labor and scale efficiency of enterprises. Innovation is the main driving force of new economic growth. In this mode of knowledge-based economic growth, knowledge is the most important factor of economic growth. Knowledge-based industry, high-tech industry and intellectual industry are the main growth points and pillar industries of new economic growth with higher growth rate than the traditional economy. To develop the new economy is not to negate the traditional economy completely, nor is the industrial economy

---

① 季正松. 论新经济的特点及其与传统经济的联系 [J]. 镇江高专学报, 2003 (1): 13-16.

to the agricultural economy. The traditional economy is still the important foundation for the whole social economy. Although the proportion of traditional economy is declining, it will not disappear. It still has the necessity and space to exist. The traditional economy provides the necessary material basis for the new economy. The new economy is just to replace the traditional economy with new ways and new products to meet the needs of human beings, or to fill the gap of human needs. Once the traditional economy's produces are produced or managed by the new economic mode, the traditional economy will be transformed into the new economy.

随着互联网的快速兴起，人类已全面进入信息社会，新的经济学理论必然反映信息时代的诸多特征，解决经济社会活动面临的新问题。如何让"新经济"理论更好地指导服务于社会经济实践，需要对新经济的内涵、特征及发展规律等有更为深刻的认识。

With the rapid rise of the Internet, human beings have entered the information society in an all-round way. New economic theories are bound to reflect many characteristics of the information age and solve new problems in the economic and social activities. How to make the theory of "new economy" better serve the social and economic practice? A deeper understanding of the connotation, characteristics and development law of the new economy is needed.

在我国经济高质量发展的过程中，"新经济"无疑是推动经济高质量发展不可或缺的重要力量。促进"新经济"发展是建设现代化产业体系、建设社会主义现代化国家的必然要求，同时也是应对新时代背景下我国所面临的不平衡不充分的社会主要矛盾的有效路径①。党的十九大报告提出"加快建设创新型国家"，明确"创新是建设现代化经济体系的战略支撑"。近年来，我国经济由高速增长阶段转向高质量发展阶段，新一轮信息技术革命的不断深化、新产业雨后春笋般出现、新商业模式源源不断涌现、新产品摩肩接踵面世，对"新经济"的理论研究随之升

---

① 任保平，何苗. 我国新经济高质量发展的困境及路径选择 [J]. 西北大学学报（哲学社会科学版），2020（1）：40-48.

温。新动能即新动力作用于经济运行而产生的前进能量，是指以互联网、物联网、大数据、云计算等新一代信息技术应用为基础，一系列相关技术突破为支撑，大量新产业、新业态、新模式快速涌现并汇聚而成的产业发展新势能①。从这个角度讲，发展"新经济"是培育"新动能"的重要措施，而"新经济"的核心又是"新技术"。归根结底，新技术的创新是发展新经济、培育新动能的根源所在。

In China's high-quality economic development, "new economy" is undoubtedly an indispensable force to promote high-quality economic development. To promote the development of "new economy" is the inevitable requirement of building a modern industrial system and socialist country, and is also the effective way to deal with the unbalanced and inadequate social contradictions faced by our country in the new era. The report of the 19th National Congress of the Communist Party of China put forwards "accelerating the construction of an innovative country", and made it clear that "innovation is the strategic support for the construction of a modern economic system". In recent years, China's economy has changed from the development stage of high-speed to high-quality. With the deepening of a new round of information technology revolution, the emergence of new industries, new business models and new products, the theoretical research on the "new economy" is heating up. New growth driver refers to the forward energy from the new power of economic operation by using new-generation information technology such as Internet, Internet of things, big data, cloud computing, and the support of a series of related technological breakthroughs. A large number of new industries, new form of business, and new models are emerging and converging rapidly. From this point of view, the development of "new economy" is an important measure to cultivate "new growth drivers". The core of "new economy" the "new technology". In conclusion, the innovation of new technology is the root of developing new economy and cultivating new growth drivers.

---

① 周跃辉. 经济新动能重塑发展新优势［N］. 成都日报，2019-05-29（007）.

▷▷▷第一节 新经济的内涵与定义
Section One Connotation and Definition of New Economy

一、新经济的内涵
1. Connotation of New Economy

第一阶段:"新经济"一词最早是由美国《时代周刊》1983年在一篇封面文章中提出的。13年后,1996年12月30日出版的美国《商业周刊》发表了一组文章,对新经济首次进行了定义:新经济是指借由经济全球化浪潮所产生的,由信息技术革命驱动,以高科技产业为龙头的经济体系。其特征是实际GDP大幅增长,公司运营利润上升,失业率降低,通货膨胀率降低,进出口之和占GDP的比例上升,GDP增长中高科技的贡献度比重上升[①]。这个定义是为20世纪90年代初到2001年互联网泡沫期间的美国经济量身定制的。它有两大背景:一是以互联网大规模商用为代表的信息技术革命;二是以产业分工向纵深推进、产业链急剧跨国延伸和国际贸易突飞猛进为主要特征的全球化。

The first stage: The term "new economy" was first put forward in a cover article of *Time* in 1983. Thirteen years later, *Business Week* published a series of articles on December 30, 1996, which defined the new economy for the first time: the new economy refers to the economic system generated by the tide of economic globalization, driven by the information technology revolution and led by high-tech industries. It is characterized by the substantial growth of real GDP, the increase of company operating profit, the decrease of unemployment rate and inflation rate, the rise of the proportion of the sum of import and export in GDP, and the increase of the contribution of high technology in GDP growth.

[①] "新经济"与产业的颠覆性变革 [EB/OL]. (2018-06-29) [2021-03-01]. http://finance.ccy.com.cn/c/2018062969624.html.

This definition is customized for the US economy during Internet Bubble from early 1990s to the 2001. It has two backgrounds： one is the information technology revolution represented by the large-scale commercial use of the Internet； the other is the globalization characterized by the deepening of industrial division, the rapid transnational extension of industrial chain and the rapid development of international trade.

第二阶段：理论界对"新经济"概念的宽泛化阐释。根据党中央提纲挈领式的描述，理论界开始对新经济展开研究。学者们普遍认为，在中国经济新常态的背景下，"新经济"的内涵较为广泛，是各项高科技迅速发展所引起的衍生产业的发展、经济动力来源的转换等现象。国内对"新经济"的理解经历了几个阶段。首先，党中央对"新经济"的战略部署。习近平总书记 2014 年在国际工程科技大会的讲话中提到当前世界正处于新经济发展阶段，2015 年又再次提到世界新一轮产业与科技革命正在催生当下的新技术、新经济、新业态，为中国的经济发展创造发展机遇。2016 年李克强总理在十二届全国人大四次会议上提出"要培育新动能、发展新经济，促进新技术、新产业、新业态成长"，同年将"新经济"写入政府工作报告中。2016 年全国人大十二届四次会议，李克强总理首次详解"新经济"的内涵："新经济"涉及一、二、三产业，不仅仅是指三产中的"互联网+"、物联网、云计算、电子商务等新兴产业和业态，也包括工业制造当中的智能制造、大规模的定制化生产等，还涉及第一产业当中像有利于推进适度规模经营的家庭农场、股份合作制，农村一、二、三产融合发展，等等①。

The second stage： extensive interpretation of the concept "new economy" in the theoretical circle. According to the description of the Party Central Committee, theorists began to study the new economy. Scholars generally believe that under the background of "new normal" of China's economy, the connotation of "new economy" is more extensive, which means the phenomena

---

① 李克强：中国经济不会"硬着陆"［J/OL］. 人民网，中国商务新闻网. 中国经贸，2016（6）：14-15.

such as the development of derivative industries and the transformation of economic power sources caused by the rapid development of various high technologies. Domestic understanding of "new economy" has gone through four stages. The first stage: the Central Committee of CPC strategic plan for the "new economy". General Secretary Xi Jinping said in his speech at the International Conference on Engineering Technology in 2014 that the world is entering a new stage of economic development. In 2015, it was mentioned again that the new round of industrial and technological revolution in the world was giving birth to new technology, new economy and new form of business, creating opportunities for China's economic development. In 2016, Premier Li Keqiang proposed at the fourth session of the 12th National People's Congress that "we should cultivate new growth driver, develop new economy, and promote the growth of new technologies, new industries, and new form of business". In the same year, he wrote "new economy" into the government work report. In the same time, Premier Li Keqiang first expounded the connotation of the new economy: the new economy involves the primary, the secondary and tertiary industry, not only referring to the new tertiary industries such as "Internet plus", Internet of things, cloud computing, e-commerce, but also including intelligent manufacturing in industrial manufacturing, large-scale customized production. It also involves family farms conducive to promoting moderate scale operation, joint-stock cooperative system, and the integration of three industries.

　　"新经济"的兴起是由于新一轮科技和产业革命带动新的生产、交换、消费、分配活动,这些活动表现为人类生产方式进步和经济结构变迁、新经济模式对旧经济模式的替代①。"新经济"的实质是通过升级经济结构从而创造新的生产关系,挖掘新增长点,推动中国的经济发展。上述对新经济概念的认识,边界过于宽泛,内涵过于笼统,标准过于模糊,使得人们难以精准地开展政策设计。

————————

① 大财喜已资管家.国内新经济发展的主要特点及国际对比[EB/OL].(2020-08-15)[2021-01-10].https://xueqiu.com/2703057174/156721961.

The rise of "new economy" is due to a new round of scientific and technological and industrial revolution, which leads to new activities of production, exchange, consumption and distribution. These activities are manifested in the progress of the human mode of production, the change of economic structure, and the replacement of the old economic model by the new economic model. The essence of "new economy" is to create new production relations, to tap new growth points and to promote China's economic development by upgrading economic structure. The above understanding of the concept of new economy is too broad in boundary, too general in connotation and too vague in standard to carry out accurate policy design.

第三阶段：实践界对"新经济"的具体化描述。目前，不少城市都展开了对新经济的相关部署。如上海提出发展新技术、新产业、新业态、新模式"四新"经济；深圳构建世界级的电子信息产业生态圈；杭州打造"互联网+"创新创业中心。由于各地发展新经济的侧重点不同，人们对新经济的理解呈现具体化倾向：有人认为，所谓"新经济"，就是知识经济、信息经济、虚拟经济；有学者用互联网经济、物联网经济、大数据经济概括新经济；也有地方政府工作人员将"新经济"理解为数字经济、智能经济、共享经济；等等①。以上关于新经济的认识，都是"管中窥豹"式的碎片化描述，并没有形成新经济的整体性、系统性观点。

The third stage: the concrete description of "new economy" in practice. At present, many cities have made the relevant plan of the new economy. For example, Shanghai proposes the development of "Four New" economy – new technologies, new industries, new form of business and new models; Shenzhen builds a world-class electronic information industry ecosystem; Hangzhou creates "Internet plus" innovation and entrepreneurship center. Due to the different emphases of developing new economy in different regions, scholars'

---

① 每日经济新闻. 从三个关键词看成都的新经济"内胆"[EB/OL]. (2018-05-18) [2021-01-10]. https://www.sohu.com/a/232115640_115362.

understanding of new economy tends to be specific：some people think that the so-called "new economy" is knowledge economy, information economy and virtual economy；some scholars summarize new economy as Internet economy, Internet of things economy and big data economy；some local government staff understand "new economy" as digital economy and intelligent economy, sharing economy and so on. The above understanding of new economy does not form a holistic and systematic view of new economy due to their one-sided description.

第四阶段：关于新经济的"成都定义"。近年来，成都立足自身实际，结合国际国内先进城市发展经验，决定聚焦数字经济、智能经济、绿色经济、创意经济、流量经济、共享经济"六大形态"，着力构建服务实体经济、智慧城市建设、科技创新创业、人力资本协同、消费提档升级、绿色低碳建设、现代供应链创新"七大应用场景"，致力于打造新经济话语引领者、场景培育地、生态创新区，建设最适宜新经济发展的城市。目前，"新经济"已成为成都高质量发展的强力推动者、高品质生活的重要创造者和高效能治理的有力参与者①。随着实践的展开，成都对"新经济"的认识将逐步系统化和深化。

The fourth stage："Chengdu's Definition" of new economy. In recent years, based on its own reality and combined with the development experience of international and domestic advanced cities, Chengdu has decided to focus on the "six major forms" of digital economy, intelligent economy, green economy, creative economy, flow economy and sharing economy, and strive to build a real service economy, smart city construction, scientific and technological innovation and entrepreneurship, human capital collaboration, consumption upgrading, green and low-carbon construction and modern supply chain innovation, the "seven application scenescapes". Chengdu is committed to lead new economic discourse, build scenescapes cultivation places, ecological innovation zones, and construct the most suitable city for new economic development. At present,

① 钟华林，刘畅. 看成都如何"最适宜新经济成长"［N］. 经济日报，2018-04-26（007）.

"new economy" has become a strong promoter of high-quality development, an essential creator of high-quality life and a strong participant in Chengdu's efficient governance. With the development of practice, Chengdu's understanding of "new economy" is gradually systematic and deepened.

二、新经济的定义
2. Definition of New Economy

一是"新经济"是一个动态性的迭代概念。新经济是一个动态的概念——新经济总是相对于传统经济而言的，属于历史的范畴，在不同的历史阶段，新经济有不同的具体内涵。与以往历次工业革命相比，第四次工业革命是以指数级而非线性速度展开。在这一时期，技术更替迅速、种类繁多，新技术与专利几乎每天都在形成，经济形态总是处于永不停息的升级状态。我们现在看到的绝大多数产品/服务都曾经是新经济，但随着大规模生产、同类商品和竞争者的涌现以及更新的产品/服务出现，它们便逐渐沦为传统经济的一部分。因此，新经济要"代表前沿、代表方向、代表趋势、代表未来"。

First, "new economy" is a dynamic and iterative concept. New economy is a dynamic concept — new economy is always relative to the traditional economy. In different historical stages, new economy has different specific connotations. Compared with the previous industrial revolution, the fourth industrial revolution was carried out at an exponential and nonlinear speed. During this period, technology changed rapidly in varieties. New technologies and patents were formed almost every day, and the economic form was always in a constant state of upgrading. Most of the products / services used to be new economy, but with the emergence of large-scale production, similar goods and competitors, and of newer products / services, they gradually become part of the traditional economy. Therefore, the new economy should "represent the frontier, direction, trend and future".

　　二是"新经济"是一种经济形态。经济形态存在于一个经济体的部分产业、部分领域之中，而非整个经济体。新经济只是整体经济的一部分而不是全部——新经济必须以传统经济为支撑、为基础、为配套，而不可能完全脱离传统经济单独存在。新经济既存在于第三产业，也存在于第二产业乃至第一产业，并且使三次产业之间界限趋于模糊。凡是能满足人民日益增长的美好生活需要的、自带需求的新供给都可以属于新经济，它可能表现为产品，也可能表现为服务，更可能表现为产品和服务的融合状态。

　　Second, "new economy" is an economic form. Economic form exists in some industries and fields, not in the whole economies. New economy is only a part, but not the whole of economy – it must be supported, based on supported by the traditional economy, and it cannot completely separate from the traditional economy. The new economy exists not only in the tertiary industry, but also in the secondary industry and even in the primary industry and makes the boundaries between the three industries tend to be blurred. Any new supply that can meet the people's growing needs for a better life and bring its own demand can belong to new economy. It may be manifested as products or services, and more likely to integrate products and services.

　　三是"新经济"的核心是融合创新。与传统经济相比，新经济的突出特征就是将科学技术转化为高效的生产力，使社会生产力出现革命性的发展。数字革命通过融合应用数字化、智能化的新型技术对传统经济加以改造升级，这一革命在全球产业变革中的影响最为广泛，它在各个领域催生了如电子商务、云计算、人工智能、新能源、物联网等新产业。受益于信息技术的迅速发展，使得新技术在各个行业领域中的应用频率加速提高，并在其中不断渗透深入，形成了技术与产业、行业跨界融合的新型组织形态，即新业态。

　　Third, the core of "new economy" is integration and innovation. Compared with the traditional economy, the prominent feature of new economy is to transform science and technology into efficient productive forces, which will lead to the revolutionary development of social productive forces. The digital revolution transforms and upgrades the traditional economy by integrating and applying new digital and intelligent technologies, which has the most extensive influence on the global industrial transformation. It has spawned new industries in various fields, such as e-commerce, cloud computing, artificial intelligence, new energy, Internet of things, etc. Benefiting from the rapid development of information technology, the application frequency of new technology in various industries has been accelerated, and the penetration of new technology has been deepened, forming a new organizational form of integration of technology, industry and trade.

四是"新经济"的目标是创造需求。"创造需求"实际上是满足潜在的、客观存在而没有被既有产品/服务满足的需求。新经济能够主动发现,并使用打破常规的办法满足这类需求,或解决产品/服务应用中的痛点和难点。新经济的本质,就是进一步满足人们对美好生活的向往。只要科技在进步,人类社会的行为路径就会按照人性的特点不断优化升级,进而导致商业逻辑的改进、社会秩序的不断重组——也意味着新经济的不断涌现。

Fourth, the goal of "new economy" is to create demand. "Creating demand" is actually to meet the latent and objective needs that are not met by the existing products / services. New economy can actively discover and use unconventional methods to meet such needs or solve the difficulties in the application of products / services. The essence of new economy is to further satisfy people's yearning for a better life. As long as science and technology progress, human society's behavior will continue to optimize and upgrade according to the characteristics of human nature, which will lead to the improvement of business logic and the continuous reorganization of social order and mean the continuous emergence of new economy.

基于上述共识,本书将新经济定义为:新经济既不仅仅是一种经济现象,也不完全是一种技术现象,而是一种由技术到经济的演进范式、虚拟经济到实体经济的生成连接、资本与技术的深度黏合、科技创新与制度创新相互作用的经济形态。

Based on the above consensus, this book defines the term as: the new economy is an economic phenomenon and not entirely a technological phenomenon. It is an economic form with the evolution paradigm from technology to economy, the generation and connection from virtual economy to real economy, the deep bonding between capital and technology, and the interaction between scientific and technological innovation and institutional innovation.

▷▷▷ 第二节 新经济发展的特征及必要条件
Section Two Characteristics and Necessary Conditions of New Economic Development

一、新经济发展的特征
1. Characteristics of New Economic Development

从技术特点来看，新经济发展依托的技术是指数级增长、数字化进步、融合式创新。新经济更注重创新，视其为推动发展的第一动力，将新技术视为创新实现过程中最关键的要素，更加注重知识、技术等要素的投入，实行内涵式的扩大再生产。与传统工业革命下的技术相比，新经济所依托的技术发生了本质变化，具体表现为"指数级的增长、数字化的进步和融合式的创新"。新技术将以摩尔定律的速度快速更迭，并向各个领域广泛渗透，从而引发传统生产生活方式的颠覆性变革。

From the perspective of technical characteristics, the development of new economy relies on exponential growth, digital progress and integrated innovation. In the new economy, it pays more attention to innovation and regards it as the first driving force to promote development. The new technology is considered as the most critical factor in the process of innovation. It pays more attention to the input of knowledge, technology etc., and implements connotative expanded reproduction. Compared with the technology under the traditional industrial revolution, the technology on which the new economy relies has undergone essential changes, which are embodied in "exponential growth, digital progress and integrated innovation". New technologies will change rapidly with the speed of Moore's law and infiltrate into various fields, which will lead to a subversive change in the traditional modes of production and life.

从创新内涵来看，新经济发展涉及的创新是涵盖技术、业态、模式、制度的全面创新。新经济的创新不再局限于科技创新，而是向业态创新、模式创新、制度创新的全面拓展。相应地，创新投入也不局限于传统的研发投入，还包括知识资本、无形资产的投入（专利、技术、版权、诀窍、发明、创意、管理、信息以及高智力人力资本等），且无形资产投入远超过有形资产投入。

From the perspective of innovation connotation, the innovation involved in the new economy development is comprehensive, covering technology, format, mode and system. The innovation of the new economy is no longer limited to that of science and technology, but extends to that of business forms, modes and systems. Correspondingly, innovation investment is not limited to traditional R&D investment, but also including investment in intellectual capital and intangible assets (patents, technology, copyright, know-how, invention, creativity, management, information and high intelligence human capital, etc.), among which the investment in intangible assets is far more than that in tangible assets.

从发展逻辑来看，新经济发展依赖新场景的助推。新场景是新经济发展的新逻辑，用场景破除技术与实体经济的供需对接矛盾，为技术找到商业化应用落点，为产业找到转型升级的解决方案，重点在培育新产业来带动城市发展。从技术视角看，场景是推动创新应用的新孵化平台；从企业视角看，场景是寻求改变人类生活方式的新试验空间；从产业视角看，场景是推动产业爆发的新生态载体；从消费视角看，场景助力消费升级，释放市场需求，为消费者提供更多美好生活新体验①。

From the perspective of development logic, the development of new economy depends on the boost of new scenescapes. New scenescapes are the new logic of new economic development. It can break the contradiction between supply and demand of technology and real economy, find the commercial application for technology and the solution of industry transformation and upgrading, and focus on cultivating new industries to drive urban development. From the perspective of technology, scenescapes are new incubation platforms to promote innovative applications; from the perspective of enterprises, scenescapes are new experimental space to change the way of human life; from the perspective of industry, scenescapes are new ecological carriers to promote industrial explosion; from the perspective of consumption, scenescapes help consumption upgrade, releases market demand, and provides consumers with more new experiences of a better life.

从产业形态来看，新经济发展呈现出跨界融合、边界模糊的特征。新经济与以往行业分类相对清晰的工业经济、服务经济不同。伴随信息技术的深度应用和互联网向传统产业领域的广泛渗透，基于不同应用创新大量涌现，制造服务融合、生产服务融合、服务跨行业融合、线上线下融合层出不穷，传统的三次产业边界趋于模糊，催生出形形色色的跨界融合"新物种"。

From the perspective of industrial form, new economy development presents the characteristics of cross-border integration and fuzzy boundary. The new economy is different from the industrial economy and service economy with clearly classification in the past. With the in-depth application of information technology and the wide penetration of Internet into traditional industries, a large number of innovations based on different applications have emerged, including the integration of manufaction and service, production and service,

---

① 长城战略咨询. 新经济应用场景供给的探索：城市机会清单［EB/OL］.（2019－09－03）［2021－02－22］. https://www.sohu.com/a/338350330_176572.

cross-business service, online and offline. The boundaries of three traditional industries tend to be blurred, giving birth to a variety of "new species" with cross-border integration.

从运作模式来看，新经济的发展呈现平台化、共享化的特征。互联网时代"共享"的特征明显，经济行为进一步公共化，各类要素通过嵌入开放式的网络平台，实现研发公共化（个体将创意、设计分享到网络）、销售公共化（从电商到微商，网络平台进一步促进供求的广域、快速和无缝对接）、数据信息公共化（如维基百科、百度百科等）。这带来了经济运作模式的重大变化，企业可依托免费平台提供增值服务实现盈利。

From the perspective of operation mode, the development of new economy presents the characteristics of platformization and shared. The characteristics of "sharing" in the Internet era are obvious, and the economic behavior is further public. Various factors are embedded in the open network platform to realize the publicity of R&D (individuals share their creativity and design on the network), the publicity of sales (from e-commerce to We-chat commerce, and the network platform further promotes the wide, fast and seamless connection of supply and demand), and the publicity of data and information (such as Wikipedia, Baidu Encyclopedia, etc.), which has brought about significant changes in the mode of economic operation. Enterprises can rely on the free platform to provide value-added services to achieve profits.

从创新主体来看，新经济的发展实现了从封闭式的研究机构走向个体的开放式创新。传统经济中的创新主体主要是高校、科研机构、企业中的技术研发人员，新经济中的创新主体拓展到创客、个体，并带动各类风险投资、私募基金、加速器、孵化器等主体参与，形成生生不息的"热带雨林"。如，深圳形成了诸多创业服务资源集聚的众创空间，集聚了天使汇、飞马旅、大家投等各领域各类型的创业服务机构，是一种典型的众创经济。

From the perspective of innovation subject, the development of new economy has realized the transformation from closed research institutions to open individual innovation. In the traditional economy, the main body of innovation is the R&D personnel in universities, scientific research institutions and enterprises. In the new economy, the main body of innovation extends to individual entrepreneur, with the participation of various venture capital, private equity funds, accelerators and incubators, forming an endless "tropical rain forest". For example, Shenzhen has formed the "maker space" gathering many entrepreneurial service resources, such as institutions in various fields of Angel Crunch, Pegasus Group, and Dajiatou (Chinese Angel List). This is a typical crowd making economy.

从经济驱动力来看，新经济是典型的需求导向、用户牵引模式。互联网时代的新经济是一种突出需求导向、通过用户来牵引和驱动的经济，这与传统经济中强调生产者生产能力和规模经济的发展模式截然不同。进入互联网时代后，新型的商业模式逐渐打破传统模式，以消费者需求为基点，共享经济、平台经济等模式逐渐兴起，各级经济主体之间的界线不复存在。现在的商业模式以顾客为主、服务为主，以新盈利理念为核心，颠覆了传统消费模式，迎合新的消费理念。比如，"互联网+银行"的结合带来了支付宝等第三方支付平台的兴起，"互联网+医疗"的结合创造出了移动就医问诊平台。

From the perspective of economic driving force, the new economy is a typical demand-oriented and user-driven mode. The new economy in the Internet era is quite different from the traditional economy emphasizing the producer's production capacity and scale economy. After entering the Internet era, new business modes gradually break the traditional ones. Based on the consumers demand, shared economy, platform economy and other modes gradually rise, and the boundaries between economic entities at different levels no longer exist. The current business mode is customer-oriented and service-oriented, with the new profit concept as the core, subverting the traditional

consumption model and catering to the new consumption concept. For example,
the combination of "Internet plus banking" has brought the rise of the third-party
payment platform such as Alipay. The combination of Internet plus medical care
has created a mobile medical inquiry platform.

二、新经济发展的必要条件
2. Necessary Conditions of New Economic Development

新技术是新经济发展的奠基石。在传统经济中，主要依靠要素规模化效应推动经济向前发展，依赖低成本资源和生产要素的高强度投入，采用外延式的生产方式，科技进步和创新对经济增长的贡献率偏低。在新经济中，更注重创新，视其为推动发展的第一动力，将新技术视为创新实现过程中最关键的要素，更加注重知识、技术等要素的投入，实行内涵式的扩大再生产。高质量创新要素是"新经济"发展的动力源，但高质量创新要素的培养并不是一蹴而就的，不论是技术、知识，还是信息、数据，都需要经过较长时间的积累、沉淀、挖掘、优化、检验，才能使之成为高价值特征的战略资源。

New technology is the cornerstone of new economic development. The
traditional economy mainly depends on the large-scale effect to promote economic
development, relying on low-cost resources and high-intensity input of production
factors and adopting the extensive production mode, with low contribution rate of
scientific and technological progress and innovation to economic growth. The new
economy attaches more attention to innovation and regards it as the first driving
force to promote development, considers new technology as the most critical factor
in the process of innovation, pays more attention to the input of knowledge,
technology and other factors, and implements connotative expanded reproduction.
High-quality innovation factors are the power source of the development of "new
economy", but the cultivation of high-quality innovation factors is not achieved
overnight. Whether it is technology, knowledge, information or data, it needs a
long time of accumulation, precipitation, exploiting, optimization and testing to

make it a strategic resource with high value.

　　新产业和新业态是新经济发展的孵化池。第四次工业革命（数字革命）将融合应用智能化、数字化的新型技术，以对传统经济改造升级，这一革命在全球产业变革中的影响最为广泛，它催生了如电子商务、云计算、人工智能、新能源、物联网等新产业。受益于信息技术的迅速发展，新技术在各个行业领域中的应用频率也加速提高，并在其中不断渗透深入，形成了技术与产业、行业跨界融合的新型组织形态，简称"新业态"。互联网、大数据等新型信息技术与第一、二、三产业逐渐融合，创造出智慧城市、智慧交通、智慧旅游、智慧农业、生物农业、观光农业、远程授课、移动办公、跨境电子商务等新业态。新经济的发展逻辑是，通过技术的应用发展来"孵化"新产业和新业态，通过实践培育新动能，再由新产业和新业态"孵化"新经济。

New industries and new forms of business are the incubators of new economic development. The fourth industrial revolution (Digital Revolution) will integrate new intelligent and digital technologies to transform and upgrade the traditional economy. This revolution has the most extensive impact on the global industrial revolution, and has spawned new industries such as e-commerce, cloud computing, artificial intelligence, new energy, Internet of things and so on. Benefiting from the rapid development of information technology, the application frequency of new technology in various industries has been increased, and the penetration of new technology has been deepened, forming a new organizational form of cross-border integration of technology, industry and trade. The Internet, big data and other new information technologies are gradually integrated into the primary, secondary and tertiary industries, creating new forms of business such as smart city, smart transportation, smart tourism, smart agriculture, biological agriculture, sightseeing agriculture, distance teaching, mobile office, cross-border e-commerce, etc. The development logic of new economy is to "incubate" new industries and new forms through the application and development of technology, cultivate new growth driver through practice, and then "incubate" new economy through new industries and new forms.

　　新模式是实现新经济发展的重要手段。在传统经济中,传统商业模式是在生产商与消费者之间逐次传递的,不能跨越任何一个商业主体,在各级经济主体之间形成沟通限制,并且多以线下交易为主,实行"一手交钱一手交货"的方式,更注重效益,不以客户满意度为经营标准。进入互联网时代后,新型的商业模式逐渐打破传统模式,以消费者需求为基点,共享经济、租赁经济等商业模式逐渐兴起,各级经济主体之间的界线不复存在,形成以顾客为主、服务为主的新盈利理念,颠覆了传统消费模式,迎合了新的消费理念。

　　The new mode is an important means to realize the development of new economy. In the traditional economy, the traditional business mode happens between producers and consumers, which can't cross any business entity and form communication restrictions between economic entities at different levels. It mainly focuses on offline transactions and implements the mode of "give money and get goods". It pays more attention to the level of efficiency without taking customers' satisfaction as the prior standard. After entering the Internet era, the new business mode gradually breaks the traditional one. Based on the consumers' demand, the sharing economy, leasing economy and other business modes gradually rise. The boundaries no longer exist between different economic entities. The new profit-making concept of customer-orientation and service-orientation is considered as the core, subverting the traditional consumption mode and catering to the new consumption concept.

▷▷▷第三节　新动能助力中国经济
高质量发展的机制机理

Section Three　Mechanism of High-Quality Development
of China's Economy with the Help of New Growth Drivers

提到新动能不得不说新经济，新经济与新动能究竟为何种关系？从广义上讲新动能具有三层含义：其一是指新动力作用于新经济运行系统而产生的推动经济前进的能量，这里新动能＝新动力＋新经济；其二是指新动力作用于原有经济运行系统而产生的推动经济前进的能量，这里新动能＝新动力；其三是指原有动力作用于新经济运行系统而产生的推动经济前进的能量，这里新动能＝新经济。就第一层含义而言，新动能可从新动力和新经济两个方面助力中国经济高质量发展；就第二层含义而言，新动能是促进新经济发展的动力机制；就第三层含义而言，培育新动能与发展新经济互为因果。因此，无论从哪个层面讲，培育新动能都是中国经济高质量发展的重要举措，具体而言：

In terms of new growth drivers, we have to talk about new economy. What is the relationship between new economy and new growth drivers? The new growth driver refers to the energy to promote economic development. In a broad sense, the new growth driver has three meanings: first, it is generated by the new power acting on the new economic operation system, which means new growth driver equals new power plus new economy; second, it is generated by the new power acting on the original economic operation system, which means new growth driver equals new power; third, it is generated by the original power acting on the new economic operation system, which means new growth driver equals new economy. In terms of the first meaning, the new growth driver can help China's high-quality economic development in the two aspects of new power and new economy; in terms of the second meaning, new growth driver is the driving mechanism to promote the development of new economy; in terms of the third meaning, cultivating new growth driver and developing new economy are mutually causes and effects. Therefore, no matter from which aspect, cultivating new growth driver is an important measure for China's high-quality economic development.

新动能强力提高要素增长效率。发展新经济培育新动能要求以人才、技术、知识、信息等新要素高质量供给为主，可从源头直接提高要素供给效率。新经济与新动能倒逼金融资本提高效率；新动能可通过生产资料智能化、流程再造等提高劳动要素效率；应用新技术可提高资源流转效率，从而间接提高要素效率。

The new growth driver strongly improves the efficiency of factor growth. The development of new economy and cultivation of new growth driver require high-quality supply of new factors such as talents, technology, knowledge and information, which can directly improve the efficiency of factor supply from the source. New economy and new growth driver force financial capital to improve efficiency. New growth driver can improve labor factor efficiency through production intelligence and process reengineering. Application of new technology can improve resource transfer efficiency, thus indirectly improving factor efficiency.

新动能加速推动产业体系现代化。新动能以人才、技术、信息和知识要素为主要投入要素，可迅速形成新共性产业技术，促进不同产业间相互融合，催生新的产业形态，培育壮大高技术前沿产业。新动能加剧产业集聚，在集群化的产业生态中，可以接受来自各产业的技术外溢效应、人才流动效应、交易成本降低效应等，有利于新产业的内部培育与外部引进，达到产业结构合理化的预期。

New growth drivers will accelerate the modernization of the industrial system. With talents, technology, information and knowledge as the main input factors, new growth drivers can rapidly form new common industrial technology, promote the integration of different industries, give birth to new industrial forms, and cultivate and expand high-tech frontier industries. New growth drivers intensify industrial gathering. In the industrial ecology of gathering, it can accept the effect of technology spillover, talents flow and transaction cost reduction from various industries, which is conducive to the internal cultivation and external introduction of new industries, to achieve the expectation of rationalization of industrial structure.

新动能全面助力消费转型升级。数据智能化引导企业以消费者为主体,以适应不同消费者的消费需求为出发点,以个性化定制模式代替标准化大量生产模式。从供给端发力,创造新的消费模式,不断满足消费者多样化的需求。依托互联网和个性化大数据技术,将个性化发展融入新兴服务业中。利用大数据技术,精准分析和识别国内外消费的潮流趋势,瞄准细分需求,打造多元品牌,满足品牌化消费需求。

The new growth driver will extensively help the transformation and upgrading of consumption. Data intelligence guides enterprises to take consumers as the main body, to adapt to the consumption needs of different consumers as the starting point, and to replace the standardized mass production with personalized customization. It creates new consumption patterns on the basis of the supply, and constantly meets the diverse needs of consumers. It relies on the Internet and personalized big data technology and integrates personalized development into the emerging service industry. Use big data technology to accurately analyze and identify the trend of consumption at home and abroad, so as to target the demand of segmentation, create multiple brands and meet the demand of brand consumption.

新动能高效优化投资结构。新技术改变了信息的传播路径、加工与组织层次,显著改善了信息不对称问题,为新兴基础设施建设与维护等提供新的投资机会,促使资本流向前沿高端产业。新动能驱动下,投资风险降低,投资领域多样化,有助于新领域的种子企业获得资金支持。在金融深化改革与支持新经济发展的政策背景下,有助于资本与新科技融合。新经济的发展与新动能的培育,有助于破除中西部地区空间发展与开放限制，在一定程度上改变外商投资的投资倾向。

The new growth driver optimizes the investment structure efficiently. New technology has changed the transmission path, processing and organization level of information, significantly improved information asymmetry, provided new investment opportunities for the construction and maintenance of new infrastructure, and promoted the capital flow to frontier high-end industries. Driven by the new growth driver, the investment risk is reduced and the investment fields are diversified, which helps the seeded enterprises in new fields to obtain financial support. With the policy of deepening financial reform and supporting the development of new economy, it is conducive to the integration of capital and new technology. The development of new economy and the cultivation of new growth driver will help to break the restrictions of spatial development and opening up in the central and western regions and change the investment tendency of foreign investment to a certain extent.

新动能深度协调区域平衡发展。新动能驱动产权改革，促使产权要素进农村。随着农业新动能的发展，产权改革越来越深入，"三权"的资产性不断被盘活，有利于现代化农业产业体系的建立。新动能打破地理空间限制，促进中西部逐渐实现全面发展。新技术的渗透、新产业的培育在一定程度上打破了中西部地理空间限制，发挥相较于东部地区的后发优势，提升生产效率，促进经济社会全面发展。新动能全面激发传统产业转型升级，有助于振兴东北。东北老工业基地通过培育人才新动能、技术新动能、消费新动能，形成新的经济增长点，有助于实现振兴发展。

The new growth driver deeply coordinates the balanced development of the regions. The new growth driver promotes the reform of property and introduces it to the countryside. With the development of new drivers in agriculture, the reform of property develops in-depth. The assets of "three rights" (rights of land owning, contracting and managing) are constantly revitalized, conducive to the establishment of modern agricultural industrial system. The new growth driver will break the geographical and spatial restrictions and promote the gradual realization of all-round development in the central and western regions. The penetration of new technologies and the cultivation of new industries will break the geographical and spatial restrictions of the central and western regions to a certain extent, give full play to the late-rising development advantages compared with the eastern regions, improve the production efficiency, and gradually promote the comprehensive economic and social development. The new growth driver stimulates the transformation and upgrading of traditional industries in an all-round way, which is conducive to the revitalization of Northeast China. The northeast old industrial base forms new economic growth points by cultivating new growth drivers of talents, technology and consumption, which helps realize revitalization and development.

CiNED

第二章
新经济发展的国内外实践

Chapter Two
Practice of New Economy Development
at Home and Abroad

　　历次工业革命的演进都是以转换经济发展的动能为基础，推动了一系列新技术和新工艺的广泛应用，催生了大量新兴产业的出现和经济结构的变革。从全球来看，各国经济发展普遍面临传统能源日益枯竭以及环境恶化等问题，特别是自 2008 年国际金融危机爆发以来，经济发展动力不足的问题日益凸显，各国都开始了对经济增长动力转换的探索。中国自改革开放以来，进入了加速工业化阶段，目前总体上处于工业化和城市化的中期，在新一轮工业革命的浪潮中，中国在推动经济创新发展、绿色发展的同时，正在积极寻求经济增长动力的转换。一系列的新变化表明，提升经济发展质量需要进一步挖掘技术进步的红利，不断探寻新旧动能转换的实现路径，进而实现经济的高质量发展①。

The evolution of all previous industrial revolutions is based on the transformation of the driver of economic development, which promotes the wide application of a series of new technologies and crafts and gives birth to a large number of new industries and the change of economic structure. Globally, the economic development in all countries is generally faced with the problems of traditional energy depletion and environmental deterioration. Especially since the outbreak of the international financial crisis in 2008, the problem of insufficient economic development driver has become increasingly prominent, and all countries have begun to exploit the transformation of economic growth driver. Since the reform and opening up, China has entered the stage of accelerating industrialization. At present, it is generally in the middle stage of industrialization and urbanization. In the wave of a new round of industrial revolution, while promoting economic innovation and green development, China is actively seeking the transformation of economic growth power. A series of new changes show that to improve the quality of economic development, China need to further exploit the profit of technological progress, and constantly explore the realization path of the transformation of new and old drivers, to achieve high-quality economic development.

---

① 张红凤，吕杰. 新旧动能转换及实现路径 [N]. 光明日报，2018-09-06 (007).

▷▷▷ 第一节 国外发达国家实践
Section One Practice of Developed Countries Abroad

一、德国：以"工业4.0"重构产业生态
1. Germany：Reconstructing Industrial Ecology with "Industry 4.0"

"工业4.0"缘于2008年金融危机。当时德国提出，工程和制造业等核心行业要做出改变，变得更有效率，才能够渡过金融危机。历时三年讨论，2011年落地。"工业4.0"经历了三个发展阶段：柔性化、定制化生产，企业从产品平台向服务平台演进，物联网技术让工业互联网成为现实。德国认为，未来7年，最重要的技术趋势是数字孪生，虚拟世界和物理世界彻底打通，员工能力和商业模式彻底重构，但任何一家企业都不可能凭一己之力做到这些，聚焦核心、打造生态，是领导型企业的普遍做法。德国"工业4.0"侧重以下几个方向。第一，运用新的技术变革，其中最重要的技术是数字孪生。产品在物理世界真实存在之前就已经在虚拟数字世界中存在，一旦有了数字孪生，就可以虚拟设计产品，可以模拟市场，可以把产品配置成客户需要的样子，可以设计产品性能和经验，所有的一切都可以在数字化世界中完成，不需要任何物理世界中的操作。第二，要重新思考产品的构成要素，重新考虑产品如何设计和验证，重新思考如何验证这些产品，让这些产品能够实现新的功能。例如客户买的不是机车，而是交通能力，这是完全不同的商业模式。如果企业提供高质量及时的交通，而且有很好的客户体验，就可以获得溢价，这就变成一个服务行业，与制造行业不一样，卖出产品之后通过服务获得利润。第三，"工业4.0"进入了新的层面，就是自动化升级，随之而来的变化是新工种和对新工作能力的需求，因为"工业4.0"的领导者在创造新的工作岗位。对于领导者来说，他们把供应链带回国内，也意味着需要重新去培训员工来做一些很重要的新工作，工作种类在发生改变。对于德国来说，制造业是强项，在B2B方面非常

强，但是 B2C 行业不是很强，将来会用人工智能、机器学习和机器人来搭建基础架构，实现定制产品和服务①。

"Industry 4. 0" came from the financial crisis in 2008. At that time, Germany proposed that core industries such as engineering and manufacturing should make changes and become more efficient in order to survive the financial crisis. It was launched in 2011 after three years of discussion. "Industry 4. 0" has experienced three stages of development: flexible and customized production; evolution of enterprise from product platform to service platform; industrial Internet realized by using Internet of things technology. Germany believed that in the next seven years, the most important technology trend is the digital twin. The virtual world and the physical world will be completely opened up, and the employees' ability and business mode will be completely reconstructed. However, no enterprise can do this on its own. The common practice of leading enterprises is to focus on the core and build ecology. Germany's "Industry 4. 0" focuses on the following directions. The first is to use new technological changes, the most important one of which is the digital twin. Products exist in the virtual digital world before they exist in the physical world. Once there is a digital twin, products can be designed virtually, markets can be simulated, products can be configured as customers need, and product performance and experience can be designed, all of which can be completed in the digital world without any operation in the physical world. Second, it should rethink the components of products, how to design and verify products, and how to verify these products so that these products can achieve new functions. For example, what customers want are not vehicles, but the transportation capacity. This is a completely different business model. If an enterprise provides high-quality and timely transportation, and has a good customer experience, it can get a premium and become a service industry. Unlike the manufacturing industry,

① 春晓财经. 工业 4. 0 在德国的进展及未来 [EB/OL]. (2018-10-10) [2021-02-23]. http://www.123gobook.com/706.html.

it will make profits through services after selling products. Third, "Industry 4.0" has entered a new level of automation upgrading, followed by changes such as the demand for new types of work and new working abilities, because the leaders of "Industry 4.0" are creating new jobs. Leaders bring the supply chain back home country, which means that they need to retrain their employees to do some critical new jobs, and types of their jobs are changing. For Germany, manufacturing industry is a strong point. It is solid in B2B, but not in B2C industry. In the future, artificial intelligence, machine learning, and robots will be used to build infrastructure and realize customized products and services.

二、美国：以新能源、先进制造和大数据引领新经济发展
2. The United States: Leading the Development of New Economy with New Energy, Advanced Manufacturing and Big Data

新能源革命对美国经济产生了深远影响。以含油砂、重油、气变油以及其他液态油为代表的非常规能源，重塑了美国的能源格局，并在就业和政府收入方面对美国经济产生了深远影响。如烃类能源的生产会促进石油化工、化肥、合成树脂、铁、钢材、玻璃、造纸以及塑料加工等依赖天然气生产的行业的发展，并会在服务业、建筑业、运输业、贸易领域产生更深远的影响。

The new energy revolution has had a profound impact on the American economy. Unconventional energy, such as oil sands, heavy oil, steam-turned oil and other liquid oil, has reshaped the energy pattern of the United States, and has had a profound impact on the U.S. economy in terms of employment and government revenue. For example, the production of hydrocarbon energy will promote the development of industries that rely on natural gas production, such as petrochemical industry, chemical fertilizer, synthetic resin, iron, steel, glass, papermaking and plastic processing, and will have a more far-reaching impact on the industry of service, construction, transportation and trade.

先进制造业带动了美国经济的发展。先进制造业以其涉及领域广、产品附加值高的特点，带动了美国经济的发展。制造业在美国历史上发挥着重要作用，是支撑美国综合国力保持世界领先的重要基石。但一段时间以来，制造业的日趋弱势与以金融为代表的虚拟经济的相对强势，增加了美国经济的不稳定性，也加剧了贫富差距，助长了两极分化。2008 年爆发的金融危机使美国人意识到，虚拟经济需要坚实的实体经济作为支撑。为此，美国政府提出了"再工业化"和"重振美国制造业"的战略，试图通过引导制造业企业的回流来增强美国经济的厚度，创造更多就业机会。

Advanced manufacturing industry drives the development of American economy. Advanced manufacturing industry, with its wide range and high added value of products, has driven the development of American economy. The manufacturing industry plays an important role in the history of the United States and is an important cornerstone to support the United States' comprehensive national strength and maintain its leading position globally. However, for some time, the manufacturing industry's weakness and the relative strength of virtual economy typically in finance have increased the instability of American economy, widened the gap between the rich and the poor and led to polarization. After the financial crisis in 2008, Americans realize that the virtual economy needs solid real economy as support. Therefore, the U. S. government puts forward the strategy of "reindustrialization" and "revitalizing the U.S. manufacturing industry", trying to enhance the strength of the U.S. economy and create more employment opportunities by guiding the return of manufacturing enterprises.

大数据产业为经济发展提供了新动能。数字经济时代孕育着海量的数字资源。电子支付的普及、网上购物的兴起、社交媒体的活跃，以及新型可穿戴设备，造就了指数级增长的数据资源。根据麦肯锡全球研究所的报告，大数据的应用每年可为美国带来 6 100 亿美元的产值。其中，在零售业和制造业领域，每年带动产值的增加额可达到 1 550 亿~3 250

亿美元；在医疗保健和政府服务领域，每年也会带来约 2 850 亿美元的成本结余，间接促进了经济增长①。

Big data industry provides new growth drivers for economic development. The era of digital economy is pregnant with massive digital resources. The popularity of electronic payment, the rise of online shopping, social media dynamics, and new wearable devices have created exponential growth of data resources. According to McKinsey Global Research Institute, the application of big data can bring 610 billion US dollars of output value every year. Among them, retail and manufacturing, the annual increase in output value can reach 155 billion–325 billion US dollars; in the fields of health care and government services, the annual cost balance will also bring about 285 billion US dollars, indirectly promoting economic growth.

三、英国：顶层规划引领智慧城市建设
3. UK：Top-Level Plan Leading the Construction of Smart City

2013 年，英国伦敦出台《智慧伦敦规划》，旨在"利用先进技术的创造力来服务伦敦并提高伦敦市民生活质量"②。规划提出将人、技术与数据有效整合，以集成、创新的方式解决城市治理问题。一是以人和企业为核心，创建"对话伦敦（Talk London）网上社区"，鼓励和帮助"伦敦人"参与社会治理。二是促进数据整合与共享，构建一站式数据开放平台——"伦敦数据仓库"，实现交通、安全、经济、旅游等跨部门跨行政区数据的整合与共享。三是发展数字技术与人工智能，创设市长出口计划，组织智慧城市领域的中小技术企业参加贸易使团赴海外开拓新市场。四是加强数字技术与城市基础设施的融合，在公共交通系统使用非接触式支付卡（CPCs）提高通行效率，将采集到的数据用于优化交通管理。伦敦智慧城市建设成效显著，在 2018 年"IESE 城市动态

① 赵建. 美国经济复苏之谜：新周期、新能源还是新技术 [J]. 国际金融，2018（11）：26-33.
② 王操，李农. 上海打造卓越全球城市的路径分析：基于国际智慧城市经验的借鉴 [J]. 城市观察，2017（4）：5-23.

指数"排行榜中获评"全球最佳智慧城市"。

In 2013, London issued the "Smart London Plan", aiming to "use the creativity of advanced technology to serve London and improve Londoners' quality of life". The plan proposes to effectively integrate people, technology and data to solve urban governance problems in an integrated and innovative way. The first is to create the online community "Talk London" with people and enterprises as the core to encourage and help "Londoners" to participate in social governance. The second is to promote data integration and shared, build a one-stop open data platform — "London Data Warehouse", and realize the cross-department and cross-region integration and share of data among transportation, safety, economy, tourism, etc. The third is to develop digital technology and artificial intelligence, make the export plan by Mayor of London, and organize small and medium technology enterprises in the smart city to participate in trade missions to open up new markets overseas. Fourth, strengthen the integration of digital technology and urban infrastructure, use contactless payment cards (CPCs) in public transport system to improve traffic efficiency, and use the collected data to optimize traffic management. London has made remarkable achievements in the construction of smart city and was rated as "The Best Smart City in the World" in the "IESE City Dynamic Index" in 2018.

四、加拿大：政企合作开发未来城市和打造数字生活互动场
4. Canada：Cooperation Between Government and Enterprise to Develop Future City and Create Interactive Field of Digital Life

2017 年 10 月，谷歌 Sidewalk Labs 宣称，计划在加拿大多伦多市开发名为 Quayside 的"未来城"，旨在利用创新性乃至具有革新性的方法实现城市更新，解决公共空间不足、可持续发展、交通拥堵等城市问题，打造未来城市平台。一是以论证性为导向的未来城市蓝图设计，推进法规修改与基础设施建设。通过专家咨询、公众反馈等多方论证，以多媒介面向大众公开文件进展与更新，推出总体创新与发展计划。二是

全面布局城市感知系统。通过开发不包含具体器件的框架，注重打造"城市 USB 端口"，方便社区、公共场所等地快速安装感知设备，帮助城市形成为居民、企业服务的全感知网络。三是在城市设计上注重居民体验：通过设计无路边台阶街道，方便行人与自行车汇入；同时将街道与多伦多的轻轨系统相连，实现出行无感连结；通过路边感应器设计，收集相关交通数据，管理多运输方式流量情况，为未来自动驾驶汽车打下基础①。

In October 2017, Google Sidewalk Labs announced that it plans to develop a "future city" named Quayside in Toronto, Canada. It aims to use innovative methods to realize urban renewal, solve urban problems such as insufficient public space, sustainable development and traffic congestion, and build a future urban platform. The first is the blueprint design of the future city oriented by argumentation, revision of laws and regulations and infrastructure construction. Through multi-party argumentation such as expert consultation, public feedback, it declares the progress and update of documents to the public through multi-media and launches the overall innovation and development plan; the second is to comprehensively layout the city perception system. Developing a framework with no specific devices, it focuses on building "urban USB port" to facilitate the rapid installation of sensing devices in communities and public places, and help the city form a full sensing network to serve residents and enterprises. The third is to pay attention to residents' experience in urban design, facilitating the blending of pedestrians and bicycles through the design of no sidewalk street, connecting the streets with the light rail system of Toronto to achieve insensate links, and collecting relevant traffic data to manage the flow of multiple modes of transportation through the design of roadside sensors to lay a foundation for future self-driving cars.

---

① 成都市新经济发展委员会. 把握技术大变革趋势以科技新引领城市转型研究报告 [R]. 2019.

▷▷▷ 第二节　国内先进城市实践

Section Two　Practice of Advanced Cities in China

一、北京："四大动能"助推新经济发展

1. Beijing：Four Drivers Boosting New Economy Development

（一）北京市新经济发展概况

（1）Survey of New Economy Development in Beijing

近几年来，北京市在新发展理念的指引下，大力坚持创新发展，深入贯彻落实《国家创新驱动发展战略纲要》，持续推进经济体制机制改革和政策的先行先试，建设中关村人才管理改革试验区，促进聚焦在新一代信息技术、新材料、新能源等"高精尖"经济领域的发展，充分发挥双创服务平台孵化"硬科技"等项目的作用，在北京加快建设全国科技创新中心、发展新经济、形成新旧动能转换"加速度"方面，取得了一定的成效。

In recent years，under the guidance of the new development concept，Beijing has vigorously adhered to innovative development，thoroughly implemented the "National Innovation-Driven Development Strategy Outline"，continuously promoted the reform of economic system and mechanism and the pilot of policies，built Zhongguancun Talents Management Reform Pilot Zone，promoted the development of "high-end" economic fields focusing on the new generation of information technology，new materials，new energy，etc.，and given full play to the innovation and entrepreneurship service platform to incubate "hard technology". It has made some achievements in accelerating the construction of a national science and technology innovation center，developing the new economy，and forming the "acceleration" of the transformation from old to new growth drivers.

北京市新经济增加值突破万亿元。北京市统计局发布的数据显示，2018 年新经济实现增加值 10 057.4 亿元，破万亿元大关。基于互联网经济规模以上的服务业实现了营业收入 1.4 万亿元。2018 年，北京市新设立的企业中，信息服务业、科技服务业企业占比超过 30%，注册资本达到了 7 311.4 亿元，同比增长 13.5%。此外，北京市的网上零售业发展也取得了优异业绩，限额以上批发零售业网上零售额达到 2 632.9 亿元，比 2017 年增长了 10.3%。有关资料显示，2019 年上半年北京市的新经济增加值比 2018 年增长 8.1%，占北京地区生产总值的 1/3 左右。恒大研究院发布的《2018 年中国独角兽地域分布》显示，北京的独角兽企业已达到 70 多家，约占全国四成，包括今日头条、滴滴出行、京东数科、快手、京东物流等。其中独角兽企业排名前 20 的榜单中北京就占了 9 家。可见，北京市的独角兽企业对新经济的发展有巨大的推动作用。

The added value of Beijing's new economy exceeded one trillion *yuan*. According to the data released by Beijing Municipal Bureau of Statistics, the new economy's added value in 2018 reached 1, 005. 74 billion *yuan*, breaking the trillion *yuan* line. The service industry based on the Internet economy got 1. 4 trillion *yuan* revenue. In 2018, among the newly established enterprises in Beijing, enterprises of information service and technology service accounted for more than 30%, and the registered capital reached 731. 14 billion *yuan*, rising by 13. 5% year on year. In addition, there is an outstanding achievements in the development of online retail industry in Beijing. The online retail volume of wholesale and retail industry above quota reached 263. 29 billion *yuan*, an increase of 10. 3% over 2017. According to relevant data, in the first half of 2019, the added value of Beijing's new economy increased by 8. 1% over 2018, accounting for about one third of Beijing's GDP. According to the "Regional Distribution of Unicorns in China" released by Hengda Research Institute in 2018, there were more than 70 unicorns enterprises in Beijing, accounting for 40% of the country's total, including Tou Tiao, Di Di, JD

Digits, Kwai Shou, JD Logistics, etc. Among them, Beijing accounts for 9 of the top 20 Unicorns. It is obvious that the unicorn enterprises in Beijing have played a major role in promoting the development of the new economy.

（二）北京市"四大动能"助推新经济发展

（2）Four Drivers in Beijing Boosting New Economy Development

动能一：新技术。目前北京有几十家高校、百余家科研院所及 300 多家跨国公司研发中心聚集在中关村，凭借这些资源优势北京市实施了 "1+6""新四条"等诸多先行先试政策，强化中关村的企业在全球科技创新竞争格局中的重要地位，加大产业资金的投入和大力支持国际前沿技术创新成果，为北京市新经济的发展提供了强大的资金保障和技术支撑。此外，人工智能、石墨烯、靶向免疫等技术创新基本与全球水平持平甚至有超越的趋势，可见中关村的新技术引领着中国新技术发展潮流。

Driver One: New Technology. At present, there are dozens of universities, more than 100 scientific research institutes and more than 300 R&D centers of multinational companies in Zhongguancun. With these resource advantages, Beijing has implemented many pilot policies such as "1+6" and "New Four Articles" to Strengthen the Zhongguancun's enterprises's important position in the global competition pattern of scientific and technological innovation, increase the investment of industrial capital and vigorously support the innovative achievements of international cutting-edge technology, and provide a strong financial guarantee and technical support for the development of Beijing's new economy. In addition, the technological innovation of artificial intelligence, graphene, targeted immunity and so on is almost equal to and even tends to surpass the global level. It can be seen that the new technology of Zhongguacun is leading the development trend of new technology in China.

动能二：新模式。为推动新经济的发展，北京市开创了包括众包、众扶、众创、众筹四类新模式。在众包方面，中关村大力支持和培育以小米、百度、京东等为代表的"知识众包""研发众包""O2O 众包"

等众包模式，助推新经济发展。在众扶方面，中关村的制造大街和创业大街将法律、金融、知识产权、人力资源等专业化服务资源充分整合，一些行业的领军者还创办了诸如百度开放云、航天云网、联想之星等 30多家众扶平台。在众创方面，以创新工场、硬蛋等 60 多家创新性孵化器为代表的众创空间在中关村涌现，中关村示范区现有科技型企业24 607 家，占北京市新创办科技型企业总量近 30%，日均创办科技型企业 60 多家，其中有九成以上都是民营企业。在众筹方面，中关村致力于打造一个全球性的股权众筹中心，例如 36 氪、天使汇等一大批股权众筹平台和股权众筹行业组织在这里聚集，为助推新经济的发展提供了极大帮助。

Driver Two: New mode. In order to promote the development of the new economy, Beijing has created four new modes: crowd-packing, crowd-supporting, crowd-making and crowd-funding. In terms of crowd-packing, Zhongguancun strongly supports and cultivates "knowledge crowd packing", "R&D crowd packing", "o2o crowd packing" etc. like Xiaomi, Baidu and JD, to boost the development of new economy. In terms of crowd-supporting, Zhongguancun's manufacturing street and entrepreneurship street fully integrate professional service resources such as law, finance, intellectual property and human resources. Leaders in some industry have also established more than 30 crowd supporting platforms, such as Baidu AI Cloud, CASI Cloud and Legend Star. In terms of crowd-making, more than 60 innovative incubators, such as Sinovation Ventures and IngDan, have sprung up in Zhongguancun. There are 24, 607 enterprises of science and technology in Zhongguancun Demonstration Zone, accounting for nearly 30% of the newly established ones in Beijing. On average, more than 60 enterprises of science and technology are founded every day, of which more than 90% are private enterprises. In terms of crowd-funding, Zhongguancun is committed to building a global equity public-fund center. For example, a large number of equity public-fund platforms and industry organizations gather here, such as 36 Kr and Angel Crunch, helping a lot to boost the development of the new economy.

动能三：新业态。中关村根据自身发展特点致力于打造"高精尖"的经济结构，在我国率先实施了"互联网＋"战略。中关村将商业模式创新、前沿技术研发和科技金融创新相结合不断催生了新业态。互联网出行、智慧医疗、互联网教育等产业发展壮大，催生了滴滴出行、美团等一批上市前估值超过 10 亿美元的"独角兽"企业。中关村大力促进制造业与服务业融合发展，一方面利用制造业服务化的优势，另一方面加快新一代信息技术与制造业深度融合发展。在现代技术的帮助下传统产业得到改造提升，先进制造业快速发展，智能制造成为其发展的主要方向，工业互联网和消费互联网结合演化为产业互联网，新业态作为四类模式的一部分对推动新经济的发展有着重要作用，也对《中国制造2025》起着支撑引领作用。

Driver Three：New forms of business. Zhongguancun is committed to building a "high-end" economic structure according to its own development characteristics and takes the lead in implementing the "Internet Plus" strategy in China. Zhongguancun combines business model innovation, research and development of cutting-edge technology and innovation of science and technology finance, which has continuously spawned new forms of business. With the development of Internet travel, smart health care and Internet education, there emerge a number of "unicorn" enterprises with pre-IPO valuation of more than US ＄ 1 billion, such as DiDi and Meituan. Zhongguancun vigorously promotes the integration of manufacturing and service industry. On one hand, it takes advantages of manufacturing service；on the other hand, it accelerates the deep integration of new generation of information technology and manufacturing industry. With the help of modern technology, traditional industries have been transformed and upgraded. Advanced manufacturing industry has developed rapidly, and intelligent manufacturing has become the main direction. The combination of manufacture Internet and consumer Internet has evolved into industrial Internet. As a part of the four types of modes, new forms play an important role in promoting the development of new economy, and also play a supporting and leading role in "Made in China 2025".

动能四：新金融。新经济的发展离不开新金融，中关村正通过一系列措施来引领新金融的发展潮流。在当下新金融不仅包括互联网金融和金融科技，还包括了为适应目前"双创"需求的天使投资、创业投资、股权私募等。中关村大力营造良好的"双创"氛围和环境，吸引了一大批创新创业人员、投资人员在此创业和投资。有关资料显示，全国有80%的天使投资人都活跃在中关村。同时，中关村的企业通过并购的方式来掌握创新主导权。企业并购的案例约有600多起，并购金额达到2 958.5亿元，并购案例和金额的数量均大幅增长，取得了历史性的突破。同时，中关村还主动顺应互联网金融发展的新要求，寻求监管与创新二者之间的平衡点，努力争取将探索开展行业准入先行先试的风险控制到最小。例如，围绕征信、支付、数据、交易等关键环节，利用人工智能、大数据等新兴技术，搭建互联网金融信用信息、大数据交易、风险控制等服务平台和基础设施，完善互联网金融应用环境，促进行业自律，营造良好的政策环境，发挥新金融对促进新经济发展的积极作用。

Driver Four: New finance. New economy cannot develop without new finance. Zhongguancun is leading the development trend of new finance through a series of measures. At present, new finance not only includes Internet finance and financial technology, but also includes angel investment, venture capital, private equity etc. to meet the current demand of "innovation and entrepreneurship". Zhongguancun has made great efforts to create a good "entrepreneurship and innovation" atmosphere, attracting many innovative entrepreneurs and investors to start businesses and invest here. Data shows that 80% of angel investors in China are active in Zhongguancun. At the same time, the enterprises in Zhongguancun take the leading role of innovation through M & A. There are more than 600 M & A cases, and the amount of money has reached 295.85 billion Yuan. The number of M & A cases has increased significantly as well as the amount of money, making a historic breakthrough. At the same time,

Zhongguancun also actively conforms to the new requirements of the development of Internet finance, seeks the balance between regulation and innovation, and strives to minimize the risk of exploiting and carrying out the pilot industry access. For example, centering on credit investigation, payment, data and transaction, it uses new technologies such as artificial intelligence and big data to build service platforms and infrastructure for Internet financial credit information, big data transaction and risk control, improve the application environment of Internet finance, promote industry self-discipline, create a good policy environment, and give full play to the positive effect of new finance on new economy development.

二、上海："四新"经济之城
2. Shanghai：City of "Four New" Economy

（一）上海市新经济发展的概况

（1）Survey of New Economy Development in Shanghai

早在 2013 年，上海市经信委就提出了新技术、新产业、新业态、新模式的"四新"概念。把上海作为"四新"经济的发展代表城市之一，得益于上海金融、教育、互联网和政策方面的优势，加之上海长年对留学海归人士的强大吸引力，上海创新创造能力强、经济发展的综合能力强。

In 2013, Shanghai Municipal Commission of Economy and Information put forward the "Four New" concept of new technology, new industry, new form and new mode. Shanghai is considered as one of the representative cities of "Four New" economy development, due to its advantages in finance, education, Internet and policy, its charm to overseas returnees over the years, and its strong innovation and creativity and comprehensive capacity in economic development.

近年，上海的"新经济"在"四新"基础上结合经济、金融、航运、贸易、科创中心建设，符合现代化国际大都市要求，反映了自贸区建设成果，突显了融合性、动态变化性、轻资产性、高成长性、需求主导性、基础环境依赖性的特点。2017 年 3 月份，上海市政府出台《关于加快推进本市"四新"经济发展的指导意见》，进一步营造全社会鼓励"四新"经济发展的氛围，各区进一步优化产业结构，积极推动经济高质量发展。例如：长宁区坚持转型，2016—2018 年，长宁智能互联网产业 298 家重点企业完成税收数平均增长 21.2%，集聚包括美团、拼多多等龙头企业在内共 4 491 家企业；航空服务业入驻企业总数达 250 家，包括东航、春秋等 5 家总部型基地航空公司，占上海基地航空公司总数的 60%，152 家行业重点企业完成税收数平均增长 21.1%①。上海重视 5G 技术的发展。2018 年，为探索与激发上海市面向 5G 时代的新经济潜力，上海市政府成立了上海 5G 创新发展联盟。5G 创新发展联盟将作为政府与企业间沟通的桥梁和纽带，坚持创新驱动，以集成优化创新资源配置为核心，以建立健全"产学研用"协同创新机制为手段，汇聚通信相关资源，突出协同配合，加强国际合作，打造贯穿创新链、应用链的新一代信息技术生态系统。预计到 2021 年，上海市 5G 发展将实现"十百千"的目标，聚焦 10 大垂直领域，形成 100 项行业应用标杆，培育 1 000 个创新应用项目；5G 产业将实现"三个千亿"的目标，即5G 制造业、软件和信息服务业、应用产业规模均达到 1 000 亿元。2017年《上海"新经济"指数报告》显示，近年来，上海新经济指数稳步增长，新经济发展速度正逐步进入上升通道，经济转型升级初见成效。该报告从"新投入、新产业、新动能、新发展"这四个维度来衡量新经济②。上海市政府发布的《2018 年上海市国民经济和社会发展统计公报》显示，新兴产业发展良好。2018 年新经济新动能对上海市工业的拉动作用进一步发挥，工业战略性新兴产业完成总产值 10 659.91 亿元，比上年增长 3.8%；其次是新一代信息技术产业完成总产值 3 576.02 亿元，比上年增长 5.8%；然而新材料产业完成总产值 2 559.14 亿元，比上年负增长 1.9%。所以，除新材料制造业外，工业战略性新兴产业各

---

① 舒抒. 长宁：新"2 号线经济"求索新动能 [N]. 解放日报，2019-06-24.
② 张煜. 上海"新经济"发展步入上升通道 [N]. 解放日报，2017-12-18.

行业增速均领先本市工业。

In recent years, Shanghai's " new economy", with the combination of economy, finance, shipping, trade, the construction of science and technology innovation center on the basis of Four News, meets the requirements of modern international metropolis, reflects the achievements in building free trade zone, and highlights the characteristics of integration, dynamic change, light assets, high growth, demand leading, and basic environment dependence. In March 2017, the Shanghai municipal government issued " Guides for Accelerating 'Four New' Economy Development", further creating an atmosphere for the whole society to encourage the "Four New" economy development. All districts further optimize the industrial structure and actively promote high-quality economic development. Take Changning District as an example. It adheres to the transformation. From 2016 to 2018, 298 key enterprises in Changning's intelligent Internet industry completed an average increase of 21.2% in tax revenue, including 4,491 enterprises such as the leading enterprises of Meituan and Pinduoduo. There are 250 enterprises in the aviation service industry, including five headquarters base airlines such as China Eastern Airlines and Spring and Autumn Airlines, accounting for 60% of the total number of Shanghai base airlines, and 152 key enterprises in the industry completed an average increase of 21.1%. Shanghai attaches importance to the development of 5G technology. In 2018, in order to explore and stimulate the new economic potential of Shanghai in the 5G era, Shanghai municipal government established Shanghai 5G innovation and development alliance, which would act as a bridge and link between the government and enterprises, adhering to the driven role of innovation, taking the integration and optimization of innovation resource allocation as the core, establishing and improving the collaborative innovation mechanism of industry, university, research and application, gathering communication-related resources, highlighting collaborative cooperation, strengthening international cooperation, and building a new generation of information technology ecosystem through innovation chain and application chain. It is estimated that by 2021, Shanghai's 5G development will achieve the "Ten Hundred Thousand" goal, focusing on 10 vertical fields, forming 100 industry application benchmarks, and cultivating 1,000 innovative application projects; the 5G industry will achieve the "Three Hundred Billion" goal, that is, the scale of 5G manufacturing industry, software and information service industry, and application industry will reach 100 billion Yuan. According to "Shanghai 'new economy' Index Report" in 2017, Shanghai's new economy index in recent years has grown steadily. The development speed of the new economy is gradually entering the upward channel, and the economic transformation and upgrading have achieved initial results. The report measures the new growth economy from four dimensions of "new investment, new industry, new driver and new development". According to "The Statistical Bulletin of Shanghai's National Economic and Social Development in 2018" issued by Shanghai municipal government, emerging industries are developing well. In 2018, new economy and new growth drivers played a further role in stimulating Shanghai's industry. The total output value of strategic emerging industries was 1,065.991 billion Yuan, up 3.8% over the previous year; the new generation information technology industry made a total output value of 357.602 billion Yuan, up 5.8% over the previous year; however, the total output value of new materials industry was 255.914 billion Yuan, up 1.9% over the previous year. Therefore, in addition to the new material manufacturing industry, the growth rate of strategic emerging industries is ahead of the city's industries.

（二）上海发展新经济的举措

（2）Measures for Shanghai to Develop New Economy

近几年，上海大力推动新技术、新产业、新模式、新业态"四新"经济发展，让新动能逐渐接棒，呈现新经济蓬勃发展、新动能培育加强的态势。上海发展"四新"经济，采取了以下措施：

In recent years, Shanghai has been vigorously promoting the development of "Four New" economy, including new technology, new industry, new mode and new form of business, so the new growth drivers gradually take over, showing a trend of vigorous development of new economy and strengthening cultivation of new growth drivers. Shanghai has taken the following measures to develop the "Four New" economy:

1. 坚持市场在资源配置中的主导作用

1）Adhering to the Leading Role of the Market in Resource Allocation

上海"四新"经济的"新"，不但体现在技术和模式上，更体现在发展路径上。首先一个特征是放弃政府主导。不同于过去某些新兴产业的发展还带有较强的政府主导意志，"四新"经济的发展主要依靠市场需求的力量，并且淡化了产业定位。"四新"经济本身代表着产业相互融合、渗透的趋势，没有一个固定的框框。只有充分留白，允许企业"盲人摸象"，才能实现"八仙过海、各显神通"的效应。例如：钢铁业龙头宝钢集团，近年来就跨界切入互联网领域，玩起了钢铁电商，设立了欧冶云商，在信息服务、物流服务、加工服务等各个方面，全方位满足终端客户需求①。

The "new" is not only embodied in technology and mode, but also reflected in the development pattern. The first feature is to abandon the government's dominance. Unlike the development of some new industries in the past dominated by the government, the development of "Four New" economy mainly depends on the power of market demand. Moreover, it weakens the industrial positioning. The "Four New" economy itself represents the trend of mutual integration and penetration of industries, without a fixed framework. Only by leaving enough space and allowing the blind to feel the elephant, can the effect be realized. For example, in recent years, Baosteel Group, the leader of the iron and steel industry, has entered into the field of Internet, developed iron and steel e-commerce, and set up the Ouyeel cloud business to

① 何欣荣，陆文军. 上海："四新"经济翩翩起舞让新动能逐渐接棒［EB/OL］.（2016-07-13）［2021-02-20］. http://www.xinhuanet.com/politics/2016-07/13/c_1119214017.htm.

meet the needs of end customers in all aspects of information services, logistics services, processing services, etc.

2. 以智能化革命创新驱动经济发展

2) Driving Economy Development with Intelligent Revolution and Innovation

政策先行，推动新一代人工智能发展。中国从 2015 年开始先后颁布了《中国制造 2025》《新一代人工智能发展规划》等重要国家级战略规划，上海市积极响应国家政策部署，于 2019 年发布了《关于本市推动新一代人工智能发展的实施意见》，提出了实施人工智能的战略。上海龙头科技企业通过收购初创企业、成立专门人工智能研究团队，独角兽企业聚焦于人工智能及其应用，人工智能企业吸金能力逐年攀升，且资本更加倾向于后期阶段融资，产业企业发展日益成熟。在国家战略布局、龙头企业聚焦、资本聚集的环境下，上海以其资金、技术、人才等创新资源，在人工智能发展中占有绝对优势，目前上海正在谋求转型打造全球科创中心，人工智能是其核心突破点①。总体来说，上海经济增长对投资依赖较低，创新驱动力较强。要继续深入推进"四新经济"、智能制造、产业创新、工业强基等系列工程，要率先走出制造业高端发展、创新发展、转型发展之路，打造属于上海的人工智能战略。

The earlier formulated policies promote the development of a new generation of artificial intelligence. Since 2015, China has successively promulgated important national strategic plans, such as "Made in China 2025" and "New Generation Artificial Intelligence Development Plan". In response to the national policy, Shanghai issued "Implementation on Promoting the Development of New Generation Artificial Intelligence in Shanghai" in 2019, putting forward the strategy of implementing artificial intelligence. Shanghai's leading science and technology enterprises acquire start-ups and set up special artificial intelligence research teams. Unicorn enterprises focus on artificial

① 陈学海. 人工智能战略解读 把握上海创新发展驱动力 [EB/OL]. (2018-10-11) [2021-01-20]. https://sh.news.anjuke.com/news-480552.html.

intelligence. The profits of these artificial intelligence enterprises are increasing year by year and more capital tends to finance in the later stage, so the industrial enterprises become more and more mature. On the condition of national strategic layout, leading enterprises gathering and capital accumulation, Shanghai has an absolute advantage in the development of artificial intelligence with its innovative resources such as capital, technology and talents. At present, Shanghai is seeking transformation to build a global science and technology innovation center, and artificial intelligence is its core breakthrough point. On the whole, Shanghai's economic growth is less dependent on investment and more driven by innovation. Shanghai should continue to promote the "Four New Economy", intelligent manufacturing, industrial innovation, industrial base etc. Shanghai should take the lead in the developing high-end, innovation and transformation of manufacturing industry, and building an AI strategy belonging to Shanghai.

3. 以大数据金融创新引领新经济发展

3) Leading the Development of New Economy with Big Data Financial Innovation

2019 年，经上海市经济与信息化委员会批准，依托复旦大学建立了公共服务平台——上海大数据金融创新中心。中心将全面服务于上海市国际金融中心的建设，为中国产业的健康良性发展以及金融创新的深化做出贡献。以数据分析驱动金融商贸创新，加强数据资源共享开放。此项举措，聚集了科技产业优势资源，积极响应了习近平总书记在党的十九大报告中所提出的国家战略，与政府企业密切沟通，着力打造"产学研"合作模式①。通过扩大开放聚集全球资源要素，促进创新链与产业链深度融合，发挥资金及创新资源优势，促进共性技术研发取得突破，推动人工智能行业渗透应用场景进一步发展，最终形成具有国际影响力的生态圈和产业链。

---

① 邬迪. 上海大数据金融创新中心在复旦揭牌成立［EB/OL］.（2017-11-03）［2021-01-15］. http://news.eastday.com/eastday/13news/auto/news/china/20171103/u7ai7185959.html.

In 2019, approved by Shanghai Economic and Information Commission, Shanghai Big Data Financial Innovation Center was established — a public service platform relying on Fudan University. The center will fully serve the construction of Shanghai international financial center and contribute to the good development of Chinese industry and the deepening of financial innovation. Data analysis is used to drive financial and trade innovation and data resource shared and opening are strengthened. This measure gathered the advantageous resources of the science and technology industry and responded positively to the national strategy stated in Xi Jinping's report in The 19th National Congress of CPC, to strengthen the communication between government enterprises and focus on building the cooperation mode of industry, University and research. An ecosystem and industrial chain with international influence has formed through expanding the opening up to gather global resource factors, promoting the deep integration of innovation chain and industrial chain, giving full play to the advantages of capital and innovation resources, making breakthrough in technology research and development of commonality, promoting the penetration of artificial intelligence industry into application scenescapes.

4. 培育产业专业孵化器集聚基地

4）Cultivating Industrial Incubator Cluster Base

在新经济、新动能的发展推动下，建设"四新"经济的专业孵化器和产业集聚基地，大力发展市场化、专业化、集成化、网络化的众创空间等新型孵化器及科技创业苗圃等企业创业基地。加强外界投资进入各类"四新"经济孵化培育载体，支持各类创新型孵化器与加速器、大学科技园、创意园等载体合作对接。依托优势产业园区、高校、科研院所、创新型"四新"企业等载体，打造出"四新"企业，重点在上海张江国家自主创新示范区（简称"张江示范区"）的各个分园以及经市政府批准纳入市张江高新技术产业开发区管理委员会管理范围的市级高新技术产业园区。由此进一步提升科技孵化器、加速器作用，打造新载体促进"四新"产业化,加快打造了一批"四新"经济创新集聚区,聚焦"四新"经济重点领域,不断为新经济集聚新动能。

Driven by the development of new economy and new growth driver, it builds professional incubators and industrial agglomeration bases for the "Four New" economy, vigorously develops new incubators such as market-oriented, professional, integrated and networked maker space, and enterprise entrepreneurship bases such as science and technology entrepreneurship nursery. It strengthens external investment in all kinds of "Four New" economic incubation carriers, and supports the cooperation of various innovative incubators with accelerators, university science and technology Parks, creative parks and other carriers. Relying on advantageous industrial parks, universities, scientific research institutes, innovative "Four New" enterprises and other carriers, Shanghai will build "Four New" enterprises, focusing on the sub parks of Shanghai Zhangjiang National Independent Innovation Demonstration Zone (hereinafter referred to as Zhangjiang Demonstration Zone) and the municipal high-tech industrial parks approved by the municipal government and managed by Zhangjiang High-tech Industrial Development Zone Management Committee. Therefore, it has further enhanced the role of science and technology incubators and accelerators, created new carriers to promote the "Four New" industrialization, accelerated the construction of a number of gathering areas with "Four New" economic innovation, focused on the key points of the "Four New" economy, and continuously gathered new growth driver for the new economy.

5. 搭建整合创新资源的公共服务平台

5) Building Public Service Platform with Innovative Resources

上海加大科研基础设施、大型科研仪器向社会开放力度,加强领军企业的创新资源共享。充分发挥本市优质高校科研基础设施、科研院所、实验室等资源优势;对接企业技术转移转化需求,强化技术创新供需对接服务,加强类似于创新创业培训、知识产权交易、标准化专业服务等公共服务平台建设,构建网络化、特色化、专业化的科技创新公共服务支撑体系，充分发挥创新能力突出、资源整合能力强的"四新"领军企业核心作用。着力推进产业联盟协同创新，鼓励企业与高校院所、产业联盟共建研发机构和开展研发合作，建立"产学研用"合作机制；充分发挥产业联盟等社会组织平台作用，促进有效对接。通过搭建开放的互联网信息查询应用平台和专业数据分析系统、加快经济信用体系建设和经济信息资源的开发利用，强化管理，以制度创新促进市场环境优化，逐步构建以信用中介服务机构为主体的市场信用服务体系，为加快培育和发展"四新"经济提供基础保障。

Shanghai has increased the opening of scientific research infrastructure and large-scale scientific research instruments to the public and has strengthened the shared of innovation resources among leading enterprises. It gives full play to the city's high-quality university research infrastructure, research institutes, laboratories and other resource advantages, meets the needs of enterprises' technology transfer and transformation, strengthens the docking service between supply and demand for technological innovation, enhances the construction of public service platforms such as innovation and entrepreneurship training, intellectual property trading, and standardized professional services, and builds a networked, characteristic, and specialized public service support system for scientific and technological innovation, and realize the core role of "Four New" leading enterprises with prominent innovation and strong resource integration ability. Efforts should be made to promote the collaborative innovation of industrial alliance, encourage enterprises to build R&D institutions and carry out R&D cooperation with colleges and universities and industrial alliance, establish the cooperation mechanism of industry university research and application, give full play to the role of industrial alliance and other social organization platforms and promote their effective link. By building an open Internet information query application platform and professional data analysis system, accelerating the construction of economic credit system and the development and utilization of economic information resources, strengthening management, promoting the optimization of market environment with institutional innovation, and gradually building a market credit service system with credit intermediary service agencies as the main body, basic guarantee can be provided for accelerating the cultivation of "Four New" economic development.

三、深圳：新兴产业加速新旧动能转换

3. Shenzhen: New industries Accelerating the Transformation of New and Old Drivers

（一）深圳市新经济发展概况

(1) Survey of New Economy Development in Shenzhen

自 2017 年起，我国经济发展态势由高速走向高质量。在这个背景下，深圳经济的发展方向也聚焦于高质量发展。深圳经济的增长速度名列广东省前列，深圳新旧动能转换速度和经济高质量发展迅速，相关方面专利数量在全国排名前列（国际 PCT 专利申请居国内第一），超越硅谷的专利数量，是新旧动能转换的典型代表之一。

Since 2017, China's economic development has changed from high speed to high quality. In this context, the development direction of Shenzhen's economy also focuses on high-quality development. Shenzhen's economic growth speed ranks in the forefront of Guangdong Province. Shenzhen's new and old driver transferring speed and high-quality economy are developing rapidly. The number of patents in related fields ranks in the forefront of China (the number of international PCT patent applications ranks first in China), more than that in Silicon Valley, which typically represents the transfer of new and old drivers.

深圳的产业发展具有结构合理、体量大，创新能力强等特点。且在互联网、通信、AI、机器人、物联网、生物医药等新产业领域都有世界级的龙头企业，深圳的研发投入占 GDP 的比重达 4.2%。并且，深圳吸引了大量国际知名科技企业入驻，苹果、谷歌、空客、微软、高通、英特尔等知名企业在深圳都成立了研发中心或实验室。深圳主要大力培育发展人工智能、第三代半导体、医疗健康、新材料等创新型产业，重视

创新创业发展。深圳从新旧动能的转换、新动能的激发与培育入手，不仅实现了数字经济、智能经济等新经济的高速发展，也实现了新经济的高质量发展。

The industrial development of Shenzhen is characterized by reasonable structure, large volume and firm innovation. Besides, there are world-class leading enterprises in Internet, communication, AI, robotics, Internet of things, biomedicine and other new industries. Shenzhen's R&D input accounts for 4.2% of GDP. In addition, Shenzhen has attracted a large number of international well-known technology enterprises. Such well-known enterprises as Apple, Google, Airbus, Microsoft, Qualcomm and Intel have set up R&D centers or laboratories in Shenzhen. Shenzhen focuses on the cultivation and development of innovative industries such as artificial intelligence, third-generation semiconductors, health care and new materials, and attaches great importance to the innovation development and entrepreneurship. Starting from the transformation, stimulation and cultivation of new growth drivers, Shenzhen has not only realized the rapid development of new economy such as digital economy and intelligent economy, but also realized the high-quality development of new economy.

深圳市新经济整体发展态势较好，2019 年深圳全年战略性新兴产业增加值合计 10 155.51 亿元，比上年增长 8.8%，占地区生产总值的 37.7%，较 2012 年提高了 7.7 个百分点。通过 PCT（Patent Cooperation Treaty）提交国际专利申请是企业进行海外专利布局的重要途径。数据显示，2019 年深圳 PCT 国际专利申请量达 17 459 件，约占全国申请总量的 30.6%，占广东全省总量的 70.6%，连续 16 年居全国大中城市第一名，其中华为公司以 4 637 件居全球企业第一①。深圳在科技创新上聚焦核心电子器件、高端通用芯片等产业技术关键共性领域，将 155 个项目列入 2019 年技术攻关储备，拟资助资金达 5.9 亿元，深圳计划围

---

① 余思毅. 广东省人民政府参事魏达志：开放型经济时代，深圳"先行"剑指全球［EB/OL］.（2020-08-26）［2021-01-10］. http://www.guba.com/column/266783.html.

绕基因组学、超材料、大数据、石墨烯等前沿领域，补齐基础研究方面的短板和建设高质量创新平台，建设"十大诺奖实验室""十大基础科研机构""十大科技基础设施"。截至 2019 年 6 月，深圳已建成 9 家诺奖实验室。

The development of new economy in Shenzhen is overall good. In 2019, the added value of new strategic industries in Shenzhen totaled 1, 015. 551 billion Yuan, an increase of 8. 8% over the previous year and increase of 7. 7% over 2012, accounting for 37. 7% of the regional GDP. Through PCT (Patent Cooperation Treatment), international patent application is an important way for enterprises to carry out overseas patent layout. Data shows that in 2019, the number of PCT international patent applications in Shenzhen reached 17, 459, accounting for 30. 6% in China and 70. 6% in Guangdong Province, continuously ranking first in large and medium-sized cities in China for 16 years, among which Huawei ranks first in the world with 4, 637 applications. In terms of scientific and technological innovation, Shenzhen focuses on key common areas of industrial technology, such as core electronic devices and high-end general chips, including 155 projects in the technological research reserve in 2019, with a planned funding of 590 million Yuan. Shenzhen plans to make up for the shortcomings in basic research and build a high-quality innovation platform around the frontier fields of genomics, metamaterials, big data, graphene, etc., so as to build a "Top 10 Laboratories for Nobel Prize", "Top 10 Basic Research Institutions" and "Top 10 Science and Technology Infrastructure". By June 2019, nine laboratories for Nobel Prize have eseablished.

（二）深圳发展新经济的举措

（2）Measures for Shenzhen to Develop New Economy

1. 以战略新兴产业为新经济增长"主引擎"

1）Strategic New Industries as "Main Engine" of New Economy Growth

从 2009 年开始，深圳先后颁布实施生物、互联网、新能源、新材料、文化创意、新一代信息技术、节能环保七大战略性新兴产业规划及其配套政策，深圳以七大战略性新兴产业和未来产业为主体的新兴产业为新经济增长的"主引擎"、培育新动能的主要场地。深圳重视培育发展未来产业，落实生命健康、机器人、可穿戴设备和智能装备等未来产业规划和政策，建设新经济发展增长点。正是得益于新兴产业的快速发展，深圳新经济才能在新常态下实现有质量的稳定增长，新旧动能才能被激活并加速转换。

Since 2009, Shenzhen has successively promulgated and implemented plans and supporting policies of seven new strategic industries, including biology, Internet, new energy, new materials, cultural creativity, new generation information technology, energy conservation and environmental protection. Shenzhen takes seven new strategic industries and future industries as the "main engine" of new economic growth and the main site for cultivating new growth driver. Shenzhen attaches great importance to the cultivation and development of future industries, implements plans and policies for future industries such as life and health, robots, wearable devices and intelligent equipment, and builds new economic growth points. Thanks to the rapid development of new industries, Shenzhen's new economy can achieve qualitative and stable growth under the new normal, and the new and old driver can be activated and the transformation can be accelerated.

2. 以消费升级支撑零售新模式

2）Supporting the New Retail Model with Consumption Upgrading

深圳聚焦以消费升级为支撑的新零售业态和以互联网为依托的智慧零售，激发新动能。当前深圳大力支持新零售尤其是智慧零售的发展，支持企业打造多功能、一体化、线上线下相结合的专业消费市场，并鼓励商贸企业应用互联网、物联网、大数据、区块链等新技术去发展新零售项目，对符合条件的市场及项目按实际投资额的20%给予资助，企业每年度资助金额最高可达2 000万元。有关统计资料显示，2019年上半年，深圳22个标杆购物中心共引进30个首店品牌，其中全球首店1家、亚洲首店1家、全国首店4家、华南首店9家、深圳首店15家。

而从业态占比来看，2019 年上半年引进的首店品牌，餐饮类依旧占比最高，共 15 家，占 50%；其次为服饰类，共 5 家，占 17%；此外，如美妆个护、运动休闲、鞋包、童装、服务配套、生活家居、电子数码等均引入 1~2 家首店品牌①。

Shenzhen focuses on new retail forms supported by consumption upgrading and smart retail based on Internet to stimulate new growth driver. At present, Shenzhen strongly supports the development of new retail, especially smart retail, favors enterprises to build a multi-functional, integrated, online and offline professional consumer market, and encourages business enterprises to develop new retail projects by applying new technologies such as Internet, Internet of things, big data, block chain, etc., and gives 20% financial support of the actual investment amount to qualified markets and projects, with the maximum amount of 20 million Yuan every year. Statistics show that in the first half of 2019, thirty brands opened their first stores in 22 benchmark shopping centers in Shenzhen, including 1 global first-store brand, 1 Asian first-store brand, 4 Chinese first-store brands, 9 South-China first-store brands and 15 Shenzhen first-store brands. In terms of the proportion of business types, catering still accounts for the highest proportion of the first-store brands in the first half of 2019, with a total of 15, accounting for 50%, followed by clothing, with a total of 5, accounting for 17%. In addition, 1 or 2 first-store brands are introduced in the fields, such as cosmetics, sports and leisure, shoes and bags, children's clothes, services, furniture, electronic digital, etc.

3. 打造巩固产业供应链核心地位

3) Building and Consolidating the Core Position of Industrial Supply Chain

深圳借助"互联网+"，为生产型制造业提供服务，这种全新的新型业态，不仅破解了诸多发展瓶颈，还创造出全新价值。深圳企业创捷供应链构建出"产业互联网+供应链金融生态圈"的新模式，聚集了大批

---

① 关键. 新零售：激发深圳经济增长新动能 [N]. 深圳商报，2019-08-02 (05).

产业相关的上、中、下游企业，导入手机项目数千个，各类芯片、软件、配套供应商几千家，以及大批制造商和方案设计商，成为行业"黑马"。与深圳资深的供应链产业相比，创捷供应链只是一个例子。目前，中国80%以上的供应链管理公司总部聚集在深圳，供应链企业达1万多家，并且前海"亚太供应链管理中心"的定位，巩固深圳力争成为亚太供应链中心的地位①。

With the help of "Internet plus", Shenzhen has provided services for the production-oriented manufacturing industry. This brand new form not only solves many bottlenecks in development, but also creates new value. The Chuangjie supply chain in Shenzhen has constructed a new mode of "financial ecosystem of industrial Internet plus supply chain", which has gathered large numbers of industries related to upstream, middle and downstream enterprises, and included thousands of mobile phone projects, suppliers for various chips, softwares and other parts, and a large number of manufacturers and designers, and become "unexpected winner" in the industry. Compared with the senior supply chain industry in Shenzhen, Chuangjie supply chain is just an example. At present, more than 80% of China's supply chain management companies have their headquarters in Shenzhen, with more than 10,000 supply chain enterprises. Moreover, Qianhai's positioning as "Asia Pacific Supply Chain Management Center" strengthens Shenzhen's position as an Asia Pacific Supply Chain Center.

---

① 深圳特区报. 新常态新经济新活力 [EB/OL]. (2016-07-31) [2021-01-10]. http://m. people.cn/n4/2016/0731/c1300-7312839.html.

CiNED

第三章
新经济发展带来的挑战与机遇

Chapter Three
Challenges and Opportunities Brought
by Development of New Economy

　　历经改革开放 40 余年的快速发展，中国经济取得了举世瞩目的成就。但随着劳动力等要素资源红利逐步消失，自然资源与环境约束逐渐加大，我国经济面临的中长期动能问题日益凸显。加之美国等先发国家对中国等后发国家的兴起、壮大开始采取各类措施进行打压、制裁，国际贸易形势愈加不利，中国所面临的经济与贸易环境加剧变化。在新的时代背景下，新技术对经济发展和就业的挑战日益扩大和加深。新科技竞争关乎国家和民族的前途命运，世界各国积极抢占全球新科技战略制高点，完善新型基础设施和制度环境，抢抓新型技术国际化标准主动权，大国科技竞争日趋白热化①。

　　After more than 40 years of rapid development of reform and opening up, China's economy has made remarkable achievements. However, with the gradual disappearance of the dividend of labor and other factor resources and the increasing constraints of natural resources and environment, the medium-term and long-term problems about drivers in China's economy is becoming increasingly prominent. In addition, the United States and other early developing countries began to take various measures to suppress and sanction the rise and growth of China and other later developing countries. The international trade situation is becoming more and more unfavorable, and the change of China's economic and trade environment is intensifying. In the new era, the challenge of new technology for economic development and employment is expanding and deepening. The competition of new science and technology is related to a nation's future and destiny. Countries worldwide actively occupy the strategic commanding height of new global strategy on science and technology, improve new infrastructure and institutional environment, seize the initiative of new technology internationalization standards. Therefore the competition of science and technology among big countries is becoming increasingly intense.

---

① 张宇，李艳春．从新动能看中国经济中长期问题：案例与对策 [J]．新经济导刊，2020（3）：42-44.

▷▷▷第一节 新经济发展带来的现实挑战

Section One　Realistic Challenges Brought
by Development of New Economy

一、对传统经济模式及产业带来的挑战

1. Challenges for Traditional Economic Model and Industry

新经济改变了传统经济模式，打乱了传统产业秩序，使各个产业重新分配资源，而传统经济模式具有自身的发展方式和运营模式。随着新经济的发展，尤其是互联网的发展，以新产业、新动能、新模式为代表的新的增长点应运而生，新经济模式和传统经济模式具有明显的不同，使得新经济对传统经济模式产生了巨大冲击与影响。

The new economy has changed the traditional economic model, disrupted traditional industries order, and made various industries redistribute resources. The traditional economic mode has its own mode of development and operation. With the development of the new economy, especially the development of the Internet, new industries, new growth driver and new models have emerged. The new economic model is obviously different from the traditional one, making the new economy have a significant impact on the traditional economic model.

传统企业的品牌、形象等优势的树立需要几年甚至几十年，传统贸易通常会受到各种条件的制约，如时间、空间等，常常也要经历各种复杂的环节。而新经济条件下，更多企业可以利用互联网、大数据、物联网等技术优势树立企业良好的形象与品牌，为客户提供相对于传统企业更优质的服务。不仅如此，新经济的发展，使企业竞争的不确定性大大增加。在传统企业的竞争领域内，通过深入的市场调研，企业可以较为直观地了解竞争对手的发展现状，并对比竞争双方优劣势，进而及时调整自身发展战略。而新经济领域内的市场竞争更为复杂，竞争对手既有来自转型升级后的同行企业，也有跨界融合出现的黑马，仅仅通过市场

调查无法全面了解竞争对手的具体情况。新经济条件下的服务模式被大众所接受，并成为一种主流消费模式，从而极大地冲击了传统企业的服务模式。

It takes several years or even decades for traditional enterprises to establish their brand, image and other advantages. Traditional trade is usually restricted by various conditions, such as time, space, etc, and often has to go through various complicated situations. Under the new economic conditions, more enterprises can make use of the Internet, big data, Internet of things and other technical advantages to establish a good image and brand and provide customers with better services than traditional enterprises. Moreover, the development of new economy has greatly increased the uncertainty of enterprise competition. In the field of competition of traditional enterprises, through in-depth market research, enterprises can more directly understand the development status of competitors and adjust their own development strategy in time by comparing the advantages and disadvantages of competitors. The market competition in the field of new economy is more complex. Competitors are not only from peer enterprises after transformation and upgrading, but also from potential black horses through cross-border integration. So enterprises cannot understand the specific situation of competitors only through market research. The service mode under the new economy is accepted by the public and has become a mainstream consumption mode, which has a great impact on the service mode of traditional enterprises.

二、对行业监管带来的挑战
2. Challenges for Industry Supervision

近年来，作为新经济头部企业的阿里、腾讯、美团，频频陷入滥用市场支配地位的争议漩涡之中，如被商家及用户举报疫情下提高佣金、垄断经营、强制"二选一"、大数据"杀熟"等。尽管相关行政主管部门对上述破坏市场秩序的行为做出了行政处罚，但各平台的无序扩张行为仍未能得到有效抑制，耕植于企业内核的垄断基因仍在敦促其开展各类不正当竞争。从近年来互联网巨头的"野蛮"生长史来看，在带来社会进步、市场活跃、科技发展的同时，巨头们的垄断地位滥用，已经对实体经济的健康发展和中小企业的创新和生存构成了威胁。2020 年 12 月 11 日，中共中央政治局会议提出"要强化反垄断和防止资本无序扩张"。市场监管总局在《关于平台经济领域的反垄断指南（征求意见稿）》中明确规定平台不得要求交易相对人"二选一"，禁止平台通过不合理的搜索降权、下架商品、限制经营、屏蔽店铺、提高服务收费等手段强制平台内经营者接受。

In recent years, some leading enterprises in the new economy like Alibaba, Tencent and Meituan, have frequently fallen into the dispute whirlpool of abusing their dominant position in the market, for example, businesses and users reports their practice of increasing commission under the COVID-19, monopolizing operation, compelling consumers to choose "one out of two" and "making money from acquaintances" by using big data. Although the relevant administrative departments have imposed administrative penalties on acts above-mentioned of disrupting market order, the disorderly expansion of various platforms has not been effectively restrained, and the monopoly gene cultivated in the core of enterprises is still urging them to carry out all kinds of unfair competition. From the "barbaric" growth history of Internet giants in recent years, we can see social progress, active market and technological development, while the giants' abuse of monopoly has posed a particalar threat to the healthy development of the real economy and the innovation and survival of small and medium-sized enterprises. On December 11, 2020, the conference of the Political Bureau of the CPC Central Committee proposed to "strengthen anti-monopoly and prevent disorderly expansion of capital". The State Administration of Market Supervision clearly stipulates in the "Guidelines on Anti-monopoly in the Field of Platform Economy (Draft for Comments)" that the platform shall not require the trading counterpart to "choose one from two" and prohibit the platform from forcing the operators in the platform through unreasonable means such as reduction of searching rights, removing goods from shelves, restricting operation, shielding shops, and increasing service charges.

在前所未有的互联网行业反垄断风暴之下，新经济头部企业亟须重新反思其市场定位及应尽的社会责任。政府加强反垄断监管，不断健全数字规则，将有效推动创新、促进共治，保障各类市场主体平等参与市场竞争，推动整个行业保持创新活力，实现健康发展。

Under the unprecedented anti-monopoly storm in the Internet industry, the leading enterprises in the new economy need to rethink their market positioning and social responsibility. The government strengthens anti-monopoly supervision and continuously improves digital rules , which will effectively promote innovation, enhance co-governance, ensure equal participation of all kinds of market players in market competition, and promote the whole industry to maintain innovation vitality and achieve healthy development.

三、对传统经济统计带来的挑战
3. Challenges for Traditional Economic Statistics

（一）对新经济界定的挑战
(1) Challenges for Definition of New Economy

如果不能准确地界定新经济，就无法准确进行经济统计。关于"新经济"的含义，有很多争议，目前还没有形成一个被国际社会普遍接受的、通用的、统一的基本概念，导致难以准确界定哪些行业或生产活动属于新经济的范围。2016 年，我国国家统计局在总结前期经验的基础上，初步形成了新产业、新业态、新商业模式"三新"统计调查制度，以客观地反映新旧动能转化的情况。该项制度包括了目前新经济所涉及的绝大部分领域，比如高新技术产业、战略性新兴产业、高技术服务业、互联网金融、科技孵化器、众创空间、众筹等，还有城市综合体、各地的开发园区[①]。

If we cannot accurately define new economy, we cannot accurately carry out economic statistics. There are many controversies about the meaning of "new economy". At present, there is no universally accepted, general and unified basic concept in the international community, which makes it difficult to accurately define which industries or production activities belong to the scope of new economy. In 2016, by summing up the previous experience, China National Bureau of Statistics initially formed the "Three New" statistical investigation system of new industries, new form of business and new business models, to objectively reflect the transformation of new and old drivers. The system includes most of new economy fields, such as high-tech industry, new strategic industry, high-tech service industry, Internet finance, technology incubator, public-innovative space, public-funding, etc, as well as urban complexes and development parks.

（二）对统计调查方法的挑战

（2）Challenges for Statistical and Survey Methods

由于新的经济活动不断涌现，就业统计、生产数据等多方面统计工作面临不少新的问题，很多情况统计实践与实际活动相矛盾。以共享经济为例，传统的生产统计以法人单位和个体经营户为主要调查对象，但共享经济，如共享住房、共享汽车、共享车位、共享图书、共享日用品等，参与其中的都不是法人单位或个体经营户，而往往是居民个人，因此传统的生产统计调查方法很难完整地采集到相应的生产数据。

Due to the continuous emergence of new economic activities, there are also problems in employment statistics, production data and other aspects of statistical work. At the same time, many cases of statistical practice and actual activities are contradictory. Take the sharing economy as an example, the traditional production statistics mainly focus on the legal entities and self-employed

---

[①] 国新网. 国家统计局建立"三新"统计调查制度 [EB/OL]. (2016 - 07 - 15) [2021 - 01 - 10]. http://www.scio.gov.cn/xwfbh/xwbfbh/wqfbh/33978/34841/zy34845/Document/1484010/1484010.htm.

households. However, in the sharing economy, such as sharing housing, cars, sharing parking spaces, sharing books, sharing daily necessities and so on, the participants are not legal entities or self-employed households, but often individual residents. Therefore, it is difficult to completely collect the corresponding production data in traditional production statistics.

▷▷▷ 第二节　新经济发展带来的新动能机遇
Section Two　Opportunities of New Growth Drivers Brought by Development of New Economy

2020 年 8 月 24 日，习近平总书记在经济社会领域专家座谈会上提出：我们要坚持供给侧结构性改革这个战略方向，扭住扩大内需这个战略基点，使生产、分配、流通、消费更多依托国内市场，提升供给体系对国内需求的适配性，形成需求牵引供给、供给创造需求的更高水平动态平衡。新经济，涉及新一代信息技术、新兴服务业、网络零售、新材料、新能源、节能环保、生物、高端装备制造、新能源汽车等相关产业。根据中央经济工作会议部署，调整经济结构，转变经济发展方式，创新经济发展模式，成为经济工作的重大任务和重要方向。新经济的发展必将通过充分发挥新兴技术的众多优势，结合国内超大规模市场优势，实现生产、分配、流通、消费更加高效快速循环，从而加快形成以国内大循环为主体、国内国际双循环相互促进的新发展格局。

In August 24, 2020, at the Expert Symposium in Economic and Social Fields, General Secretary Xi Jinping put forward: We must adhere to the strategic direction of supply side structural reform, seize the strategic base of expanding domestic demand, make production, distribution, circulation and consumption rely more on the domestic market, enhance increase the adaptability of the supply system to domestic demand, and form a higher level of dynamic balance for demand-oriented supply and supply-creating demand. New economy involves a new generation of information technology, new service industry, online retail, new materials, new energy, energy conservation and environmental protection, biology, high-end equipment manufacturing, new energy vehicles and other related industries. According to the deployment of the central economic work conference, adjusting the economic structure, changing the mode of economic development and innovating the mode of economic development have become the major task and important direction of economic work. The development of new economy is bound to take full advantages of new technologies and domestic super large-scale market to realize more efficient and rapid circulation of production, distribution, circulation and consumption, to accelerate the formation of a new development pattern with large domestic circulation as the main body and domestic and the double circulation domestically and internationally.

一、新兴信息技术产业发展动能
1. Development Drivers of New Information Technology Industry

信息技术已经成为推动全球产业变革的核心力量，并且不断集聚创新资源与要素，与新业务形态、新商业模式互动融合，快速推动农业、工业和服务业的转型升级和变革。前瞻产业研究院发布的《新一代信息技术产业发展前景预测与投资战略规划分析报告》的统计数据显示，2017 年中国信息消费市场规模已达到 4.5 万亿元，2018 年中国信息消费市场规模已达到 6.3 万亿元，市场整体规模年均增长率约为 15.38%，预计 2022 年将达到 8.6 万亿元。

Information technology has become the core force to promote the global industrial transformation, and constantly gather innovative resources and factors, interact and integrate with new forms of business and new business models, to rapidly promote the transformation, upgrading and reformation of agriculture, industry and service industry. According to the statistics of "Analysis Development Prospect Forecast and Investment Strategy Planning of New Generation Information Technology Industry" released by Qianzhan Industry Research Institute, the scale of China's information consumption market reached 4. 5 trillion Yuan in 2017, 6. 3 trillion Yuan in 2018, and the average annual growth rate of the overall market scale is about 15. 38%, which expected to reach 8. 6 trillion Yuan in 2022.

当前，新兴信息技术正成为驱动我国经济发展的重要力量。云计算、大数据、人工智能、物联网、移动互联网等新兴信息技术的发展，正加速推进产业分工细化和经济结构调整，重塑经济竞争格局。新兴信息技术产业发展主要表现如下。

At present, new information technology is becoming an important driving force for China's economic development. The development of cloud computing, big data, artificial intelligence, Internet of things, mobile Internet and other new information technologies is accelerating the refinement of industrial division and the adjustment of economic structure, reshaping the economic competition pattern. The development of new information technology industry is mainly manifested in the following aspects.

软件产业发展势头迅猛。软件和信息技术服务业处于高速发展的成长期，进入 21 世纪以来，中国软件和信息技术服务业取得了明显进步，目前正处于高速发展的成长期。经初步统计，2018 年全国软件和信息技术服务业规模以上企业 3.78 万家，软件产业实现业务收入 6.3 万亿元，同比增长 14.2%；各地区在软件企业数量、软件人才数量等方面也都取得了快速增长，软件产业高质量发展成效初显。初步统计，2018 年软件和信息技术服务业实现利润总额 8 079 亿元，同比增长 9.7%。2019 年，我国软件业市场业务收入近 68 000 亿元，市场规模也进一步扩大。根据 2018 年工业和信息化部和国家发展和改革委员会发布的《扩大和升级信息消费三年行动计划（2018—2020 年）》，2020 年，我国信息消费规模将达 6 万亿元，年均增长 11%以上，信息技术拉动相关领域产出达到 15 万亿元①。

---

① 中商产业研究院. 2019 年中国软件业市场现状分析及发展趋势预测［EB/OL］. (2019-06-17) ［2021-01-08］. https://www.askci.com/news/chanye/20190617/1005091147772.shtml.

The software industry develops rapidly. Software and information technology service industry is in the growth period of rapid development. Since entering the 21st century, China's software and information technology service industry has made significant progress and is now in the growth period of rapid development. According to preliminary statistics, in 2018 there were 37,800 Enterprises above designated size in the software and information technology service industry in China, and the software industry achieved a business income of 6.3 trillion Yuan, a year-on-year increase of 14.2%; the number of software enterprises and software talents in various regions also achieved rapid growth, and the high-quality development of the software industry has achieved initial results. According to preliminary statistics, in 2018 the total profit of software and information technology service industry was 807.9 billion Yuan, with a year-on-year growth of 9.7%. In 2019, the market revenue of China's software industry will be nearly 6,800 billion Yuan, and the market scale will expand again. According to the "Three-year Action Plan for Expanding and Upgrading Information Consumption (2018—2020)" issued by Ministry of Industry and Information Technology and National Development and Reform Commission in 2018, China's information consumption scale will reach 6 trillion Yuan by 2020, with an average annual growth of more than 11%, and the output of related fields driven by information technology will reach 15 trillion Yuan.

"多网融合"趋势愈发明显。"三网融合"从广义上来讲就是电信网、计算机网和有线电视网三大网的物理合一，其主要表现为技术上趋于一致，使用统一的 IP 协议，在网络层面上实现互联互通，实现高层业务应用的融合。而"四网融合"，是在现有"三网融合"的基础上加入电网。目前，国家电网已经和中国联通、中国移动、中国电信等运营商合作，推出各项服务，包括无线电力抄表、路灯控制、设备监控、负荷管理、智能巡检、移动信息化管理。

The trend of "Multi-network Integration" is more and more prominent.

"Three Network Integration" is the physical integration of telecommunication network, computer network and cable TV network. It is mainly manifested in the convergence of technology, the use of unified IP protocol, the realization of interconnection at the network level and the integration of high-level business applications. The "Four Network Integration" is to join the power grid on the basis of the existing "Three Network Integration". At present, State Grid has cooperated with China Unicom, China Mobile, China Telecom and other operators to launch various services, including wireless power meter reading, street lamp control, equipment monitoring, load management, intelligent inspection and mobile information management.

二、新兴服务业发展动能
2. Development Drivers of New Service Industry

新兴服务业是新的经济形态。近年来，我国服务业占比加速提升，引擎作用凸显；服务业投资较快增长，成为带动投资的主动力；服务业创业持续活跃，成为新增企业的主力军；服务业就业人数增加，成为吸纳城乡居民就业的主渠道；服务业税收快速增加，对财税增长贡献显著。2019 年，服务业增加值为 53.42 万亿元，比上年增长 6.9%。未来五年服务业在国民经济中的比重还将继续上升，预计 2023 年将达到 65.67 万亿元。服务业的发展趋势表现为以下突出特征。

The emerging service industry is a new economic form. In recent years, the proportion of China's service industry has accelerated and its role as an engine has become prominent; the investment in service industry has increased rapidly, which has become the driving force of investment; the entrepreneurship in service industry has continued to be active, which has become the main force of new enterprises; the number of employment in service industry has increased, which has become the main channel for the employment of urban and rural residents; the tax revenue in service industry has increased rapidly, which has made a significant contribution to the growth of finance and taxation. In 2019, the added value of the service industry is 53. 42 trillien billion Yuan, an increase of 6. 9% over the previous year. In the next five years, the proportion of service industry in the national economy will continue to rise, and it is expected to reach 65. 67 trillion Yuan in 2023. The following aspects characterized the development trend of the service industry.

由处处对抗转向合作共赢。近年来，传统企业与新兴互联网企业进入了焦灼的"对抗期"，尤其是电商对实体零售行业的冲击，互联网金融和传统银行的博弈也较为激烈。然而，近期的一系列事件表明，传统业态与新兴业态，正在不约而同地走向一种积极的联合，甚至是融合。应该看到，在变革的阵痛过后，几乎每一个实体零售企业都在努力"触网"，打造线上平台，并与互联网巨头、电商巨头展开合作。更值得注意的是，电商巨头们也在向传统零售业中的优质资源靠拢，积极向线下拓展。传统零售业在大数据、智能物流和智能生产的推动下，迎来了"新零售"的新局面①。

From confrontation to win-win cooperation. In recent years, traditional enterprises and emerging Internet enterprises have entered an anxious "confrontation period", especially shown in the impact of e-commerce on the physical retail industry, the fierce game between Internet Finance and traditional banks. However, a series of recent events show that traditional and emerging formats are moving towards a positive combination or even integration. It should be noted that after the pain of reforming, almost every entity retail enterprise is trying to "Touch the Internet", build an online platform, and cooperate with Internet giants and e-commerce giants. What's more, the e-commerce giants are also moving closer to the high-quality resources of the traditional retail industry and actively expanding their offline business. Driven by big data, intelligent logistics and intelligent production, the traditional retail industry has ushered in a new situation of "New Retail".

---

① 高蕊. 服务业企业发展新趋势值得关注［N］. 经济日报，2018-04-12（02）.

由单一点对点功能转向复合平台功能。当前，很多传统服务业大企业都以自有服务和特定服务群体为基础，从封闭的企业组织转变为开放的平台，并积极在产业链领域"攻城略地"，构建具有企业特色的平台生态圈。比如，苏宁易购就致力于成为连接供应商和客户的桥梁，通过系统化的服务和资源的集成，打造多产业布局、线上线下共融、从商品展示到物流再到金融服务全过程的智慧零售服务平台①。

From single point-to-point to composite platform function. At present, many large enterprises in traditional service industry are based on their own services and specific service groups, transforming from closed enterprise organizations to open platforms and actively "occupying the land" in the field of industrial chain to build a platform ecosystem with their own characteristics. For example, Suning E-buy is committed to becoming a bridge between suppliers and customers. Through systematic service and resource integration, it creates a smart retail service platform with a multi-industry layout, online and offline integration, and the whole process from commodity display to logistics to financial services.

由跟随者转向引领者。服务业企业大都分离于制造业，并随着制造业的繁荣、更多服务需求的产生逐渐发展。近年来，"互联网+"对经济生活各领域影响深远，产业互联已成气候。"科技+""金融+""物流仓储+""大数据+"等新业态，重塑了服务业企业的商业模式，以资本为纽带、以数据为要素的服务业企业正走向"大联合""大融通"。在此背景下，企业之间的关系正从供求关系、合作伙伴等传统的上下游关系，转变为"引领平台"和"被引领者"的服务关系。服务业企业成为连接着生产端和消费端的"中央处理器"，并在更高的维度上打通行业壁垒、重塑产业格局。

Change from followers to leaders. Most of the service enterprises are separated from the manufacturing industry. With the prosperity of the manufacturing

---

① 高蕊. 中国服务业大企业成长五大趋势［J］. 中国经济报告，2017（9）：72-76.

industry, more service demand gradually emerges and develops. In recent years, Internet plus has a far-reaching impact on all economic life fields, and industrial Internet has become a trend. New form of business such as "science and technology plus", "finance plus", "logistics and warehousing plus", "big data plus" have reshaped the business model of service enterprises. The service enterprises with capital as the link and data as the factor are moving towards "great union" and "great integration". In this context, the relationship between enterprises is changing from the traditional upstream and downstream relationships such as supply and demand, partnership to the service relationship of "leading" and "being led". Service enterprises become the "central processor" connecting production and consumption, further breaking through the industry barriers and reshaping the industrial pattern.

三、新兴网络零售业发展动能
3. Development Drivers of New Online Retail Industry

在经济增速放缓、消费者需求升级、新技术开始广泛应用的形势下，网上零售已屡创纪录，成为新的经济增长点。国家统计局公布的数据显示，2019 年，社会消费品零售总额 411 649 亿元，比上年名义增长 8.0%。其中，全国网上零售额 106 324 亿元，比上年增长 16.5%。其中，实物商品网上零售额 85 239 亿元，增长 19.5%，占社会消费品零售总额的比重为 20.7%；在实物商品网上零售额中，吃、穿、用类商品分别增长 30.9%、15.4% 和 19.8%。随着市场竞争的升级和新技术的应用，消费升级显现，线上购物的崛起，也开始倒逼传统消费渠道进行服务和品质的升级。国内的消费结构目前正在发生积极的变化，逐渐向多元化、品质化、个性化的方向发展。其具体表现为：

Under the situation of slowing-down economic growth, upgrading consumer demand and wide application of new technologies, online retail has repeatedly set records and become a new economic growth point. According to the data released by National Bureau of Statistics, the total retail sales of social consumer goods reached 41,164.9 billion Yuan in 2019, an increase of 8.0% over the previous year. The national online retail sales reached 10,632.4 billion Yuan, an increase of 16.5% over the previous year. The online retail sales of goods amounted to 8,523.9 billion Yuan, rising by 19.5%, accounting for 20.7% of the total retail sales of social consumer goods, among which the sales of goods to eat, wear and use increased by 30.9%, 15.4% and 19.8% respectively. With the upgrading of market competition and the application of new technologies, consumption upgrading appears, and the rise of online shopping also forces traditional consumption channels to upgrade service and quality. At present, the domestic consumption structure is undergoing positive changes, and is gradually developing in the direction of diversification, quality and personalization. The specific performance is as follows:

线上线下相互嵌入。"新零售"背景下的线上线下融合区别于电商与实体零售对立时期的O2O。目前，"新零售"正处于O2O发展的窗口期，发展趋势以数据为核心，以先进技术为支撑，实现线上线下资源全面整合，多业态叠加，全链条打通，如盒马鲜生的"线上+线下、餐饮+商品、标品+非标品"综合零售形态。

Online and offline are embedded in each other. The online and offline integration under the background of "New Retail" is different from O2O in the period of opposition between e-commerce and physical retail. At present, "new retail" is in the window period of O2O development, with data as the core and advanced technology as the support, to realize the comprehensive integration of resources online and offline, the superposition of multiple formats and the connection of the whole chain, such as Hema's comprehensive retail form of "Online plus offline, catering plus commodity, standard plus non-standard".

线上线下物流同步跟进。线上线下深度配合是"新零售"的核心，两者与物流的同频共振是"新零售"发展的保障，以阿里、京东、苏宁等为代表的"新零售"主导企业实质上也在围绕两个关键方面进行布局。就采取的形式而言，线上线下协同，或布局线下实体企业，或链通实体企业业务，或开设多业态的自营实体；两者与物流的协同，或扩充自营物流网络，提高物流智能化、自动化水平，利用数据技术赋能物流，或搭建物流网络支点，软硬结合整合社会物流资源①。

Logistics follow up simultaneously online and offline. The deep cooperation between online and offline is the core of "New Retail", and the resonance between the two and logistics is the guarantee for the development of "New Retail". The leading enterprises of "New Retail" represented by Ali, JD and Suning are also laid out around the two key aspects. The forms includes online and offline collaboration, layout of offline physical enterprises, chain connection of physical business, establishment of self-operated entities with multi-forms, collaboration among online, offline and logistics or expansion of self-operated logistics network to improves the level of logistics intelligence and automation, empowerment of logistics with or data technology construction of logistics network branches to integrate social logistics resources.

---

① 韩彩珍，王宝义. "新零售"的研究现状及趋势 [J]. 中国流通经济，2018（12）：20－30.

CiNED

第四章
新经济发展的成都理念与方案

Chapter Four
Concept and Plan of New Economy
Development in Chengdu

随着新一轮信息技术革命的深化，新产业、新商业模式、新产品如雨后春笋般地涌现，尤其在我国经济由高速增长阶段转向高质量发展阶段，抢抓新技术带来的变革机遇、促进经济高质量发展尤为重要。2016年3月，成都应时而谋、顺势而为，将发展新经济首次写入政府工作报告，新经济发展思路及路径逐步清晰并日臻完善，如图4-1所示。当前，成都新经济呈现出高速增长、迅猛崛起的蓬勃势头。2017年以来，成都新经济从量到质实现全方位突破，新经济企业从24.6万家增至43.3万家，独角兽企业从0家增加到7家，新经济总量指数居全国第二、新职业人群规模居全国第三。新冠疫情前经济增速连续12个季度保持8%左右，疫情下成为全国复工复产复市最快、秩序活力恢复最好的城市之一，2020年第一季度GDP回落幅度在7座新一线城市中最低，表现出强大的经济韧性。

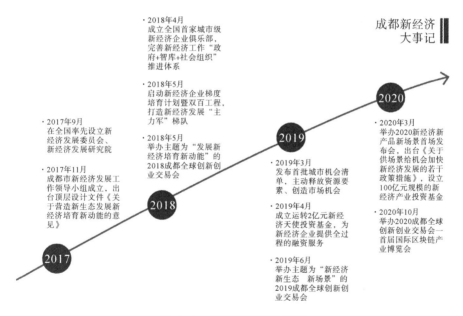

图4-1　成都新经济大事记

Figure 4-1　Events of New Economic Development in Chengdu

With the deepening of a new round of information technology revolution, new industries, new business models and new products are springing up. Especially in the stage of China's economy from high-speed growth to high-quality development, it is particularly important to seize the opportunity of change brought by new technology and promote high-quality economic development. In March 2016, Chengdu took the opportunity to develop the new economy and wrote it into the government work report for the first time. The new economy development paths are gradually clear and improving, as shown in Figure 4-1. At present, Chengdu's new economy is showing a vigorous impetus of rapid growth and rise. Since 2017, Chengdu's new economy has achieved an all-round breakthrough from quantity to quality. The number of new economy enterprises has increased from 246,000 to 433,000, and the number of Unicorn enterprises has increased from 0 to 7. The new economic aggregate index ranks second in China, and the scale of the new professional population ranks third in China. Before the outbreak of COVID-19, Chengdu's economic growth rate remained about 8% in the 12 quarters continuously. During the pandemic, Chengdu has become one of the cities with the fastest recovery of work, production and market, and the best recovery of order and vitality. The first quarter of 2020 had the lowest GDP decline rate among the seven new first-tier cities, showing strong economic resilience.

为加强对新经济发展工作的组织领导，建立完善部门协同、区（市）县联动的工作机制，成立了由市长挂帅、38 个市级相关部门和 22 个区（市）县参与的成都市新经济发展工作领导小组。为大力发展和培育新经济，加快形成以制度创新推动新经济加速发展的工作格局，在全国率先成立了协调服务新经济发展的专门机构——成都市新经济发展委员会，统筹推进新经济发展相关工作。成立了成都新经济发展研究院，搭建包括共享经济在内的新经济发展研究智库，为成都市新经济发展提供态势感知、趋势预测、政策设计、决策判断、平台运营、对外合作、生态建设等方面的服务和支撑。

To strengthen the organization and leadership of the new economic development, Chengdu has established and improved the working collaboration between department and district (city) or county and established a leading group of Chengdu new economy development headed by the mayor and participated by 38 municipal departments and 22 districts (city) or counties. In order to vigorously develop and cultivate new economy and form the work pattern of promoting the development of the new economy through institutional innovation, Chengdu New Economy Development Committee, the first specialized agency in China to coordinate and serve the development of the new economy, was established to coordinate and promote the work related to the development of the new economy. Chengdu New Economy Development Research Institute was established to build a new economic development research think tank including shared economy, providing services and support for Chengdu's new economic development in the aspects of situation awareness, trend prediction, policy design, decision-making, platform operation, foreign cooperation and ecological construction.

2017 年 9 月，成都在全国率先设立新经济发展委员会、新经济发展研究院。

In September 2017, Chengdu took the lead in setting up the committee and the research institute of new economy development.

2017 年 11 月，成都市新经济发展工作领导小组成立，出台顶层设计文件《关于营造新生态发展新经济培育新动能的意见》。

In November 2017, the leading group for new economy development in Chengdu was established, and the top-level design document "Opinions on Creating New Ecology, Developing New Economy and Cultivating New Growth Driver" was issued.

2018 年 4 月，成都成立全国首家城市级新经济企业俱乐部，完善新经济工作"政府+智库+社会组织"推进体系。

In April 2018, Chengdu established China's first city-level new economy enterprise club to improve the "government + think tank + social organization" promotion system of new economy work.

2018 年 5 月，成都启动新经济企业梯度培育计划暨双百工程，打造新经济发展"主力军"梯队。

In May 2018, the new economy enterprise gradient mechanism and cultivation plan（or double hundred project）were launched to build the "main force" of new economy development.

2018 年 5 月，成都举办主题为"发展新经济培育新动能"的 2018 成都全球创新创业交易会。

In May 2018, Chengdu Global Innovation and Entrepreneurship Fair was held with the theme of "Developing New Economy and Cultivating New Growth Driver".

2019 年 3 月，成都发布首批城市机会清单，主动释放资源要素，创造市场机会。

In March 2019, Chengdu issued the first list of urban opportunities t to actively release resource factors and create market opportunities.

2019 年 4 月，成都成立运转 2 亿元新经济天使投资基金，为新经济企业提供全过程的融资服务。

In April 2019, the new economy angel investment fund of 200 million Yuan was set up to provide the whole process of financing services for new economy enterprises.

2019 年 6 月，成都举办主题为"新经济新生态新场景"的 2019 成都全球创新创业交易会。

In June 2019, Chengdu Global Innovation and Entrepreneurship Fair was held with the theme of "New Economy, New Ecology and New Scenescapes".

2020 年 3 月，成都举办 2020 新经济新产品新场景首场发布会，出台《关于供场景给机会加快新经济发展的若干政策措施》，设立 100 亿元规模的新经济产业投资基金。

In March 2020, Chengdu held the first press conference of new economy, new product and new scenescapes. "Policies and Measures on Providing Scenescapes and Opportunities for New Economy Development" was issued, and a new economy industry investment fund of 10 billion Yuan was set up.

2020 年 10 月，成都举办 2020 成都全球创新创业交易会，即首届国际区块链产业博览会。

In October 2020, Chengdu Global Innovation and Entrepreneurship Fair was held, namely First International Block Chain Industry Expo.

▷▷▷第一节　新经济发展的成都理念
Section One　Concept of New Economy Development in Chengdu

新经济作为一项开创性工作，成都积极探索、大胆创新，创造性开展工作，初步形成了一套新经济发展的理念。

Thinking new economy as a pioneering work, Chengdu has actively explored, boldly innovated and creatively carried out its work, initially forming a set of new economic development concepts.

一、一个定义
1. One Definition

新经济不仅仅是一种经济现象，也不完全是一种技术现象，而是一种由技术到经济的演进范式、虚拟经济到实体经济的生成连接、资本与技术深度黏合、科技创新与制度创新相互作用的经济形态①。当前，在全球新一轮科技革命与产业变革的历史性机遇下，新技术、新业态、新模式层出不穷，新经济催生新动能不断积聚。创新驱动发展有两条重要路径：一方面是推动传统产业转型升级，实现新旧动能、增长动力接续转换；另一方面是发展新经济、培育新动能，打造高质量发展新引擎。因此，新经济不仅包括战略性新兴产业、也包括传统产业的转型升级，是以科技为根本动力，数据为核心要素，互联网为主要支撑的数字化平台经济。

---

① 范锐平. 学习新思想发展新经济加快建设新时代现代化经济体系［EB/OL］.（2017-12-03）［2021-01-10］. http://www.qstheory.cn/llqikan/2017-12/03/c_1122049256.htm.

The new economy is not only an economic phenomenon, but also a technological phenomenon. It is an economic form with the evolution paradigm from technology to economy, the generation and connection from virtual economy to real economy, the deep adhesion between capital and technology, and the interaction between scientific and technological innovation and institutional innovation. At present, under the historic opportunity of a new round of global scientific and technological revolution and industrial change, new technologies, new forms of business and new models emerge endlessly, and the new economy promotes the accumulation of new growth drivers. There are two important paths for innovation-driven development. One is to promote the transformation and upgrading of traditional industries and realize the continuous transformation of new and old drivers and growth forces. The other is to develop new economy, cultivate new growth drivers and create a new engine of high-quality development. Therefore, the new economy includes not only strategic emerging industries, but also the transformation and upgrading of traditional industries. It is a digital platform economy with science and technology as the fundamental driving force, data as the core factor, and Internet as the main support.

二、二维世界
2. Two-Dimensional World

新经济既包括线下的物理世界，也包括线上的虚拟世界。新经济的发展让人们实现了从互联网的线下向线上迁徙，扩展了发展空间，也实现了从物理世界向数字世界的迈进，提高了认知的维度。

The new economy includes both the physical world offline and the virtual world online. The development of new economy makes people migrate from offline to online, expanding the development space. It brings about advances from the physical world to the digital world, improving the cognitive dimension.

三、三个转变

3. Three Changes

一是从"政府配菜"向"企业点菜"转变。在政策制定中要突出"用户思维"，让企业家参与政策制定；要注重精准匹配，聚焦新经济企业全生命周期，建立新经济企业梯度培育机制；要强化政策落实，让企业有实实在在的获得感。二是从"给优惠"向"给机会"转变。一方面要在出现新的应用市场后，以包容的态度管理、服务新生业态，允许新经济企业创新尝试、允许试错纠错；另一方面要以整体场景思维整合公共资源要素，主动释放城市机会、培育新兴产业，为新经济企业提供发展机会和接入端口。三是从"个别服务"向"生态营造"转变。要推动政府管理向政府治理转变，推进包容审慎监管体制改革，深化"放管服"改革，持续优化营商环境。

First, the change from "government allocating dishes" to "enterprise ordering dishes". Policy-making should consider "users' thought" and entrepreneurs' participation, attach importance to accurate matching and focus on the whole life cycle of new economy enterprises to establish gradient cultivation mechanism of new economy enterprises, strengthen the implementation of policies so that enterprises have a real sense of acquisition. Second, the change from "giving preferential treatment" to "giving opportunity". On one hand, after the emergence of new application market, manage and serve new forms of business with an inclusive attitude and allow new economy enterprises to innovate and to make and correct mistakes; on the other hand, integrate public resource factors with overall scenescape thinking, actively release urban opportunities, cultivate emerging industries, and provide development opportunities and access ports for new economy enterprises. Third, the change from "individual service" to "ecological construction". It is necessary to promote the change from government's governance to management, promote the reform of inclusive and prudent supervision system, deepen the reform of "deregulation, supervision and service", and continuously optimize the business environment.

四、四个特征
4. Four Features

新经济具有四个明显的特征，一是聚合共享。随着互联网技术发展和普及，海量分散的各类资源通过网络聚合起来，促进信息流、资金流、物流、人流重新聚合和供需双方高效配置，打破了工业社会崇尚资源与财富占有的理念，更加注重最佳体验与物尽其用。二是跨界融合。新一代信息技术快速发展，颠覆了产业组织方式和企业商业模式，推动价值链上下游的分工转变为价值网络上的交互与协同、产业内部的精耕细作转变为跨界的组合式创新，以技术应用、模式创新为内核的跨界融合成为显著特征。三是快速迭代。新一轮科技革命和产业变革带来颠覆式技术创新，互联网思维、技术、产品、模式等变革升级时间远远短于传播普及时间，快速迭代倒逼产业更加专精、更加开放、更加主动高效适应，否则就顾此失彼、被动应对。四是高速增长。技术创新推动新技术、新产品、新业态、新模式爆发式井喷，促进新经济指数型增长。企业不再是缓慢由小变大，而是跃迁式快速成长，在独角兽群体中 3～5 年就会成长出现一个引领世界的企业。

The new economy has four obvious features: The first is aggregation and sharing. With the development and popularization of Internet technology, a large number of scattered resources are aggregated through the network to promote the re-aggregation of information flow, capital flow, logistics and people flow and the efficient allocation of supply and demand, breaking the concept of advocating resources and wealth possession in industrial society, and paying more attention to the best experience and making the best use of things. The second is cross-border integration. The rapid development of the new-generation information technology has subverted the mode of industrial organization and enterprise business model, promoted the labor division in the upstream and downstream of the value chain to change into interaction and collaboration in the value network, and transformed intensive cultivation within the industry into cross-border combinatorial innovation. The cross-border integration with technology application and model innovation as the core has become a prominent feature. The third is speeding up iteration. A new round of scientific and technological revolution and industrial change has brought about disruptive technological innovation. The transformation and upgrading time of Internet thinking, technology, products and mode is far shorter than the time of communication and popularization. Rapid iteration forces us to be more specialized, open, active and efficient to adapt, otherwise economy will lose the other and respond passively. Fourth, rapid growth. Technological innovation promotes the explosion of new technologies, new products, new form of businesses and new models, and promotes the exponential growth of the new economy. Enterprises no longer proliferate from small to large but grow rapidly by leaps and bounds. In the unicorn group, a world-leading enterprise will grow in 3−5 years.

五、五条路径
5. Five Paths

一是坚持以新技术为驱动，聚焦前沿技术，打破转化壁垒，让科技成果尽快转化为现实生产力。二是坚持以新组织为主体，推动各类创新组织、创新企业迅速成长，培育扶持一批独角兽企业，聚集一批新经济领域高端领军人才。三是坚持以新产业为支撑，顺应新产业发展趋势，推动工艺流程、产业场景、创意设计和生产要素组合再造，大力发展高新技术产业，打造一批新经济聚集区。四是坚持以新业态为引擎，推动信息技术与工业化、城镇化、农业现代化加速融合，建立"互联网＋"创新联盟，大力发展互联网金融、精准医疗、互联网教育、IP经济等新业态。五是坚持以新模式为突破口，加速发展平台服务模式，创新发展共享服务模式，积极引入共享经济企业在蓉设立分支机构。"五新"之中，新经济因新技术而衍生，是基础、是驱动力量，具体表现为新技术、新组织、新产业、新业态、新模式，"五新"共同构成集成、协调、系统的新经济发展路径。

First, persist in taking new technology as the driving force, focus on cutting-edge technology, break down transformation barriers, and transform scientific and technological achievements into real productive forces as soon as possible. Second, adhere to the new organization as the main body, promote the rapid growth of various innovative organizations and enterprises, cultivate and support a number of Unicorn enterprises, and gather a number of high-end leading talents in the field of new economy. Third, adhere to the support of new industries, conform to the development trend of new industries, promote the combination and reconstruction of technological process, industrial scenescapes, creative design and production factors, vigorously develop high-tech industries, and create a number of new economy communities. Fourth, adhere to the new form of business as the engine, accelerate the integration of information technology with industrialization, urbanization and agricultural modernization, establish an "Internet plus" innovation alliance, and vigorously develop new form of business such as Internet finance, precision medicine, Internet education, IP economy and so on. Fifth, adhere to the new mode as a breakthrough, accelerate the development of platform service mode, innovate and develop the shared service mode, and actively introduce shared economy enterprises to set up branches in Chengdu. Among the "Five New", the new economy derived from new technology, which is the basis and driving force. It is embodied in new technology, new organization, new industry, new form of business and new mode. The "Five New" constitutes an integrated, coordinated and systematic new economic development path.

六、六大形态

6. Six Formats

重点发展数字经济、智能经济、绿色经济、创意经济、流量经济、共享经济，着力构建具有全球竞争力和区域带动力的新经济产业体系。

Importance should be attached to the development of digital economy, intelligent economy, green economy, creative economy, flow economy and shared economy, to build a new economic and industrial system with global competitiveness and regional driving force.

七、七大应用场景
7. Seven Application Scenescapes

重点提升服务实体经济能力、推进智慧城市建设、推进科技创新创业、推进人力资本协同、推进消费提档升级、推进绿色低碳发展、推进现代供应链创新应用，着力培育新经济发展的市场沃土。

Focus on improving the ability to serve the real economy. Promote the construction of smart city, scientific and technological innovation and entrepreneurship, the coordination of human capital, consumption upgrading, green and low-carbon development, and the innovative application of modern supply chain, and strive to cultivate a fertile market for new economy development.

▷▷▷第二节　新经济发展的成都方案
Section Two　Plan of New Economy Development in Chengdu

一、实施新经济企业梯度培育计划，打造新经济发展"爆发点"
1. Implement the Gradient Cultivation Plan of New Economy Enterprises and Create the "Hot Points" of New Economy Development

聚焦新经济企业全生命周期，针对各个成长阶段的"痛点"，建立新经济企业梯度培育机制，助力新经济重点企业快速成长。一是因企施策梯度培育企业。针对种子企业资金缺乏、竞争力弱等痛点，建立健全以政府股权投资为引导、社会资本为主体的初创投资筹集机制，用好用活 2 亿元的天使投资基金，助力企业跨越"创业死亡谷"；针对准独角兽企业亟须提升行业显示度和知名度的痛点，采取区域性准独角兽榜单推介、主题会议推介、点对点推介等多种形式，为准独角兽企业增信；针对独角兽企业急剧扩张和拓展的个性化需求，实行"一企一策"、全程跟踪服务，助力独角兽企业成为"城市合伙人"。二是完善配套支持政策。制定出台《成都市新经济梯度培育企业认定办法（试行）》和相应的《成都市新经济企业梯度培育若干支持政策》，明确强化人才支撑、拓宽融资渠道、加强政府采购、构建应用场景等普惠政策，以及制定针对种子企业、准独角兽企业、独角兽或行业领军企业的个性化支持政策。三是打造企业生态产业链。加快构建新经济发展"第一象限"，尽快发展具有引领性、代表性的新经济企业，支持新经济重点企业快速成长，鼓励大型国有企业、大型民营企业利用自身资源孵化新经济企业；大力发展中小企业，支持技术极客、科学家、海归等高端人群的高端创业，激发在校大学生和毕业 5 年以内高校毕业生创业热情和活力，在市场准入、减税降费、创业担保贷款等方面细化扶持政策。

Focus on the whole life cycle of new economy enterprises and establish the gradient cultivation mechanism of new economy enterprises to help the key enterprises of new economy grow rapidly by aiming at the "pains" of each growth stage. First, make specific policies and cultivate enterprises by steps. In view of the pains of lack of funds and weak competitiveness of seed enterprises, Chengdu establish and improve the fund-raising mechanism of start-up investment with government equity investment as the guide and social capital as the main body and make good use of 200 million Yuan angel investment fund to help enterprises cross the "Entrepreneurial Death Valley". Aiming at the pains of the urgent need to improve the industry visibility and popularity of the quasi unicorn enterprises, it adopts various forms such as promotion of quasi unicorn regional list, theme conference promotion, and point-to-point promotion to increase the credit of the quasi unicorn enterprises; and it implements "one strategy for one enterprise" and "whole process tracking service" for the rapid expansion and expansion of the unicorn enterprises to help unicorn enterprises become "city partners". Second, improve supporting policies. "Chengdu New

Economy Identification Method of Enterprise Gradient Cultivation for Trial" and "Support Policies of Chengdu New Economy Enterprise Gradient Cultivation" are formulated and promulgated, making clear the inclusive policies such as strengthening talents support, broadening financing channels, strengthening government procurement, and building application scenescapes. Personalized support policies are formulated for seed enterprises, quasi unicorn enterprises, unicorn or industry leader enterprises. The third is to build enterprise ecological industrial chain. Speed up the construction of the "first quadrant" of new economic development, develop leading and representative new economic enterprises as soon as possible, support the rapid growth of key enterprises, encourage large state-owned enterprises and large private enterprises to use their own resources to incubate new economic enterprises, vigorously develop small and medium-sized enterprises, support high-end entrepreneurship of high-end talents such as technology geeks, scientists and overseas returnees, and stimulate entrepreneurial enthusiasm and vitality of college students and graduates within five years, and make support policies detailed in market access, tax reduction and fee reduction, entrepreneurship guarantee loans, etc.

二、抢抓城市功能布局机遇，形成新经济发展"机会点"

2. Seize the Opportunity of Urban Function Layout to Form the "Opportunity Points" of New Economy Development

以功能布局为重点抢占城市未来发展战略主动权，积极向上争取政策红利，把握国家重大项目战略布局，努力在"城市卡位战"中抢占先机。一是争取国家层面重大试点任务。积极向上争取具有基础性、面向前沿、引领发展的国家重大项目战略布局，推动数字城市试点和国家级工业互联网平台等重大功能性平台落户成都。二是抢抓信息基础设施布局。聚焦新一代信息技术基础领域，抓住 IPv6 协议在全球开始普及的历史机遇，争取根服务器部署在成都；积极对接联通、电信、移动，争取试点建设 5G 网络，进行 5G 业务应用示范。

Focus on the functional layout, seize the initiative of the future development strategy of the city, actively strive for policy dividends, grasp the strategic layout of major national projects, and strive to seize the opportunity in the "city competition". First, strive for major pilot tasks at the national level. Actively strive for the strategic layout of national major projects with basic, frontier-oriented and leading development, and promote the settlement of major functional platforms such as digital city pilot and national industrial Internet platform in Chengdu. The second is to grasp the layout of information infrastructure. Focus on the basic field of new generation information technology, seize the historical opportunity when IPv6 protocol begins to popularize in the world, strive for the deployment of root server in Chengdu. Actively connect with Unicom, Telecom and Mobile to strive for the pilot construction of 5G network and carry out 5G business application demonstration.

三、强化创新要素资源集聚，搭建新经济服务的"连接点"
3. Strengthen the Agglomeration of Innovation Factors and Resources and Build the "Connective Points" of New Economic Services

推进新经济要素供给侧结构性改革，积极培育技术、人才、资本等效率型要素，形成具有比较优势、有利于新经济企业快速发展的要素市场。一是强化技术要素供给。加强新经济企业的技术创新核心竞争力，积极向上争取布局科学与工程研究类、技术创新与成果转化类国家创新基地。加快突破科技成果转移转化的制度障碍，推进科研院所、高校职务科技成果权属混合所有制改革，促进科技成果向现实生产力转化。探索建立知识产权交易中心，实现知识产权咨询、申报、评估、交易、保护等一站式服务。二是强化人才要素供给。与优势企业协作创办专业性大学，与一流高校围绕新经济创办一流学科，以各类高水平人才汇聚形成服务新经济发展的核心动力。实施"精准引才计划"，重点引进资源集聚能力强的创业人才和行业影响力强的创新人才，抓住"企业创始人"这类"自带流量"的人群。加强新经济企业发展所需的高级财务、

法务、人力资源、运营等管理人才培养。实施"专业人才计划",解决
企业家关心的户籍办理、安居保障、子女入学和医疗保障等方面的服务
问题。三是强化资本要素供给。鼓励优质创投机构支持创新创业项目,
定期向风投机构推荐具有发展潜质的新经济企业,根据创投机构年度收
益、返投本地项目、本地金融人才培育等情况,研究税收、投资比例等
方面的支持政策。抢抓 IPO 新政机遇,推进"上市倍增行动计划",积
极对接优质券商,做好 IPO 前的培训、辅导等服务工作,助推独角兽企
业成功上市。发展创投机构,吸引全国乃至全球知名风投机构在蓉设立
法人机构,培育一批本土天使投资人和创业投资机构,鼓励本地创投机
构建立创投联盟,打造具有全国乃至全球影响力的创投资源汇聚高地。

Promote the supply side structural reform of new economic factors and
actively cultivate efficient factors such as technology, talents, capital to form an
advantageous factor market conducive to the rapid development of new economy
enterprises. One is to strengthen the supply of technological factors. Strengthen
the core competitiveness of technological innovation of new economy enterprises
and actively strive for the layout of national innovation bases for scientific and
engineering research, technological innovation and achievement transformation.
Accelerate the breakthrough of institutional barriers in the transfer and
transformation of scientific and technological achievements, promote the reform
of mixed ownership of scientific and technological achievements in scientific
research institutions and universities, and promote the transformation of
scientific and technological achievements into real productive forces. Explore
the establishment of intellectual property trading center to realize one-stop
services of intellectual property consultation, declaration, evaluation, trading
and protection. Second, strengthen the supply of talents factors. Cooperate with
advantageous enterprises to set up professional universities and set up first-class
disciplines around new economy with first-class universities, to gather all kinds
of high-level talents to form the core power to serve the development of the new
economy. Implement the "Accurate Talents Introduction Plan", focus on

introducing entrepreneurial talents with strong resource gathering ability and innovative talents with strong influence in their fields, and retain the "self-flow" talents such as "enterprise founders". Strengthen the training of senior financial, legal, human resources, operation and other management personnel needed by the development of new economy enterprises. Implement the "professional talents program" to solve the problems of registered residence, housing security, children's enrollment and medical care. Third, strengthen the supply of capital factors. Encourage high-quality venture institutions, support projects of innovation and entrepreneurship, regularly recommend potential new economy enterprises to venture institutions, and study support policies in tax, investment ratio, etc. according to the annual income of venture institutions, local investment projects, local financial talents cultivation, etc. Seize the opportunity of the new policy for IPO, promote the "Listing Plan", actively connect with high-quality brokers, and do a good job in pre-IPO training, counseling and other services, so as to promote the successful listing of Unicorn enterprises. Develop venture institutions, attract national and even global well-known venture institutions to set up corporate bodies in Chengdu, cultivate a number of local angel investors and venture capital institutions, encourage local venture institutions to establish venture alliances, and create a high pool of venture resources with national and even global influence.

四、强化新经济平台载体作用，建设新经济发展"极核点"

4. Strengthen the Role of New Economy Platform as a Carrier and Build "Core Points" for New Economy Development

进一步加强新经济平台建设，汇流量、聚资源、抓落地。一是推动独角兽岛建设。将天府新区独角兽岛作为推动新经济发展的重要载体，开展全周期培育、全要素保障、高品质生活的产业生态圈建设，打造超级孵化器载体。高标准设置入园门槛，优选具备发展潜质和竞争力的新经济企业进园区，为其提供创业俱乐部、头脑风暴室、云服务等共享单元服务和一站式、人性化的政务服务，培育新经济企业快速达到独角兽规模并推动其 IPO 上市，促进独角兽企业"早出园"。二是加快构建校院地企合作平台。加强与四川大学、电子科技大学、西南交通大学、西南财经大学、四川农业大学、成都理工大学和中科院成都分院等高校院所的战略合作，共同建设新型研发机构、协同创新平台和科技产业园区。支持"校院企地"共建产业技术研发、转化平台和共享公共技术服务平台，建设一批"产学研"紧密结合的新型产业技术研究院。支持产业功能区和央企、省企共建产业功能区管委会或管理公司，探索"校院企地"深度融合的利益绑定机制。三是提升新经济企业俱乐部品质。进一步发挥新经济企业俱乐部提升凝聚力的"正能量"作用，汇聚各类专业机构、领军企业、产业联盟和行业协会，建立企业、协会、政府常态化交流对话平台，定期或不定期开展政府和企业深度对话，开展头脑风暴、专题培训、成果演示、资本对接等合作，做大做强新经济企业"朋友圈"，实现本地新经济企业互惠共赢、抱团发展。

Further strengthen the construction of the new economy platform to gather flow and resources. First, promote the construction of Unicorn Island. Take Unicorn Island in Tianfu New Area as an important carrier to promote the development of new economy, carry out the construction of industrial ecosystem with full cycle cultivation, full factor guarantee and high-quality life, and build a super incubator carrier. Set the entry threshold with high standards, select new economy enterprises with development potential and competitiveness to enter the park, provide them with shared unit services such as entrepreneurial club, brainstorming room, cloud service and one-stop, humanized government services, cultivate new economy enterprises to quickly reach the scale of Unicorn and promote their IPO, and promote Unicorn enterprises to "leave the park early". The second is to speed up the construction of cooperation platform between universities, colleges, local enterprises. Strengthen strategic cooperation with Sichuan University, University of Electronic Science and Technology, Southwest Jiaotong University, Southwest University of Finance and Economics,

Sichuan Agricultural University, Chengdu Institute of Technology and Chengdu Branch of Chinese Academy of Sciences, and jointly build new R&D institutions, collaborative innovation platform and science and Technology Industrial Park. Support universities, enterprises and local governments to jointly build industrial technology research and development, transformation platforms and shared public technology service platforms, and build a number of new industrial technology research institutes closely integrating industry, university and research. Support the industrial functional areas, central enterprises and provincial enterprises to jointly build the management committee or management company of the industrial functional areas and explore the interest binding mechanism of the deep integration of universities, enterprises and local governments. Third, improve the quality of new economy enterprise club. Chengdu will further give play to the "positive energy" role of the new economy enterprise club in enhancing cohesion, gather all kinds of professional institutions, leading enterprises, industry alliances and industry associations, and establish a normalized exchange and dialogue platform for enterprises, associations and governments, Carry out in-depth dialogue between the government and enterprises on a regular or irregular basis, carry out brainstorming, special training, achievement demonstration, capital docking and other cooperation, expand and strengthen the "circle of friends" of new economy enterprises, and realize mutual benefit and win-win development of local new economy enterprises.

五、以话语引领为重点，营造新经济发展的"话语点"
5. Focus on Discourse to Create "Discourse Points" for New Economy Development

围绕"成都，最适宜新经济发展的城市"，持续形成新经济发展强大舆论氛围。一是强化对新经济发展的决策咨询研究。积极开展新经济决策咨询研究，为成都新经济发展提供态势感知、趋势预测、政策设

计、决策判断、平台运营、对外合作、生态建设等服务和支撑，打造新
经济"智囊团"。适时举办新经济高端论坛、研讨会等，打造新经济
"发声器"。二是持续出台新经济政策。按照持续推出《关于营造新生
态发展新经济培育新动能的意见》配套政策的思路，及时出台并对外发
布"六大形态""七大应用场景"实施方案，对有关内容和相关政策进
行解读。三是做好新经济热点宣传。围绕未来新经济发展中可能出现的
互联网巨头反垄断监管、企业爆发式成长、行业重大投融资事件、本地
颠覆性技术诞生等热点，提前谋划安排系列报道，持续发出成都新经济
的"最强音"，营造新经济发展的城市良好氛围。

The continuous discussion, "Chengdu, the most suitable city for new economy development", form a strong public opinion atmosphere for new economy development. One is to strengthen the decision-making consultation research on the development of new economy, to provide services and support for Chengdu's new economic development, such as situation awareness, trend prediction, policy design, decision-making judgment, platform operation, foreign cooperation, ecological construction, and build a new economic "think tank". And timely hold new economy high-end forum, seminar, etc., to create new economy "sounder". The second is to continuously introduce new economic policies. In accordance with the idea of continuously launching the supporting policies of "Opinions on Creating New Ecology, Developing New Economy and Cultivating New Growth Driver", the implementation plans of "six forms" and "seven application scenescapes" were timely introduced, released, and interpreted. The third is to publicize the issues of the new economy. Around the possible explosion points of new economy development in the future, such as anti-monopoly supervision of Internet giants, explosive growth of enterprises, major investment and financing events in the industry, and the birth of local disruptive technology, it is necessary to plan and arrange a series of reports in advance, continue to produce the "loudest voice" of Chengdu's new economy, and create a good atmosphere for the city's new economic development.

CiNED

第五章

发展新经济培育新动能的
要素支撑体系

Chapter Five
Support System of Factors in Developing New
Economy and Cultivating New Growth Drivers

随着新一轮科技革命和产业变革的到来，经济要素已经从土地、资本、劳动力等传统要素转向新经济时代的人才、技术、资本、数据等新要素上。以企业为中心，人才、技术、资本、数据是最直接的要素支撑，为企业注入源源不断的活力，对新经济活动的作用最直接。营商环境犹如企业生长系统中的土壤、阳光和水，能够促进新经济企业快速成长、开花结果，吸引更多企业落户。为加快建设最适宜新经济发展的城市，构建有利于新经济发展的要素生态，《中共成都市委 成都市人民政府关于营造新生态发展新经济培育新动能的意见》明确提出"构建有利于新经济发展的要素生态和供给体系"。从企业的需求出发，坚持人才是第一资源、科技是第一生产力的思想，将人才、技术、土地、资本、数据等促进产业发展的核心要素作为重中之重，围绕新经济要素出台专项政策，优化要素生态，形成精准的政策体系，磁场效应开始显现。

With the advent of a new round of scientific and technological revolution and industrial change, economic factors have changed from traditional factors such as land, capital and labor force to new factors such as talents, technology, capital and data in the new economic era. With the enterprise as the center, the most direct supporting factors are talents, technology, capital and data, which inject continuous vitality into enterprises, and play the most direct role in the new economy activities. The business environment is like the soil, sunshine and water in the enterprise growth system, which can promote the rapid growth, blossom and fruit bearing of new economy enterprises and attract more enterprises to settle down. In order to speed up the construction of the most suitable city for the development of new economy and build the factor ecology conducive to the development of new economy, Opinions of Chengdu Municipal Party Committee and Chengdu Municipal People's Government on Creating New Ecology, Developing New Economy and Cultivating New Growth Driver clearly put forward that Chengdu will build the factor ecology and supply system conducive to the development of new economy. From the needs of enterprises, talents should be considered as the first resource, science and technology should be considered as the first productivity. The core factors of to promote industrial development such as talents, technology, land, capital and data as the most import. The magnetic field effect begins to appear after issuing special policies around the new economic factors, optimizing the factor ecology and forming an accurate policy system.

▷ ▷ ▷ 第一节　人才支撑

Section One　Talents Support

　　人才是新经济发展的关键支撑。新经济作为一种可持续发展的经济，在技术特征、组织结构、产业组织等方面有别于传统经济，更强调以创新为核心，以智力为支撑。智力的体现是以人为载体，创新也只能以人为载体。为此，作为新经济运行活性支撑——人的作用性质没有改变，但人力或人才的作用机制相应发生了变化。新经济跨界、互联互通的特征，要求更多的创新企业家和复合型人才。在新经济时代，国际经济竞争的本质是潜在的智力资本的竞争。积极培养、引进、使用各类人才，强化制度设计和政策创新，最大限度释放人才的积极性和创造力是助力新经济发展的引擎①。随着新经济迅速发展，持续增长的经济状况，快速壮大的新经济企业，为社会提供了大量就业机会，但人才需求短期缺口问题凸显。同时，新经济人才培养存在难度大、周期长的特点。在新经济形态下，创新知识产品需要一定的科技含量和创造才能，而在这一要求下，对人才的要求就更加突出。事实上，这一类人才的培养难度极大，由于需要一定科技能力和研发水平，因此对人才的知识储备要求极高，对实践能力也提出了一定要求②。

Talents are the key support for the development of new economy. As a sustainable economy, new economy is different from the traditional economy in

---

① 孙安会. 释放人才创新潜能 [J]. 国企管理, 2017 (11): 50-51.
② 刘建成. 我国新经济人才供求失衡的成因及对策分析 [J]. 经济师, 2002 (3): 124-125.

technical characteristics, organizational structure and industrial organization. It emphasizes innovation as the core and intelligence as the support. Human is the carrier of the intelligence, as well as of the innovation. Therefore, as the active support of new economy, the nature of human's role has not changed, but the mechanism of human or talents has changed. The characteristics of cross-border and interconnection of new economy require more innovative entrepreneurs and versatile talents. In the new economic era, the essence of international economic competition is the competition of potential intellectual capital. The engines to help the development of the new economy are actively cultivating, introducing and using all kinds of talents, strengthening the system design and policy innovation, and maximizing the enthusiasm and creativity of talents. With the rapid development of the new economy, the sustained economic growth and the rapid growth of new economy enterprises provide a lot of employment opportunities for the society, but the short-term shortage of talents demand is prominent. At the same time, the personnel's training for new economy is very difficult and long-termed. In the new economic form, the innovation of knowledge products requires a certain scientific and technological content and creative ability, so the requirements for talents are more prominent. In fact, the cultivation of this kind of talents is very difficult. Due to the need for a certain scientific and technological ability and R&D level, talents are required for their knowledge reserve and practical ability.

2018 年 3 月，成都市经济和信息化局、成都市财政局印发《成都市实体经济新经济领域人才奖励实施办法》，对农业、工业、交通运输业、商务服务业等具有基础性、支撑性、稳定性、引领性的实体经济领域的人才进行奖励。奖励的对象是从 2017 年《成都实施人才优先发展战略行动计划》实施后，新进入成都市工作满一年及以上的人才。申报人及所在单位应同时具备与所在单位签订了 3 年以上的劳动合同、所在单位在成都市注册且税收解缴关系在成都市的企业、所在单位属本办法下的实体经济领域或新经济领域、上一年度缴纳个人所得税后年收入 50 万元以上（民营企业人才上一年度缴纳个人所得税后年收入 40 万元以上）、申报人已足额缴纳了个人所得税和申报人没有受到刑事处罚，或刑事处罚已经执行完毕等条件。

In March 2018, Chengdu Municipal Bureau of Economy and Information Technology and Chengdu Municipal Bureau of Finance issued "Measures for Implementation of Talents Award in New Economic Field of Real Economy in Chengdu" to reward talents in the basic, supporting, stable and leading practical economic fields such as agriculture, industry, transportation and business services. The award targets the new talents who have worked in Chengdu for more than one year after "Implementation of Talents Priority Development Strategy Action Plan in Chengdu" was implemented in 2017. The applicants should meet the following conditions: the applicants and their units shall have the labor contract signed for more than 3 years; their units should register and pay tax in Chengdu; their units belong to real economy or new economy field included in the measures; they pay the annual income of more than 500,000 Yuan after paying personal income tax in the previous year (400,000 Yuan for those in private enterprises); they have paid the individual income tax in full and have not been subject to criminal punishment, or their criminal punishment has been implemented, etc.

2019 年 6 月，BOSS 直聘研究院通过其人力资源大数据平台，抽取 2019 年 1 月 1 日至 5 月 31 日的数据，并通过对比往年数据，发布了《成都新经济人才趋势报告》。从新经济人才需求、行业分布、人才偏好及数量缺口等维度详尽分析了成都新经济人才的发展现状，并预测分析了人才流动趋势。报告显示，以成都为中心的区域人才流动频繁，人才流入和流出的城市重合度较高。成渝双城经济圈初步实现了区域内部人才的良性流动。一线城市和省内城市成为成都人才供给的重要来源，也成为成都人才寻求发展的首选。2019 年，成都对比一线城市表现为人才净流入，以成都为代表的新一线城市，依靠人才吸引优势成为大型企业成立分公司的首选。如阿里巴巴、腾讯、华为、小米、京东等头部企业均纷纷落户新一线城市。2019 年 9 月，成都新经济大数据监测平台对外发布《2019 年第三季度成都新经济发展监测报告》，报告主要围绕新经济企业高级人才需求量、新经济企业专利总量、新经济企业融资总额三个维度进行了监测和数据分析。从分析结果看，截至 2019 年 9 月，成都新经济高级人才需求总量为 99 263 人次，全国副省级城市中排名第五位。其中，高新区需求量最高，为 37 248 人；郫都区增速最快，同比增长 225.3%。

In June 2019, the direct employment research institute BOSS extracted data from January 1 to May 31, 2019 through its big data platform of human resources and released "Chengdu New Economy Talents Trend Report" by comparing the data of previous years. It analyzes the development status of Chengdu new economy talents from the perspectives of talents demand, industry distribution, talents preference and quantity gap, and forecasts and analyzes the trend of talents flow. It is shown that the flow of talents is frequent in the region centering around Chengdu, and the coincidence degree of cities from which talents flow in and out is high. Chengdu-Chongqing twin city economic circle has initially realized the benign flow of talents within regions. First-tier cities and provincial cities have become an important source of talents supply for Chengdu and also the first choice for Chengdu's talents to develop. In 2019, compared with the first-tier cities, Chengdu achieved a net inflow of talents. The new first-tier cities represented by Chengdu will become the first choice for large enterprises to set up branches due to their advantages of attracting talents. Some leading enterprises such as Alibaba, Tencent, Huawei, Xiaomi, Jingdong have settled in new first-tier cities. In September 2019, Chengdu big data monitoring platform of new economy released "Chengdu New Economy Development Monitoring Report in the Third Quarter of 2019". The report mainly monitored and analyzed the data from three dimensions: the demand for senior talents of new economy enterprises, the total amount of patents of new economy enterprises, and the total amount of financing of new economy enterprises. According to the analysis, as of September 2019, the total demand for new economy senior talents in Chengdu is 99,263, ranking the fifth among cities of the vice provincial level in China. Especially Hi-Tech Zone has the highest demand of 37,248 people and Pidu District has the fastest growth with a year on year growth of 225.3%.

2019 年 12 月，成都新经济发展研究院与 58 同城招聘研究院联合发布的《成都市新职业人群发展报告（2019）》（以下简称《报告》）显示，2019 年成都新职业从业者总体规模已突破 45 万人，也呈现出高速增长态势。《报告》指出，目前成都生活服务类新职业从业规模居全国首位，成都新职业人群总体规模排名全国第三，并且以青年从业者为主。成都新职业从业者对工作的认可度和满意度很高，对城市的归属感和文化认同感比较强烈。调查显示，成都新职业人群分布较为集中，生活服务类新职业人群占比近 90%，主要集中在出行、医美丽人、健康、餐饮、亲子等领域，如图 5-1 所示。就从业规模而言，成都生活服务类新职业从业规模居全国首位，占 19 个样本城市生活服务类从业者总量的 12.9%。

In December 2019, Chengdu New Economic Development Research Institute and 58 City Recruitment Research Institute jointly released the "2019 Chengdu New Professionals Development Report" (hereinafter referred to as Report), which shows that the overall scale of new occupation practitioners in Chengdu in 2019 has exceeded 450,000, with the trend of a high speed growth. The report points out that at present, Chengdu's scale of new occupations in life service ranks the first in China, and Chengdu's overall scale of new professionals ranks the third in China, with young practitioners as the main group. The new occupation practitioners in Chengdu have a high degree of recognition and satisfaction with their work, and a strong sense of belonging and cultural identity to the city. The survey shows that the distribution of new occupations in Chengdu is relatively concentrated, with nearly 90% of new occupations in life services, mainly in travel, medical beauty, health, catering, children's caring and education etc, as shown in Figure 5 – 1. In terms of the scale of employment, Chengdu's scale of new occupations in life service ranks first in China, accounting for 12. 9% of the total number of life service practitioners in 19 sample cities.

图 5-1　成都生活服务类新职业各行业从业规模占比

Figure 5-1 Employment in Chengdu's New Life Service Occupations

《报告》显示,人工智能工程、无人机、物联网工程引领高学历第一梯队。在学历要求较高的生产技术类人群中,本科及以上学历占比超过70%,硕士及以上学历占比也达到8.8%,主要集中在人工智能工程、无人机、物联网工程、大数据工程、云计算工程等生产技术类新职业。

According to the report, artificial intelligence engineering, UAV and IOT engineering lead the first echelon of high education. Among the production technology groups with higher education requirements, more than 70% of them have bachelor's degree or above, and 8. 8% have master's degree or above, mainly focusing on new production technology jobs such as artificial intelligence engineering, UAV, Internet of things engineering, big data engineering and cloud computing engineering.

《报告》显示，成都大部分新职业人群对目前从事的行业比较满意。满意或比较满意人群占比超过 50%，如图 5-2 所示。良好的工作满意度离不开美好生活环境的打造，成都连续 12 年蝉联"中国最具幸福感城市"榜首，表明成都在教育、医疗、卫生等方面公共服务保障完备，为居民提供了满意的生活和工作环境。

The report shows that most of new professionals in Chengdu are satisfied with the industry they are currently engaged in. More than 50% of people are satisfied or relatively satisfied, as shown in Figure 5-2. Good job satisfaction is inseparable from the creation of a better living environment. Chengdu has been ranked first in "the happiest city in China" for 12 consecutive years, which shows that Chengdu has a complete guarantee of public services such as education, medical care and health care, providing residents with a satisfactory living and working environment.

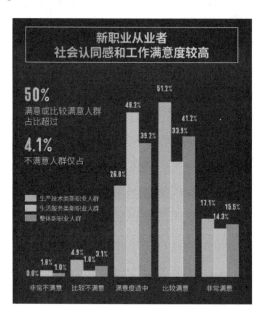

图 5-2　新职业从业者工作满意度

Figure 5-2　Job Satisfaction of New Occupation Practitioners

▷▷▷ 第二节　技术支撑

Section Two　Technological Support

当今世界，新一轮科技革命和产业变革正在重塑世界经济格局，以大数据、云计算、人工智能等为代表的新技术正在不断创新突破，以新产业、新业态、新商业模式为主要表现形式的新经济正以势不可挡之势异军突起，新技术成为牵引新经济发展的澎湃动力。党的十九大指出，我国经济正处在转变发展方式、优化经济结构、转换增长动力的攻关期，要深化供给侧结构性改革，推动互联网、大数据、人工智能与实体经济深度融合，培育新增长点，形成新动能。我国已经把这些新技术的创新发展上升为国家战略，致力于在关键技术领域取得突破。科学技术创新已经成为我国推进高质量发展、建设现代化经济体系的重要战略支撑。

In today's world, a new round of scientific and technological revolution and industrial change is reshaping the world economic pattern. New technologies such as big data, cloud computing and artificial intelligence are constantly innovating and breaking through. The new economy manifested as new industries, new form of businesses and new business models has sprung up. New technologies have become the power to drive the development of new economy. The 19th National Congress of the Communist Party of China pointed out that China's economy was in a critical period of transforming the mode of development, optimizing the economic structure and transforming the driving force of growth. It is necessary to deepen the supply side structural reform, promote the deep integration of the Internet, big data, artificial intelligence and the real economy, and cultivate new growth points to form new driving forces. China has upgraded the innovation and development of these new technologies as a national strategy and is committed to making breakthroughs in the field of key technologies. Scientific and technological innovation has become an important strategic support for China to promote high-quality development and build a modern economic system.

为深入实施创新驱动发展战略，加快推动科技成果转化为现实生产力，自 2017 年以来，成都市出台了一系列有关技术要素保障的政策文件，主要包括《成都市促进科技成果转移转化行动方案（2017—2020年）》《关于大力发展高新技术服务业支撑产业功能区及园区建设增强西部科技中心功能的实施意见》《成都市创新创业活动资助管理办法的通知》等。2020 年 9 月，成都新经济创新产品（服务）交易平台首次亮相。该平台由成都市新经济发展委员会、成都市公共资源交易中心联合搭建，旨在以城市新场景为创新企业提供大展身手的新舞台，以企业新产品为人民群众带来品质生活的新感受，为建立新的经济秩序、提升城市治理效能、满足人民美好生活向往，强化对新经济企业的支持与服务，构建创新产品推广应用新通道。

In order to further implement the innovation-driven development strategy and accelerate the transformation of scientific and technological achievements into real productive forces, Chengdu has issued a series of policies to guarantee technological factors since 2017, mainly including "Chengdu Action Plan for Promoting Transfer and Transformation of Scientific and Technological Achievements (2017—2020)", "Implementations on Vigorously Developing High-tech Service Industry to Support Construction of Industrial Functional Zones and Parks and Strengthen the Function of Western Science and Technology Center", and "Notice on Measures for Administration of Innovation and Entrepreneurship Funding in Chengdu", etc. In September 2020, Chengdu new economy innovation products (services) trading platform debuted. The platform was jointly built by Chengdu New Economic Development Committee and Chengdu Public Resources Trading Center. It aims to provide a new stage for innovative enterprises with new urban scenescapes, bring new feelings of quality life to the people with new products, and strengthen the support and service for new economy enterprises and build a new channel for the promotion and application of innovative products in order to establish a new economic order, improve urban governance efficiency and meet people's yearning for a better life.

成都新经济创新产品（服务）交易平台通过交易、服务、管理三大功能，实现供方在线发布信息、需方在线采购新经济创新产品、全过程信息化统计管理。企业可以通过平台发布新经济创新产品信息，采购人通过查阅网站获取新经济创新产品信息，并进行站内实时联系，从而撮合交易。采购人也可发布需求信息供潜在供给企业查询。目前已发布500余个新经济创新产品。未来，平台将打造为成都新经济创新产品重要的宣传推广、交易撮合、企业交流平台，持续发布新经济创新产品，推动新技术新产品新模式应用推广，助力消费升级，释放市场需求，为企业引领创新发展提供更多城市新机会，为新经济企业发展提供更多赋能渠道①。

Chengdu new economy innovative products（services）trading platform realizes online information release of suppliers, demanders' online purchase of new economy innovative products and whole-process information statistics management through three functions of trading, service and management. Enterprises can release the information of new economy innovative products through the platform. Purchasers can obtain the information of new economy innovative products through the website and make real-time contact on the website to match transactions. Purchasers can also release demands for potential suppliers to inquire. At present, more than 500 new economic innovative products have been released. In the future, the platform will be built as an important platform for publicity, trade matching and enterprise exchange of Chengdu's new economic innovative products, continuously release new products, promote the application and promotion of new technologies, new

---

① 谢燃岸，柴枫桔. 成都新经济创新产品（服务）交易平台亮相［EB/OL］.（2020-09-25）［2021-01-05］. https://www.163.com/dy/article/FND0RMQM0514D3UH.html.

products and new models, help consumption upgrade, release market demand, provide more new opportunities for enterprises to lead innovation and development, and provide more empowering channels for the development of new economic enterprises.

　　作为"新基建"之一的超算中心的落地运行，无疑将为创新驱动发展提供新的动能。截至2019年，科技部批准建立的7家国家超级计算中心，均位于我国中东部（分别是天津、长沙、济南、广州、深圳、无锡、郑州），在西部地区尚无国家级超级计算体系的布局。成都超算中心于2019年12月18日开工建设，并于2020年9月建成投运，填补了我国西部地区超级计算体系的布局空白。

The operation of Supercomputing Center, as one of the "new infrastructures", will undoubtedly provide new growth driver for innovation-driven development. As of 2019, seven national supercomputing centers has been approved by the Ministry of Science and Technology, all located in the central and eastern parts of China (Tianjin, Changsha, Jinan, Guangzhou, Shenzhen, Wuxi and Zhengzhou), none of which is from the western region. Chengdu Supercomputing Center had been under construction since December 18, 2019, and was completed and put into operation in September 2020, filling the layout gap of supercomputing system in Western China.

　　成都超算中心位于成都科学城鹿溪智谷核心区，总投资约25亿元，净用地面积约36亩（1亩＝0.066 7公顷，后同），总建筑面积约6万平方米，包含硅立方计算机、动力楼和科研楼等部分。未来将支撑成都乃至西部的科学、经济、社会各方面发展。高校、科研院所和以人工智能为代表的科技型企业，将是成都超算中心接下来的"重要客户"。成都目前有四川大学、电子科大等高校64所，中科院光电技术研究所等国家级科研机构30家，高校院所从事的科学研究都需要超算支持。以成都超算中心为依托，成都将集聚更多领军型科技创新人才，推动产出更多具有国际竞争力的科技成果，为成都建设具有全国影响力的科技创新中心提供重要支撑，大力推进成渝地区双城经济圈建设。

Chengdu Supercomputing Center is located in the core area of Luxi Wisdom Valley of Chengdu Science City, with a total investment of about 2. 5 billion Yuan, a net land area of about 5. 9 acre and a total construction area of about 60, 000 square meters, including silicon cube computer, power building and scientific research building. In the future, it will support the scientific, economic and social development of Chengdu and even the West. Universities, scientific research institutes and technological enterprises represented by artificial intelligence will be the next "important customers" of Chengdu Supercomputing Center. At present, there are 64 universities and colleges in Chengdu, such as Sichuan University and University of Electronic Science and Technology, and 30 national scientific research institutions, such as Institute of Optoelectronic Technology of Chinese Academy of Sciences. The scientific research of universities and colleges all need supercomputing support. Relying on Chengdu Supercomputing Center, Chengdu will gather more leading scientific and technological innovation talents, promote the output of more scientific and technological achievements with international competitiveness, provide important support for the construction of Chengdu as a science and technology innovation center with national influence, and vigorously promote the construction of Chengdu-Chongqing Twin Cities Economic Circle.

▷▷▷ 第三节　资本支撑
Section Three　Capital Support

随着信息技术的全方位普及，大数据、云计算、人工智能、区块链等新兴领域的行业渗透，我国正逐渐步入"新经济"发展时期，新产业、新技术、新业态、新模式的变化，对金融体系提出了新要求，进而催生了新金融，新金融本身就是新经济的重要内容。新金融绝对不是对传统金融的颠覆，而是在新的发展背景下产生的新的金融产品与服务、金融市场体系、金融监管模式等，是传统金融适应新市场环境后发生的变化。新金融的实质仍是服务实体经济发展，创新的金融产品、高效的金融服务、多层的资本市场、有效的金融监管又进一步满足了实体经济发展的资金需求，助力了新经济的健康、快速、平衡发展。截至 2019 年年末，成都市已有新经济企业 34.7 万户，同比增长 26.2%。新经济企业获得风险投资总额 159 亿元，同比增长 22.3%。

With the all-round popularization of information technology and the appearance of emerging industries as big data, cloud computing, artificial intelligence and block chain, China is gradually stepping into the development period of "new economy". The changes of new industries, new technologies, new form of business and new models put forward new requirements for the financial system, and then gave birth to new finance. New finance itself is the content of the new economy. New finance is definitely not the subversion of traditional finance, but the new financial products and services, financial market system, financial supervision mode and so on produced in the new development background, as a the change of traditional finance after adapting to the new market environment. The essence of new finance is still to serve the development of the real economy. Innovative financial products, efficient financial services, multi-layer capital market and effective financial supervision further meet the capital demand of the development of the real economy and help the healthy, rapid and balanced development of the new economy. By the end of 2019, there had been 347,000 new economy enterprises in Chengdu, with a year-on-year growth of 26.2%. The total amount of venture capital obtained by new economy enterprises was 15.9 billion Yuan, up 22.3% year on year.

为进一步加快国家西部金融建设，让金融更好地服务于实体经济，自 2017 年以来，成都市印发了一系列有关资本要素保障的政策文件，主要包括《关于进一步加快建设国家西部金融中心的若干意见的通知》《关于进一步推进政府和社会资本合作（PPP）的实施意见》《关于印发成都国家中心城市经济证券化行动计划的通知》《关于进一步激发社会领域投资活动任务分工方案的通知》等。2020 年 3 月，成都出台《关于统筹推进新冠肺炎疫情防控和经济社会发展工作 奋力完成 2020 年经济社会发展目标的意见》，提出要大力发展新经济，推动实体经济数字化转型。为鼓励新经济企业发展，成都设立了 100 亿元新经济创投基金。按照"三个三分之一"原则为新经济企业提供投融资扶持，即，投资金额的 1/3 份额所购股权按"投资额+固定收益"由被投企业核心团队回购，1/3 份额所购股权按"投资额+固定收益"由投资者收购，剩余 1/3 份额所购股权按市场化方式运作，共同分享产业发展红利。作为成都市专项扶持新经济企业的创投基金，"成都新经济创投基金"将坚持以扶持新经济产业发展为导向，提高成都市新经济企业成长起点，为其后续发展带来更加丰富的产业合作资源和更广阔的产业对接平台，打造"资本+服务+资源"的新经济企业生态闭环，成为支持成都新经济发展的"生力军"。

In order to further accelerate the financial construction in Western China and make finance better serve the real economy, Chengdu has issued a series of policies on the guarantee of capital factors since 2017, mainly including "Notice of Some Opinions on Further Accelerating the Construction of the Financial Center in Western China", "Opinions of Implementation on Further Promoting Public-Private Partnership (PPP)", and "Notice of Printing and Distributing Chengdu National Central City Economic Securitization Action Plan" and "Notice of Further Stimulating the Division of Social Investment Tasks". In March 2020, "Notice of Coordinating Prevention and Control of Novel Coronavirus Pneumonia with Economic Social Development to Achieve the Goal of Economic and Social Development in 2020" was launched in Chengdu, which encourages the development of new economy, promotes the digital transformation of the real economy. To encourage the development of new economy enterprises, Chengdu has set up a 10 billion Yuan new economy venture fund. According to the principle of "Three 1/3", Chengdu provide investment and financing support for new economy enterprises, that is, 1/3 shares of the investment amount are bought back by the core team of the invested enterprise according to "investment amount + fixed income", 1/3 shares are purchased by investors according to "investment amount + fixed income", and the remaining 1/3 shares are operated in a market-oriented way to share the industrial development dividend. As a special venture fund to support new economy enterprises in Chengdu, "Chengdu New Economy Venture Fund" will adhere to the guidance of supporting the development of new economy industry, improve the starting line of the growth of new economy enterprises in Chengdu, bring more abundant industrial cooperation resources and broader industrial docking platform for its follow-up development, and create an ecological closed loop of "capital + service + resources" for new economy enterprises, and become a "new force" to support the new economic development of Chengdu.

"成都新经济创投基金"由国内排名前十的创投管理机构——德同资本旗下成都德同西部投资管理有限公司管理，交子金融控股集团旗下成都市产业引导基金认缴出资资金占总认缴规模的20%，且不超过5 000万元。"成都新经济创投基金"的投资范围，包括优先投资受到疫情冲击面临困难的优秀成都新经济企业，已经获批的独角兽企业、准独角兽企业、瞪羚企业，与疫情防控及技术相关的企业和项目。同时，还将重点投资国家重点支持的先进设备制造、人工智能及新一代信息技术等新经济或战略性新兴产业领域。基金投资方式包括股权投资、定向增发、可转债投资、企业并购、闲置资金理财投资等在内的各种符合法律法规的对外投资活动，为企业提供全过程的融资服务，提升新经济企业的融资能力。

"Chengdu New Economy Venture Fund" is managed by Chengdu Detong Western Investment Management Co., Ltd. Detong Capital is one of the top ten venture capital management institutions in China. The subscribed capital of Chengdu industrial guidance fund of Jiaozi Financial Holding Group accounts for 20% of the total subscribed capital, and does not exceed 50 million Yuan. The investment scope of "Chengdu New Economy Venture Fund" includes priority investment in outstanding new economy enterprises in Chengdu that are facing difficulties under the impact of the pandemic, approved Unicorn enterprises, quasi Unicorn enterprises and gazelle enterprises, and enterprises and projects related to pandemic prevention and control and technology. At the same time, it will also focus on new economic or strategic emerging industries such as advanced equipment manufacturing, artificial intelligence and new-generation information technology supported by the state. Fund investment includes equity investment, private placement, convertible bond investment, enterprise merger and acquisition, idle funds financial investment and other foreign investment activities in line with laws and regulations, to provide the whole process of financing services for enterprises and enhance the financing ability of new economy enterprises.

"成都新经济创投基金"将通过基金管理机构精细到位的投后管理，有力地帮助新经济企业完成市场拓展、提质增效、创新转型。在产业的转型升级中，进一步提升品牌价值、优化运营策略，实现产业链与资源整合的协同效应，为成长型优质新经济企业提供稳定的低成本融资渠道和全方位的特色金融服务，助推新经济产业升级步伐，带动成都市新经济产业高质量发展①。

"Chengdu New Economy Venture Fund" will effectively help new economy enterprises to complete market expansion, improve quality and efficiency, innovate and transform through fine post-investment management of fund management institutions. In the process of industrial transformation and upgrading, the brand value will be further enhanced, the operation strategy optimized, the synergy effect of industrial chain and resource integration will be realized, providing stable low-cost financing channels and comprehensive featuring financial services for growing high-quality new economy enterprises, boosting the pace of new economy industrial upgrading, and driving the high-quality development of new economy industry in Chengdu.

---

① 人民网. 总规模3亿元的"成都新经济创投基金"落地［EB/OL］.（2020-02-29）［2021-01-09］. http://sc.people.com.cn/n2/2020/0229/c379469-33838581.html.

▷▷▷ 第四节　数据支撑
Section Four　Data Support

信息技术与经济社会的交汇融合引发了数据的迅猛增长，数据已成为国家基础性战略资源。坚持创新驱动发展，加快大数据部署，深化大数据应用，已成为稳增长、促改革、调结构、惠民生和推动政府治理能力现代化的内在需要和必然选择。《成都市促进大数据产业发展专项政策》明确提出，为提升信息基础设施保障能力，系统布局一批区域性、行业性数据中心，对主要面向大数据应用的互联网数据中心、云计算中心、云数据中心等给予项目用地、市场拓展、投融资服务等支持，执行优惠电价和优惠带宽资费，并给予通信资费补贴。为支持大数据平台化服务，文件提出搭建全市统一的公共数据开放平台，按照市场化机制优先开放社会公众、市场主体关注度和需求度较高的公共数据，推动数据资源的社会化开发利用。支持企业、机构和行业协会建设大数据共性技术平台，为用户提供研发设计、计量、评估、标准化、检验检测、认证认可等技术服务；支持企业、机构和行业协会搭建大数据开源社区技术创新平台，提供面向行业应用的解决方案、软件开发和平台运营服务。对购买上述平台服务的企业，按照服务费实际支出金额的 20%，给予最高 100 万元/年的补贴。为促进产业加速器发展，成都支持大数据企业、机构和行业协会建设面向行业应用的数据资源库和专业大数据服务平台，对公共数据和行业数据进行采集、整合、清洗、加工，对外开放数据并提供数据服务，形成以数据平台为核心的产业加速器，聚合产业链企业。对重点加速器按投资额的 30%一次性给予最高不超过 300 万元的补贴，每年按照运营费用的 20%给予最高 100 万元补贴。同时，支持行业协会、产业服务机构等组织开展大数据产业生态研究、行业数据收集、规划及标准制定，以及企业服务、产业对接、项目路演等活动，按项目内容和效果给予不超过 20 万元的活动补贴。

The convergence of information technology and economic society has led to the rapid growth of data, and data has become a national basic strategic resource. It has become the inherent need and inevitable choice for stabilizing growth, promoting reform, adjusting structure, benefiting people's livelihood and promoting the modernization of government's governance capacity to adhere to innovation-driven development, accelerate the deployment of big data and deepen the application of big data. "Chengdu Special Policy for Promoting the Development of Big Data Industry" clearly proposes that in order to improve the support ability of information infrastructure, a number of regional and industrial data centers should be systematically arranged; support of project land, market development, investment and financing services etc. should be given to Internet data centers, cloud computing centers, cloud data centers, etc, which are mainly oriented to big data applications; preferential electricity prices and preferential Bandwidth charges are implemented in addition to subsidies to communication charges. In order to support big data platform service, the document proposes to build a unified public data open platform in the city, give priority to open public data with high attention and demand from the public and market subjects according to the market mechanism, and promote the social development and utilization of data resources. Support enterprises, institutions and industry associations to build big data common technology platform, provide users with R&D design, measurement, evaluation, standardization, inspection, certification and other technical services; support enterprises, institutions and industry associations to build big data open source community technology innovation platform, provide industry application-oriented solutions, software development and platform operation services. Enterprises that purchase the above platform services will be given a subsidy of up to 1 million Yuan per year according to 20% of the actual amount of service fee. To promote the development of industrial accelerator, Chengdu support big data enterprises, institutions and industry associations to build data resource database and professional big data service platform for application, collection, integration, cleaning and processing of public data and industry data. Open data to the outside world and provide data services, form industrial accelerator with data platform as the core, and aggregate industrial chain enterprises. For key accelerators, a one-off subsidy of no more than 3 million Yuan will be given at 30% of the investment and a subsidy of no more than 1 million Yuan will be given annually at 20% of the operating expenses. At the same time, it supports industry associations, industry service institutions and other organizations to carry out big data industry ecological research, industry data collection, planning and standard formulation, as well as enterprise services, industry docking, project roadshows and other activities, and give subsidies of no more than 200,000 Yuan according to the content and effect of the project.

为进一步促进大数据产业快速发展，成都市采取"内育外引"的政策思路，制定出台了《成都市促进大数据发展工作方案》。针对本土大数据企业成长度不够的问题，提出加强产业政策引导，营造优质营商环境，对大数据企业实施梯度培育，给予数据、技术、资金、市场、人才等要素支持，着力培育一批数据资源富集、创新能力领先、品牌价值较高、市场拓展能力较强的大数据本土企业，助推其成长为准独角兽、独角兽或行业领军企业。支持本土大数据专业服务企业积极争取国家级大数据项目，建设国家级大数据中心。支持农业、工业制造、能源、金融等行业骨干企业利用积累的行业数据资源，提供大数据相关的产品、解决方案及服务，推动行业骨干企业转型发展。鼓励研究机构和企业合作，推动电信运营商、大型互联网企业建设大数据产业平台，培育一批基于大数据的信息消费、文化创意、先进制造等领域新兴企业。同时，为加强对大数据产业精准招商，提出按照"一核两带"规划布局，在综合研判大数据产业发展和技术演进趋势的基础上，梳理大数据产业全景图及招商地图，创新招商机制，依托招商云网和产业生态建设联盟网实现大数据产业精准招商，吸引国内外大数据人才、企业、资金、项目落户成都，促进大数据产业生态建设。以政府数据运营授权为牵引，在数据安全可管可控的前提下，支持市属国有企业利用大数据资源主动开放合作，吸引国内外知名大数据重点企业强强联合，打造大数据创新应用项目。

In order to further promote the rapid development of big data industry, Chengdu adopts the policy idea of "internal cultivation and external introduction" and formulates "Work Plan of Promoting the Development of Big Data in Chengdu". In view of the insufficient growth of local big data enterprises, it proposes to strengthen the guidance of industrial policies, create a high-quality business environment, implement gradient cultivation of big data enterprises, give support to data, technology, capital, market, talents and other factors, and strive to cultivate a number of local big data Enterprises with rich data resources, leading innovation ability, high brand value and strong market expansion ability, and boost these enterprises grow into quasi unicorn, unicorn or industry leaders. Support local big data professional service enterprises to actively strive for national big data projects and build national big data centers. Support backbone enterprises in agriculture, industrial manufacturing, energy, finance and other industries to use the accumulated industry data resources to provide big data related products, solutions and services, and promote the transformation and development of backbone enterprises. Encourage cooperation between research institutions and enterprises, promote the construction of big data industry platform by telecom operators and large Internet enterprises, and cultivate a number of emerging enterprises in information consumption, cultural creativity, advanced manufacturing and other fields based on big data. At the same time, in order to strengthen the accurate investment invitation of big data industry, Chengdu proposes that in accordance with the planning layout of "one core, two belts", on the basis of comprehensive study and judgment of the development and technology evolution trend of big data industry, the panorama and investment invitation map of big data industry should be sorted out, the investment invitation mechanism should be innovated, and the accurate investment invitation of big data industry should be realized by relying on the investment invitation cloud network and industrial ecological construction alliance network, to attract big data talents at home and abroad, enterprises, funds and projects to settle in Chengdu to promote the ecological construction of big data industry. Guided by the government's data operation authorization and under the premise of controllable data security, it supports the municipal state-owned enterprises to actively open and cooperate by using big data resources and attracts the strong cooperation of domestic and foreign well-known big data key enterprises to create big data innovative and applicative projects.

按照《成都市促进大数据发展工作方案》要求,成都市将以建设"西部数都"为核心目标,按照综合化、体系化、生态化发展路径,努力将成都打造为全国大数据治理创新领先城市、全国大数据产业生态创新示范区和国际化大数据市场集散中心。到 2020 年,重点培育 3~5 个大数据产业集聚区,推进政府数据开放数据集 1 000 个以上,打造行业大数据应用示范 20 项以上、专业性大数据服务平台和行业加速器 10 个以上,制定大数据标准规范 10 项以上;力争培育大数据独角兽企业 1 家以上,培育收入规模超 10 亿元大数据企业 5 家以上,培育收入规模超亿元大数据企业 40 家以上;集聚国内外顶尖大数据人才不少于 30 人,大数据从业人员规模达到 6 万人以上;大数据核心产业产值突破 800 亿元。

According to "Chengdu's Work Plan for Promoting Big Data Development", Chengdu will aim at building "Western Digital City" and strive to become a leading city of big data governance and innovation, and a demonstration area of big data industry ecological innovation and an international big data market distribution center according to the comprehensive, systematic and ecological development approach. By 2020, Chengdu will cultivate 3-5 big data industrial clusters, promote more than 1,000 open data sets of government data, build more than 20 industry big data application demonstrations, more than 10 professional big data service platforms and industry accelerators, and formulate more than 10 big data standards and specifications; strive to cultivate more than one big data Unicorn enterprise, and cultivate more than 5 big data enterprises with the revenue of more than 1 billion Yuan and more than 40 big data enterprises with profits exceeding 100 million Yuan, introduce no less than 30 top big data talents at home and abroad and more than 60,000 big data professionals; and exceed 80 billion Yuan of the output value of big data core industry.

CiNED

第六章
跨界融合的 "六大形态"

Chapter Six
"Six Forms" of Cross Border Integration

"六大形态"包括数字经济、智能经济、绿色经济、创意经济、流量经济和共享经济,六大形态既各有其表征,在实践中又相互嵌入,形成了推动新经济高质量发展的强大合力。"六大形态"之间的关系可做如下理解。数字经济是载体。数字经济加速推动新经济产业价值链的分解、融合,不断催生新业态,构筑新场景,为经济提质增效提供新变量,为产业转型增长构建"新蓝海"。智能经济是表现形式。人工智能技术的应用逐渐渗透到生产、服务和消费的各个层面。人工智能技术在生产中的应用提升生产质量和工作效率,在服务行业的应用为消费者提供了更丰富多彩的消费体验,人工智能产品使人民生活更加便捷。绿色经济是基本要求,新经济的发展模式是一种符合环保发展要求,注重生态文明建设,以新能源和节能环保产业推进节能减排的绿色发展模式。创意经济是新趋势。新一代信息技术的不断完善,促使生产由大规模、标准化向小规模、个性化和定制化方向转变,以更低成本的多样化产品满足顾客的个性化需求,从需求侧满足了人民对美好生活的向往。流量经济是新引擎。流量经济具有强集聚辐射性,通过吸引全球范围内的资本、知识、信息、技术和人才等要素,实现重塑供应链、整合产业链、融合价值链,进而推动产业体系的跃升和高级化。共享经济是业态形式。共享经济以互联网为媒介,通过产品所有权与使用权的分离,使交易双方均获得经济利益,提高了社会资源配置效率,使闲置资源重新产生经济效益,如图 6-1 所示。

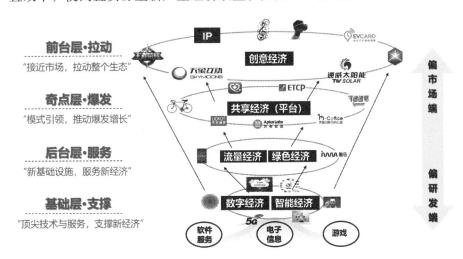

图 6-1 新经济"六大形态"

Figure 6-1 "Six Forms" of New Ecocomy

The "six forms" include digital economy, intelligent economy, green economy, creative economy, flow economy and shared economy. The six forms have their own features and interact in practice, forming a powerful force to promote the high-quality development of the new economy. The relationship between the "six forms" can be interpreted as follows: digital economy is the carrier, which accelerates the decomposition and integration of the industrial value chain of the new economy, constantly expedites new forms of business and constructs new scenescapes, provides new variables for improving economic quality and efficiency, and constructs a "new blue ocean" for industrial transformation and growth. Intelligent economy is a form of expression. The application of artificial intelligence technology has gradually penetrated into all levels of production, service and consumption. The application of artificial intelligence technology in production improves production quality and work efficiency; the application in service industry provides consumers with more colorful consumption experience; artificial intelligence products make people's life more convenient. Green economy is the basic requirement. The development mode of new economy is a green development mode that meets the requirements of environmental protection development, attaches importance to the construction of ecological civilization, and promotes energy conservation and emission reduction with new energy and industry of energy conservation and environmental protection. Creative economy is a new trend. With the continuous improvement of the new generation of information technology, the production has changed from large-scale and standardization to small-scale, personalization and customization. The diversified products with lower cost meet the personalized needs of customers and satisfy the people's yearning for a better life from the demand side. Flow economy is the new engine, which has the feature of strong agglomeration and radiation. By attracting capital, knowledge, information, technology and talents from all over the world, Chengdu can reshape the supply chain, pull together the industrial chain and integrate the value chain, to promote the leap and upgrading of the industrial system. Shared economy is a form of business. Shared economy takes the Internet as the medium. Through the separation of product ownership and use right, both parties of the transaction can obtain economic benefits, improve the allocation efficiency of social resources, and re-generate economic benefits from idle resources, as shown in Figure 6-1.

▷▷▷第一节　数字经济
Section One　Digital Economy

一、数字经济的内涵
1. Connotation of Digital Economy

党的十九届五中全会提出了加快数字化发展，推进数字产业化和产业数字化。数字经济是以数字化的知识和信息为关键生产要素的新经济形态。数字技术与实体经济融合，加速了资源要素的流动，扩展了经济发展新空间，促进了全要素生产率提升和经济可持续发展。目前，数字经济已逐渐成为推动新经济增长的新动能，发展数字经济成为促进我国经济转型和产业升级的国家战略。

The Fifth Plenary Session of the 19th CPC Central Committee proposed to accelerate the development of digitalization and promote digital industrialization and industrial digitalization. Digital economy is a new economic form with digital knowledge and information as the key production factors. The integration of digital technology and real economy accelerates the flow of resource factors, expands the new space of economic development, and promotes the improvement of total factor productivity and sustainable economic development. At present, digital economy has gradually become a new driving force to promote new economic growth, and the development of digital economy has become a national strategy to promote China's economic transformation and industrial upgrading.

目前，数字经济的内涵主要包括两大部分：一是以数字技术为核心的新兴产业，二是以数字经济为主导的新经济模式。数字经济具有数据化、平台化、技术创新、产业融合、多元共治等特征，推动数字经济的发展将进一步促进新经济的蓬勃发展。数字经济通过新技术和其他领域紧密融合，形成了5个层次和类型。一是基础型数字经济层，主要是以信息产业为主，包括电子信息制造业、信息通信业、软件服务业。二是融合型数字经济层，以信息产业投入传统产业为主，包括将信息采集、传输、仓储、处理等信息设备融入传统产业的生产、销售、流通、服务等各个环节，形成新的生产组织形式。三是效率型数字经济层，以信息技术带来的全要素生产效率提高的经济层，即以信息通信技术的使用提高全要素生产率，进而增加经济的总量部分。四是新生型数字经济层，由新产品新业态构成的经济层，即因信息通信技术与传统产业的融合，不断催生出新技术、新产品、新模式，并形成富有创新活力和发展潜力的新产业。五是福利型数字经济层，因数字技术的运用产生积极社会外部效应的经济层，即信息通信技术在社会经济领域的普及和推广，带来社会责任、公共安全和社会参与等潜在社会福利的增加而形成的新产业、新模式。

At present, the digital economy's connotation mainly includes two parts: one is the emerging industry with digital technology as the core; the other is the new economic model guided by digital economy. Digital economy has the characteristics of digitalization, platformization, technological innovation, industrial integration and multi-governance. Promoting the development of digital economy will further promote the vigorous development of new economy. Digital economy has formed five levels and types through the close integration of new technology and other fields. The first is the basic digital economy, which mainly focuses on information industry, including electronic information manufacturing, information communication and software services. The second is the integrated digital economy: information collection, transmission, storage, processing and other information equipment in the information industry will be integrated into the production, sales, circulation and service in traditional industries to form a new production organization form. The third is the efficient digital economy, which improves the total factor productivity by information technology, that is, the use of information and communication technology improves the total factor productivity, and then increases the total output of the economy. The fourth is the new digital economy which composed of new products and new form of business, that is, due to the integration of information and communication technology and traditional industries, new technologies, new products and new models have been continuously spawned, and new industries with innovative vitality and development potential have been formed. The fifth is the welfare digital economy, which comes from positive social externalities due to the application of digital technology, that is, the popularization and promotion of information and communication technology in the social and economic field, brings about the increase of social responsibility, public security, social participation and other potential social welfare to form new industries and new models.

二、数字经济的特征
2. Characteristics of Digital Economy

（一）以软件重构系统功能
（1）Reconstructing System Function with Software

所谓的"软件定义"就是指借助软件去重新定义系统的功能，通过软件给硬件赋能，从而促进行业系统运行效率最大提升。之所以说数字行业具有软件定义的特征，是因为软件定义的本质就是促进各行业产业数字化、标准化。数字产业通过软件编程实现虚拟、灵活、多样和定制化的功能，提供给客户更加智能化、定制化的服务，促进数字产业实现应用软件与硬件的深度融合。随着云计算、大数据、移动互联网、物联网等技术的迅猛发展，大部分行业的发展都离不开软件的支撑，以软件定义为特征之一的数字经济时代正与经济社会加速融合发展，软件创造了全新的经济、全新的管理和生活。数字经济必须通过软件才能实现人与人、人与物、物与物之间的连接和交流，而应用软件就是实现人际交流的窗口和渠道，通过软件来提升数字化能力，特别是在智能制造、机器人、航空航天、智慧城市、智慧医疗等重点领域尤为明显。

The so-called "software definition" refers to the use of software to redefine the functions of the system, empowering the hardware through software, to promote the maximum efficiency of the industry system. The reason why digital industry has the characteristics of software definition is that the essence of software definition is to promote the digitization and standardization of various industries. Through software programming, the digital industry realizes the functions of virtualization, flexibility, diversity and customization, provides customers with more intelligent and customized services, and promotes the deep integration of application software and hardware in the digital industry. With the rapid development of cloud computing, big data, mobile Internet, Internet of things and other technologies, the development of most industries cannot do without the support of software. The era of digital economy characterized by software definition is accelerating the integration of economic and social development. Software has created a new economy, new management and life. Digital economy can only realize the connection and communication between people, people and things, things and things through software, and application software is the window and channel to realize interpersonal communication. Software can obviously improve the digital ability, especially in some key fields such as intelligent manufacturing, robot, aerospace, smart city, smart medical.

（二）以平台支撑行业发展

（2）Supporting Industry Development with Platform

随着互联网的迅猛发展，生产服务、网络约车、电子商务等互联网平台已逐渐进入人们的生活，一定程度上也将促进运输业、零售业等进入下一个繁荣阶段。数字平台主要包括互联网生产服务平台、互联网生活服务平台、互联网科技创新平台、互联网公共服务平台。

With the rapid development of the Internet, production services, online car hailing, e-commerce and other Internet platforms have gradually entered people's lives, to a certain extent, which will also promote the transportation industry, retail industry to step into the next stage of prosperity. Digital platform mainly includes Internet production service platform, Internet life service platform, Internet technology innovation platform and Internet public service platform.

数字经济时代各行业的发展离不开大数字平台的支撑，例如智慧车联网平台依靠成熟云平台的支撑进行架构的设计和建设，以开发、智能、互动、高效为原则，充分利用物联网、大数据、分布式存储等技术，提供充电服务、设备接入、客户运营商入住、互联互通、用户支付、清算结算等综合服务，对港口行业的岸电对接、电动车行业推行"E 精灵"起到支撑作用。

In the era of digital economy, the development of various industries is inseparable from the support of big digital platform. For example, the vehicles's intelligent Internet platform relies on the support of mature cloud platform to design and construct. With the principle of development, intelligence, interaction and efficiency, it makes full use of the Internet of things, big data, distributed storage and other technologies to provide comprehensive services such as charging services, equipment access, customer operator check-in, interconnection, payment, clearing and settlement, which play a supporting role in the shore-power docking of the port industry and the implementation of "e-spirit" in the electric vehicle industry.

（三）以数据驱动要素流动

(3) Data-driven Factor Flow

数据驱动是指以数据为核心，在梳理各行业的数据资产的基础上，对其进行深度挖掘，共享共通，并以整合集成的方式驱动创新。数据具有客观性，人们可以从数据中发现规律、发现价值，从而为创新提供智力支撑，同时数据的广泛运用，也可以帮助管理者透过复杂繁多的流程看到行业业务的本质，为优化决策提供条件。

"Data-driven" refers to taking data as the core, deeply mining and sharing it, and driving innovation in the way of integration on the basis of ordering the data assets of various industries. Data is objective, from which rules and values can be discovered, thus providing intellectual support for innovation. At the same time, the wide use of data can also help managers see the nature of industry business through complex and complicated processes and provide conditions for optimizing decision-making.

依据数据的类型划分，主要包括：互联网安全服务、互联网数据服务、房地产中介服务、信息系统集成服务。互联网安全服务包括网络安全监控、网络可信度测评和网络安全等小类；互联网数据服务即指以互联网技术为基础的大数据处理、云存储、云计算、云加工（云制造）等服务；房地产中介服务即指网络房产中介网站及网络房产中介软件服务；信息系统集成服务产业主要包括信息系统设计、集成设施、运行维护及其他信息系统集成服务等。

The types of data mainly include: Internet security services, Internet data services, Internet advertising services, real estate agency services, information system integration services. Internet security services include network security monitoring, network credibility evaluation and network security, etc; Internet data services refer to big data processing, cloud storage, cloud computing, cloud processing (cloud manufacturing) and other services based on Internet technology; real estate agency services refer to network real estate agency website and network real estate agency software services; information system integration services industry mainly includes information system design, integration facilities, operation and maintenance and other information system integration services.

（四）以智能赋予万物互联

（4）Interconnection with Intelligence

近年来，在数字经济的引领下我国智能化的步伐逐渐加快，智能制造发展态势越来越突出。交通行业、电力行业、医疗行业等领域智能化的趋势逐渐显现，智能制造发展迅猛。代表性产业包括智能音响设备制造、智能影视录放设备制造、可穿戴智能设备制造、智能车载设备制造、智能无人飞行器制造、服务消费机器人制造等方面，其中智能车载设备制造的发展尤为突出。

In recent years, under the guidance of digital economy, the pace of intelligent development in China is gradually accelerating, especially in intelligent manufacturing. The intelligent trend in transportation industry, electric power industry and medical industry is gradually emerging, and intelligent manufacturing is developing rapidly. Representative industries include manufacturing of intelligent audio equipment, intelligent video recording and playing equipment, intelligent wearable equipment, intelligent vehicle equipment, intelligent unmanned aerial vehicle, service consumption robot and so on. The development of intelligent vehicle equipment manufacturing is particularly prominent.

三、数字经济的成都实践
3. Practice of Digital Economy in Chengdu

数字经济是当前新经济发展的主导形态，是数字技术应用在三次产业中形成的最广泛新经济形态，既有全新的新业态新模式新产业，也有传统产业转型升级的新业态新模式新产业。根据腾讯发布的《数字中国指数报告（2019）》，成都数字城市总指数领域排名全国第五，数字人才总量上排名全国第六、数字产业指数排名全国第五，数字文化指数排名全国第六，数字政务指数排全国第五，数字生活指数排名全国第三，数字产业十大细分行业排名均在全国前十位，产业优势十分明显。

Digital economy is the leading form of the current new economic development, and the most extensive new economic form formed by the application of digital technology in three industries. There are not only novel new forms of businesses, new modes and new industries, but also those transformed and upgraded from traditional industry. According to the "Digital China Index Report（2019）" released by Tencent, Chengdu ranks fifth in the total digital city index, sixth in the total number of digital talents, fifth in the digital industry index, sixth in the digital culture index, fifth in the digital government affairs index, third in the digital life index, and top ten sub-sectors of the digital industry in China, with obvious industrial advantages.

2018 年 3 月，作为数字经济产业牵头部门，成都市经济和信息化局等部门联合印发了《成都市推进数字经济发展实施方案》，聚焦信息技术产业 3 大重要领域：新一代信息技术基础领域、信息技术软件领域、信息技术硬件领域。13 个重点方向：IPv6、5G、数字终端、大数据、云计算、物联网、移动互联网、人工智能、网络信息安全、集成电路、新型显示、传感控制、智能硬件，推进数字经济重点产业加快发展。2020 年成都市政府工作报告提出，积极推动国家数字经济创新发展试验区建设，开展工业互联网、数字化车间和智能工厂应用试点，大力发展软件产业和软件应用，推动制造业数字化转型升级。预计到 2022 年，成都将基本形成较为完善的数字经济生态体系，预计数字经济重点领域产业规模超过 3 000 亿元，成为国内领先的数字经济发展高地。

In March 2018, as the leading department of digital economy industry, Chengdu Municipal Bureau of Economy and Information Technology and other departments jointly issued "Implementation Plan for Promoting the Development of Digital Economy in Chengdu", focusing on three important fields of information technology industry: the basic field of new generation information technology, the field of information technology software, and the field of information technology hardware, with 13 key directions: IPv6, 5G, digital terminal, big data, cloud computing, Internet of things, mobile Internet, artificial intelligence, network information security, integrated circuit, new display, sensor control, and intelligent hardware to promote the development of key industries in the digital economy. In 2020, the work report of Chengdu municipal government proposes to actively promote the construction of national digital economy innovation and development pilot zone, carry out the application pilot of industrial Internet, digital workshop and intelligent factory, vigorously develop software industry and software application, and promote the digital transformation and upgrading of manufacturing industry. It is estimated that by 2022 Chengdu will basically form a relatively complete digital economy ecosystem, with the industrial scale of key fields of digital economy over 300 billion Yuan, and become the leading digital economy development highland in China.

当前，以国民天成化合物半导体产业园为支撑的天府新区新能源新材料产业功能区，将打造从半导体核心基础材料到高端芯片、传感器、模组和终端产品制造及应用多位一体的产业集群，主要面向5G、物联网和智能电网等行业，助力成都数字经济产业生态圈创新生态链建设。在成都芯谷产业功能区，中电九天已建成智能制造创新中心、展示中心、协调中心和人才培养基地，旨在建设工业4.0体系下智能制造系统解决方案并提供智能制造云平台相关服务。2020年3月，新希望全球控股总部及天府数字经济产业园项目落户成都天府新区。2020年4月，软通动力信息技术（集团）有限公司提出，将在成都郫都区打造数字经济小镇。项目涵盖软件研发、人才培训以及基于数字经济的科技创新综合体。同年5月，《成都东部新区总体方案》出炉，简州新城将重点发展以智联新能源汽车为核心的智能经济、绿色经济，以大数据、物联网为支撑的数字经济，以智慧出行为方向的共享经济①。

At present, the industrial functional zone of new energy and new materials in Tianfu New Area, supported by National Tiancheng Compound Semiconductor Industrial Park, will build an industrial cluster from the core basic semiconductor materials to the manufacturing and application of high-end chips, sensors, modules and terminal products, mainly facing such industries

① 宋东旭，李珺. "双轮驱动"铸就成都数字经济新引擎［EB/OL］.（2020-06-09）［2021-03-01］. http://www.xinhuanet.com/enterprise/2020-06/09/c_1126092434.htm.

as 5G, Internet of things, smart grid, and help Chengdu digital economy industry ecosystem innovate ecological chain construction.

In Chengdu Chips Valley Industrial Functional Zone, CEC Jiutian has built intelligent manufacturing innovation center, exhibition center, coordination center and talents training base, aiming to build intelligent manufacturing system solutions under industry 4.0 system and provide relevant services of intelligent manufacturing cloud platform. In March 2020, New Hope Global Share Holding Headquarters and Tianfu Digital Economy Industrial Park Project were settled in Chengdu Tianfu new area. In April 2020, iSoftStone proposed to build a digital economic town in Pidu District of Chengdu. The project covers software R&D, talents training and innovation complex of science and technology based on digital economy. In May 2020, Overall Plan for the Eastern New Area of Chengdu was published, which states that Jianzhou new city will focus on the development of intelligent economy and green economy with intelligent new-energy vehicles as the core, of digital economy with big data and Internet of things as the support, and of the shared economy with smart travelling as the direction.

典型案例：打造智慧政务应用场景之新经济大数据监测平台
Typical case: Building a New Economic Big Data Monitoring Platform
for Smart Government Application Scenescapes

为推动新经济研究从"结果分析"到"趋势预测"，成都市新经济发展委员会牵头搭建了"成都新经济大数据监测平台"。该平台从2018年12月开始试运行，每季度末抓取互联网公开数据并生成监测报告。作为成都市发展新经济培育新动能工作的数字化决策辅助系统，该监测平台主要通过采集分析新经济关键量化指标数据，对成都市及各区（市）县新经济发展水平进行动态监测，同时进行成都市与国内新经济代表性城市的对标分析，对成都新经济企业进行全息画像，发掘未来的独角兽企业，提供国内外新经济发展最新资讯查询。

In order to promote the research of new economy from "result analysis" to "trend prediction", Chengdu New Economy Development Committee takes the lead in building "Chengdu New Economy Big Data Monitoring Platform". The platform has been operated for trial since December 2018. At the end of each quarter, it captures the Internet public data and generates monitoring reports. As a digital decision support system for the development of new economy and cultivation of new energy in Chengdu, the monitoring platform dynamically monitors the development level of new economy in Chengdu or its districts (counties) by collecting and analyzing the key quantitative index data of new economy. Meanwhile, it conducts bench-marking analysis between Chengdu and domestic representative cities of new economy and gets holographic maps of new economy enterprises in Chengdu to explore the future Unicorn enterprises and provide the latest information of new economic development at home and abroad.

▷▷▷ 第二节　智能经济
Section Two　Intelligent Economy

一、智能经济的内涵
1. Connotation of Intelligent Economy

智能经济是 2.0 版的数字经济。人工智能技术的应用逐渐渗透到生产、服务和消费的各个层面，在生产中的应用提高了产品质量和工作效率，在服务行业的应用为消费者提供了更丰富多彩个性化的消费体验。智能经济是以云计算、大数据、物联网、移动互联网等新一代信息技术为基础，以人工智能（AI）、虚拟现实（VR）、5G 技术、区块链等为代表的智能技术为支撑，以智能感知的信息与数字化的知识为关键生产要素，以智能产业化和产业智能化为主要形式，以智慧工厂、智慧旅游、智慧生活、智慧城市等为应用领域，推动人类社会生产方式、生活方式和社会治理方式智能化变革的经济形态。根据赛迪研究院公布的"2019

年中国智能经济发展潜力城市二十强"榜单，成都排位第 9，与武汉、南京、青岛、苏州同处智能经济第二梯队，在中西部地区处于领先水平，资源吸引力持续增强，后劲十足。

Intelligent economy is the digital economy of version 2.0. The application of artificial intelligence technology has gradually penetrated into all levels of production, service and consumption. The application in production improves production quality and work efficiency, and the application in service industry provides consumers with more colorful and personalized consumption experience. Intelligent economy is based on cloud computing, big data, Internet of things, mobile Internet and other new generation of information technology, with the support of such intelligent technology as artificial intelligence (AI), virtual reality (VR), 5G and block chain, the intelligent perception information and digital knowledge as the key production factors, the intelligent industrialization and industrial intelligence as the main forms, and the intelligent factory, intelligent tourism, intelligent life and intelligent city as the application fields to promote the intelligent transformation of human social production mode, life style and social governance mode. According to the list of "Top 20 Cities with Intelligent Economy Development Potential in China in 2019" released by CCID Research Institute, Chengdu ranks the ninth, in the second echelon of intelligent economy with Wuhan, Nanjing, Qingdao and Suzhou. It is in the leading level in the central and western regions, and its resource attraction continues to increase with great potential.

智能经济包括三个层级：一是基础层级，即新一代信息技术；二是产品层级，即智能制造（包括智能家居、智能穿戴、智能汽车、智能装备、机器人等相关产业）；三是应用层级，即智慧工厂、智慧旅游、智慧生活、智慧城市等。

Intelligent economy includes the following three levels: first, the basic level is new-generation information technology; second, the product level is intelligent manufacturing (including smart home, smart wear, smart car, smart equipment, robot and other related industries); third, the application level is smart factory, smart tourism, smart life, smart city, etc.

二、智能经济的特征

2. Characteristics of Intelligent Economy

（一）人机协同

（1）Human-machine Cooperation

人机协同是经济活动中人与智能和谐状态的体现，是智能经济发展中智能与人类生态、环境、活动和谐共生的表现。人机协同表明，在智能经济结构中，人与智能（机器、信息、传感器、人工智能等）是相互依存、相辅相成的，具有同等重要的作用[1]。感知技术成为当前人工智能产业化的主要内容，尤其是图像识别技术和语音交互类技术进入产业应用阶段。随着感知技术的成熟，机器能够以全新的人机交互模式感知人类，与人进行交互。例如制造领域，成熟的感知技术将推动传统的自动化生产设施和工业机器人向智能化升级。随着感知能力和人机协作能力的提升，未来就会呈现出人机协同生产的趋势。

Human-machine cooperation is embodied in the harmonious state of human and intelligence in economic activities, and in the harmonious coexistence of intelligence and human ecology, environment and activities in the development of intelligent economy. Human-machine cooperation shows that human and intelligence (machine, information, sensor, artificial intelligence, etc.) are interdependent and complementary as the same important role in the intelligent economic structure. Sensory technology has become the main content of AI industrialization, especially the image recognition technology and voice interaction technology at industrial application the stage. With the maturity of sensory technology, machines can perceive and interact with people in a new human-computer interaction mode. For example, in the field of manufacturing,

---

[1] 孙守迁. 智能经济构建未来形态 [J]. 杭州（党政刊），2018（36）：13-16.

mature sensory technology will promote the intelligent upgrading of traditional automatic production facilities and industrial robots. With the improvement of sensory ability and human-computer cooperation, human-computer cooperative production will be the future trend.

（二）多重融合

（2）Multi-integration

相比以往的信息技术，人工智能具有更强大的垂直渗透和横向整合能力。现如今，人工智能已逐渐渗透到各行各业，在医疗、汽车、金融、零售、安防、教育、家居等行业都有了具体的落地产品，通过"人工智能+"的方式，推动信息技术与传统产业深度融合。另外，数据作为新的生产要素，也会改变原有的产业链结构。跨界获取数据将会极大增强自身产品的竞争力，将自身数据应用于其他行业，衍生新的商业模式和产品。行业之间的界限将变得模糊，跨界、跨行业融合发展的智能经济正在成为经济发展的新形态。

Compared with the previous information technology, artificial intelligence has a stronger ability of vertical penetration and horizontal integration. Nowadays, artificial intelligence has gradually penetrated into all walks of life. There are specific products in medical, automobile, finance, retail, security, education, home furnishing and other industries. The way of artificial intelligence plus promotes the deep integration of information technology and traditional industries. In addition, as a new factor of production, data will also change the original industrial chain structure. Cross-border access to data will greatly enhance the competitiveness of the products, and new business models and products take shape by applying these data to other industries and derive. The boundaries between industries have become blurred, and the cross-border and cross-industry integrated development of intelligent economy is becoming a new form of economic development.

（三）共担共享

(3) Sharing

共担共享是智能经济中知识、资源、信息等重要生产要素的分配体现，是满足智能经济发展目标的重要保障。通过共创分享，智能经济的生产要素才能在经济活动中无限制地流通，从而最大限度地挖掘出经济价值，实现经济健康发展。从网络时代开始，基于互联网的共创分享模式已经快速地发展起来，在网络化时代，随着基于互联网的群体智能技术的发展，不同个体之间智力的分享和协同成为可能，众创、众包、众服成为组织经济活动的基本方式。在大数据驱动的基本模式下，随着智能可穿戴设备、数字孪生体技术的进一步应用，智能化应用向平台化、生态化发展，这类智能化产品的用户既是产品的使用者，也是产品创造者，智能化应用的共创分享特征将越来越明显①。

Sharing is the distribution of knowledge, resources, information and other important production factors in the intelligent economy, which is an important guarantee to meet the intelligent economy development's goals. Through co-creation and sharing, the production factors of intelligent economy can circulate freely in economic activities, to maximize the economic value and realize the healthy development of economy. At the beginning of the network era, the co-creation and shared mode based on the Internet has developed rapidly. In the network era, with the development of Internet-based group intelligence technology, it is possible for different individuals to share and coordinate their intelligence. Crowd-making, crowd-packing and crowd-service have become the basic ways to organize economic activities. In the basic mode driven by big data, with the further application of intelligent wearable and digital twin technology, intelligent applications are developing towards platform and ecology. Users of such intelligent products are not only product users but also product creators. The co-creation and shared characteristics of intelligent

① 李修全. 从五个方面看未来智能经济的发展特征［EB/OL］.（2017–12–14）［2020–10–28］. https://www.iyiou.com/analysis/2017121462192.

applications will be more and more obvious.

（四）自主优化

（4）Self-optimization

自主优化是智能的体现，是智能经济的高级表现。自主优化体现在智能经济发展成熟阶段，随着智能感知的信息不断增加和更新，面对多样化的经济态势，自主优化能够自主地适应变化，智能地完成相对应的处理，从而避免可能的风险，优化经济资源，创造经济价值。

Self-optimization is the embodiment of an intelligence and the advanced performance of intelligent economy. Self-optimization is reflected in the mature stage of intelligent economy development. With the increasing and updating of intelligent sensory information, in the face of diversified economic situation, self-optimization can independently adapt to changes and intelligently complete the corresponding processing, to avoid possible risks, optimize economic resources and create economic value.

三、智能经济的成都实践
3. Practice of Intelligent Economy in Chengdu

中国信息通信研究院《成都智能经济产业发展报告》指出，目前成都智能经济在中西部地区处于领先水平，预计到 2022 年将成为"全国智能经济发展的城市样本"。成都将重点围绕智能技术、智能产品、智能服务、应用场景四个维度，前瞻布局"云大物智"（云计算、大数据、物联网、人工智能）、工业控制、安全保障、芯片与模块、智能硬件、终端与装备、工业软件、无人系统、大数据服务、人工智能服务十大技术产业领域，聚焦工业互联网、机器人、无人机、卫星、智慧城市五大应用场景，着力实施载体建设、创新发展、企业培育、人才建设四大生态工程，推动智能经济可持续发展。其中，围绕智能经济十大技术产业领域，成都构建了"三区一环双翼"的产业发展空间。

According to "Chengdu Intelligent Economy Industry Development Report" issued by China information and Communication Research Institute,

Chengdu's intelligent economy is currently at the leading level in the central and western regions and is expected to become a "national sample city of intelligent economy development" by 2022. Chengdu will focus on the four dimensions of intelligent technology, intelligent products, intelligent services, and application scenescapes, and make a forward-looking layout of the top ten technology industries of "cloud big intelligence" (namely cloud computing, big data, Internet of things, and artificial intelligence), industrial control, security, chips and modules, intelligent hardware, terminals and equipment, industrial software, unmanned systems, big data services, and artificial intelligence services. It focuses on five application scenescapes of industrial Internet, robot, UAV, satellite and smart city, four ecological projects of carrier construction, innovation and development, enterprise cultivation and talents construction to promote the sustainable development of intelligent economy. Among them, around the top ten technological industries of intelligent economy, Chengdu has built an industrial development space of "three districts, one ring and two wings".

"三区":以成都天府新区、高新区和双流区为主体,构建智能经济综合集聚区。成都高新西区围绕芯片与模块、智能硬件、终端与装备等领域,重点布局集成电路、光电显示、智能信息终端、卫星导航等产业;高新东区围绕"云大物智"、工业控制等关键技术,重点布局云计算、大数据、人工智能、虚拟(增强)现实、智能信息终端、机器人等领域;成都天府新区、高新南区及双流区围绕"云大物智"、网络安全等关键技术,重点布局芯片与模块、智能硬件、传感控制、无人系统、人工智能、信息安全、智能服务等领域。

"Three zones": Take Chengdu Tianfu New Area, Hi-Tech Zone and Shuangliu District as the main body to build an intelligent economy comprehensive gathering zone. Chengdu West Hi-Tech Zone focuses on integrated circuit, photoelectric display, intelligent information terminal, satellite navigation and other industries in the fields of chips and modules, intelligent hardware, terminals and equipment; East Hi-Tech Zone focuses on cloud computing, big data, artificial intelligence, virtual (augmented) reality, intelligent information terminal, robot and other key technologies in the fields of "cloud computing, big data, Internet of things, artificial intelligence", industrial control and so on; Chengdu Tianfu New Area, South Hi-tech Zone and Shuangliu District focus on the layout of chips and modules, intelligent hardware, sensor control, unmanned system, artificial intelligence, information security, intelligent services and so on in the fields of the key technologies such as "cloud computing, big data, Internet of things, artificial intelligence" and network security.

"一环"：以青羊区、金牛区、武侯区、成华区和锦江区等为主体，构建智能经济"软实力"功能圈。重点布局大数据、人工智能、工业互联网、工业大数据、工业软件等关键技术产业，发展大数据服务、人工智能服务、精准医疗服务、研发设计、信息服务、金融服务、内容服务等高技术服务业。

"One Ring": build the "soft power" functional circle of intelligent economy with Qingyang District, Jinniu District, Wuhou District, Chenghua District and Jinjiang District as the main body. Focus on key technology industries such as big data, artificial intelligence, industrial Internet, industrial big data and software, and develop high-tech service industries such as big data service, artificial intelligence service, precision medical service, R&D and design, information service, financial service and content service.

"双翼"：城市东侧以青白江区、金堂县、龙泉驿区、简阳市，西侧以郫都区、崇州市、大邑县、邛崃市、蒲江县等为主体，构建成都市智能经济的"硬实力"产业带，重点发展无人机、智能网联汽车、机器人、高档数控机床、增材制造、传感控制、智能可穿戴、智能家居、卫星导航、光电技术等新兴制造业，分类分梯度承接成都全市相关制造企业转移。

"Two wings": with Qingbaijiang District, Jintang County, Longquanyi

District and Jianyang City on the east side of the city, Pidu District, Chongzhou City, Dayi County, Qionglai City and Pujiang County on the west side, the "hard power" industrial belt of Chengdu's intelligent economy is constructed, focusing on the development of UAVs, intelligent networked vehicles, robots, high-end CNC machine tools, additive manufacturing, sensor control and intelligent wearable equipment, smart home, satellite navigation, optoelectronic technology and other emerging manufacturing industries, undertaking the transfer of relevant manufacturing enterprises in Chengdu by classification and gradient.

2020 年 3 月，成都获批建设国家新一代人工智能创新发展试验区。这是国家在西部布局的首批国家级人工智能发展试验区，标志着成都在人工智能产业上迈出了新步伐。试验区将开展人工智能创新试验，探索体制机制、政策法规、人才培育等方面的重大改革，推动人工智能成果转化，重大产品集成创新以及智能空管、普惠金融、智慧医疗等场景加强应用示范。

In March 2020, Chengdu was approved to build a national new generation artificial intelligence innovation and development pilot zone. This is one of the first batches of national artificial intelligence development pilot zones in Western China, marking a new step in Chengdu's artificial intelligence industry. The pilot zone will carry out artificial intelligence innovation experiments, explore major reforms in institutional mechanisms, policies and regulations, talents cultivation, promote the transformation of artificial intelligence achievements, major product integration and innovation, and strengthen application demonstration in intelligent air traffic control, inclusive finance, intelligent medical and other scenescapes.

典型案例：提升新技术、新模式服务实体经济能力

应用场景之译迅科技

Typical Case：Improving the Ability of New Technology

and New Mode to Serve the Real Economy（Eson Tech）

译迅科技以破除语言信息壁垒为使命，致力于打造全球领先的跨语言大数据信息共享平台。依托百亿句对（约 4 000 亿字）、28 个专业细分领域的精准多语言大数据库，凭借在图文识别、智能算法、机器学习、数据检索等领域的技术优势，为用户提供快速、准确、方便、省钱的软件技术工具和信息情报系统，并以软件系统作为用户流量及数据增量的入口，构建跨国交流社群和国际朋友圈，打造全球跨语言大数据信息共享平台。

With the mission of breaking down language information barriers, Eson Tech is committed to building a global leading inter-language big data information shared platform. Relying on the 10 billion sentence pairs（about 400 billion words）, the accurate multilingual database in 28 professional subdivisions, and the technical advantages in the fields of text recognition, intelligent algorithm, machine learning, data retrieval, etc., it provides users with fast, accurate, convenient and economical software technology tools and information systems, and takes the software system as the entrance of user flow and data increment to construct a transnational communication community and international circle of friends, and build a global cross language big data information shared platform.

▷▷▷第三节 绿色经济
Section Three　Green Economy

一、绿色经济的内涵
1. Connotation of Green Economy

绿色经济的内涵主要包括三个部分：一是环境资源利用的绿色化。经济学家肯尼斯·博尔丁利用"牛仔"和"太空人"的对比图像来阐释对环境的态度变化：生活在美国西部广袤土地上的"牛仔"，总是向外推进，扩大他的可用资源，寻找新的开拓领域。因为广袤的土地能够为他提供足够的资源，也能自然净化他生产生活的废弃物，但是"太空人"生活在狭小的飞船之中，没有无限的空间予以提取资源或净化污染，他必须"精打细算"地利用循环系统以保证其在有限的空间能尽可能地生存。我们现在的地球已经变成了一艘宇宙飞船，绿色经济的提出，表明人类已经开始关注如何促使资源的循环利用和废弃物的有效处理。

The connotation of green economy mainly includes three parts: first, the green utilization of environmental resources. Economist Kenneth Ewart Boulding uses the comparative images of "cowboy" and "astronaut" to explain the change of attitude towards the environment: the "cowboy" who lives in the vast land of the western United States always pushes outward, expands his available resources, and looks for new development areas, because the vast land can provide him with enough resources, and also can naturally purify the waste of his production and life. However, the "astronaut" lives in a small spaceship, and has no unlimited space to extract resources or purify pollution. He must make good use of the recycling system to ensure that he can survive in the limited space as much as possible. Now our earth has become a spaceship.

Green economy proposes that human beings have begun to pay attention to promoting the recycling of resources and the effective treatment of waste.

二是经济运行系统的绿色化①。绿色经济是低碳排放、资源有效、兼顾社会效益的环境型经济，是新经济发展的内在要求。从广义上看，绿色经济包括数字经济、智能经济、共享经济等新经济形态。目前，成都绿色经济发展在人才和技术方面有突出优势，显现出良好的发展势头，在西部地区处于领先地位。目前，对绿色经济的理解是一种广义的理解，应关注社会、经济与环境三者的协调发展，谋求在经济发展、环境保护和社会和谐之间实现一种有机平衡。

The second is the green economic operation system. Green economy means low carbon emissions, effective resources, and social benefits. It is the inherent requirement of new economic development. In a broad sense, it includes digital economy, intelligent economy, sharing economy and other new economic forms. At present, Chengdu's green economy development has outstanding advantages in talents and technology, showing a good driver of development, and is in a leading position in the western region. The understanding of green economy is a broad understanding, which focuses on the coordinated development of society, economy and environment, and seeks to achieve an organic balance between economic development, environmental protection and social harmony.

市场机会转化为利润，而更多的利润不仅是经济系统的动力，也是社会系统更快发展所需的财政资源的来源，所以商人和政治家都喜欢它。但是正如美国环境学家爱德华·阿比所认为的那样——"为增长而增长是癌细胞的意识形态"。单纯的以追求"数量"增长为目标的经济发展方式带来了极大的危害：资源枯竭，废物超负荷，褐色经济发展难以为继②。与传统经济只关注"数量"不同，绿色经济更加关注经济发展的"质量"。把有利于环境改善和资源的节约作为其质的规定性，把

---

① Molly Scott Cato. Green Economics. London: Earthscan, 2009: 35-41.
② D. H. Meadows, D. L. Meadows, J. Randers and W. W. Behrens (1972) The Limits to Growth: A Report for the Club of Rome's Project on the Predicament of Mankind, New York: Universe Books.

人与自然的关系纳入经济学的研究范围，把人们的经济活动置于人类生态系统中，把经济系统作为人类生态系统的子系统来看待。

Market opportunities turn into profits, and more profits are not only the driving force of the economic system, but also the source of financial resources needed for the faster development of the social system, favored by businessmen and politicians. But an American environmentalist Edward Abby states, "Growth for growth is the ideology of cancer cells." The economic development mode with the goal of pursuing "quantity" growth has brought great harm: resource depletion, waste overload and unsustainable economic development. Unlike the traditional economy which only focuses on "quantity", green economy pays more attention to the "quality" of economic development. The relationship between man and nature is included in the scope of economics. People's economic activities are placed in the human ecosystem, and the economic system is regarded as a subsystem of the human ecosystem.

三是生产生活理念的绿色化。传统经济学通常从"供给"与"需求"的角度对商品生产和交换关系进行分析，绿色经济则要求对人们、人们的关系以及人们的行为和动机有更加丰富和深入的理解。我们关心的"需求"不仅仅是身体上的需求，还有心理和精神上的需求。绿色经济在人类自我精神层面主张抛弃"消费主义"，提倡可持续的生产生活理念——"富足伦理"。

Third, the concept of green production and life. Traditional economics usually analyzes the relationship between commodity production and exchange from the perspective of "supply" and "demand", while green economy requires a richer and deeper understanding of people, their relationship, behavior and motivation. The "needs" people care about are not only physical, but also psychological and spiritual. Green economy advocates abandoning "consumerism" and instead the concept of sustainable production and life — "affluence ethics".

二、绿色经济的特征

2. Characteristics of Green Economy

（一）环境友好

（1）Friendly Environment

建立在对资源环境过度消耗基础上、忽视生态保护的不可持续的经济发展模式被称为"褐色经济"。与褐色经济相对应的绿色经济，以亲环境为基本特征，追求经济发展的环境合理性，要求在较小的环境代价、较低的资源消耗下实现经济发展，即在低消耗、低排放、低污染的条件下进行生产生活。绿色经济的环境合理特性，使得绿色经济在资源配置上有利于实现社会利益的最大化。

"Brown economy" means the unsustainable economic development model based on excessive consumption of resources and environment and ignoring ecological protection. The green economy, corresponding to the brown economy, with environment protection as its basic feature, pursues the environmental rationality of economic development, and requires the realization of economic development with less environmental cost and lower resource consumption, that is, to produce and live under the conditions of low consumption, low emission and low pollution. The reasonable environmental characteristics of green economy make it beneficial to realize the maximization of social benefits in resource allocation.

（二）高效兼顾

（2）High Efficiency

社会中人的行为具有极强的"经济理性"，也就是人在既定法律和制度约束下是自利的、理性的和效用最大化的追逐者，人们从事经济活动是为了满足自己的经济福利，实现个人利益的最大化是人们从事经济活动的原生动力。发展绿色经济，并不是片面地为了保护环境来牺牲经济效率，而是要求在资源配置时，既要保护环境实现社会利益，又要通过发展低碳、循环等产业，促使经济效率的提升，有效实现个人利益。

绿色经济更主要地体现着最小资源耗费与最大经济产出、清洁生产资源循环利用及高新技术创新的生态系统的特征。只有绿色经济效率实现了最大化，才能保证生态系统在新的条件下实现和谐，也才能为社会系统的公平提供坚实的经济基础。

People's behaviors in society have a strong "economic rationality". That is, people are pursuers of self-interest, rationality and utility maximization under the constraints of established laws and systems. People are engaged in economic activities to meet their own economic welfare, whose original driving force to engage in economic activities is realizing the maximization of personal interests. The development of green economy is not to sacrifice economic efficiency unilaterally to protect the environment, but to protect the environment and realize social interests in resource allocation and promote the improvement of economic efficiency and effectively realize personal interests through the development of low-carbon, recycling and other industries. Green economy mainly embodies the characteristics of the ecosystem of minimum resource consumption and maximum economic output, clean production resource recycling and high-tech innovation. Only when the efficiency of green economy is maximized, can the ecosystem be harmonious under the new conditions and provide a solid economic foundation for the fairness of the social system.

三、绿色经济的成都实践
3. Practice of Green Economy in Chengdu

绿色发展路径中，绿色经济是关键所在。为此，成都把发展绿色经济作为推动经济高质量发展的重要抓手，把建设低碳城市作为推进绿色经济发展的重要载体，把低碳城市建设与绿色经济发展有机结合，为成都建设美丽宜居的公园城市提供绿色产业支撑。

Green economy is the key in the green development. Therefore, Chengdu takes the development of green economy as an important way to promote high-quality economic development, and takes the construction of low-carbon city as an important carrier to promote the development of green economy. It organically combines the construction of low-carbon city with the development of green economy, to provide green industry support for ieself to build a beautiful and livable Park City.

2018 年由成都市发改委牵头制定出台的《成都市推进绿色经济发展的实施方案》（以下简称《实施方案》），系统性地描绘了成都绿色经济发展的路线图：到 2022 年，绿色经济将成为成都现代化经济体系的重要支柱，绿色低碳制造业实现主营业务收入 3 000 亿元以上。

In 2018, Chengdu Development and Reform Commission took the lead in formulating "Implementation Plan for Promoting Green Economy Development in Chengdu", which systematically describes the road map of green economy development in Chengdu: by 2022, green economy will become an important pillar of Chengdu's modern economic system, and green low-carbon manufacturing industry will get more than 300 billion Yuan of main business profits.

《实施方案》从做强绿色低碳制造业、壮大绿色低碳服务业、培育绿色循环产业三个维度，提出重点发展新能源、节能环保、新能源汽车、绿色建筑、绿色物流、绿色低碳第三方服务、绿色金融、城市静脉、森林康养共"九大产业形态"，旨在全面提升绿色产品供给水平。

The plan puts forward to give priority to nine industrial forms of new energy, energy conservation and environmental protection, new-energy vehicles, green buildings, green logistics, green low-carbon third-party services, green finance, urban vein and health care, from three dimensions of strengthening green low-carbon manufacturing industry, expanding green low-carbon service industry and cultivating green recycling industry, aiming at comprehensively improving the supply of green products.

在绿色低碳制造业方面，将重点做强新能源产业，力争打造国内一流、中西部领先的新能源产业基地。与此同时，将做强节能环保产业，建成国家级节能环保产业基地，使节能环保产业成为发展绿色经济的重要支柱。新能源汽车产业方面将实施新能源汽车全产业链发展战略，建成国家重要的新能源汽车生产和示范基地。同时，做强绿色建筑产业，转变城乡建设模式和建筑业发展方式，建设国家装配式建筑示范城市。

In terms of green and low-carbon manufacturing, Chengdu will strengthen the new energy industry, and strive to build a first-class new energy industry base in China and leading in the central and western regions. At the same time, it will strengthen the energy-saving and environmental protection industry and build a national base to make the energy-saving and environmental protection industry an crucial pillar for the development of green economy. In terms of new energy vehicle industry, Chengdu will implement the whole industry chain development strategy of new-energy vehicles and build an important national production and demonstration base of new-energy vehicles. At the same time, it will strengthen the green construction industry, change the urban and rural construction mode and the development mode of the construction industry, and build a national prefabricated construction demonstration city.

在绿色低碳服务业方面，成都将重点壮大绿色物流产业，推进物流领域全过程绿色化、低碳化。壮大绿色低碳第三方服务业，培育壮大节能环保、碳交易和碳资产管理服务公司，增强绿色生产服务能力。壮大绿色金融产业，重点发展绿色信贷、绿色债券、绿色股票、绿色基金、绿色保险等产品，鼓励更多社会资本投入绿色产业。

In terms of green and low-carbon service industry, Chengdu will focus on strengthening the green logistics industry and promoting the green and low-carbon process of logistics. It will expand the green and low-carbon third-party service industry, cultivate and expand energy conservation and environmental protection, carbon trading and carbon asset management service companies, and enhance the green production service capacity. It will strengthen the green financial industry, focus developing green credit, green bonds, green stocks, green funds, green insurance and other products, and encourage more social capital to invest in the green industry.

在培育绿色循环产业方面，成都将重点培育城市静脉产业，科学规划专业性、综合性的固体废物处置设施和园区。培育森林康养产业，坚持林旅融合、医养并重，推出一批以特色医疗、疗养康复、森林康养等为主题的康养旅游产品，建设康养综合体。

In terms of cultivating green recycling industry, Chengdu will focus on cultivating urban venous industry, and scientifically plan professional and comprehensive facilities and parks to dispose solid waste. It will cultivate the forest health care industry, adhere to the integration of forest and tourism, pay equal attention to medical care and regimen, launch a several health care tourism products with the theme of featured medical treatment, convalescence and rehabilitation, and forest health care, and build a health care complex.

发展绿色经济"九大产业形态"必须有相应的空间载体。按照产业生态圈理念，《实施方案》围绕重塑绿色经济发展空间格局，重点依托产业功能区及园区，提出构建"新能源、节能环保、新能源汽车、绿色金融、森林康养"五大产业重点发展区，构建"绿色建筑、绿色低碳第三方服务、城市静脉"三大产业聚集区，落实绿色经济发展"5+3"空间版图。

To develop "nine industrial forms" of green economy must have corresponding space carrier. According to the concept of industrial ecosystem, the plan proposes to build five major industrial development zones of "new energy, energy saving and environmental protection, new energy vehicles, green finance and forest health care", and three industrial clusters of "green building, green low-carbon third-party service and urban vein", and realize "5+3" map of green economy development, by focusing on reshaping the spatial pattern of green economic development and relying on industrial functional areas and parks.

典型案例:推动生产、城市、生活绿色化应用场景
之天府新区第一污水处理厂

Typical case:First Sewage Treatment Plant in Tianfu New Area

to Promote Green Scenescapes of Production,City and Life

为把绿色低碳理念运用于城市规划建设管理的各方面,成都积极推进海绵城市、地下综合管廊建设,加强绿色能源使用和废弃物无害化处理,加大环保技术推广应用,提升城市可持续运营和发展能力。天府新区第一污水处理厂按照"环境友好、土地集约、资源利用"的理念建设,出水水质的主要指标达到地表水 IV 类水标准,优于国家关于再生水的相关标准。建设形式上,该项目的污水处理均在地下厂区内完成,地面为集环保科普、休闲游憩于一体的景观活水公园,有效提升了周边社区的环境品质。建设标准上,首先,污水厂设计出水主要指标达到地表水 IV 类水标准,优于现行最严格的国家标准;其次,污水厂建设形式为全地埋式,机械噪声全隔离,对周边无噪声污染;最后,尾气全收集全处理,达到国家一级排放标准,该标准是按照在风景名胜区建设污水处理设施标准来设置的,为国内污水厂尾气排放的最严格标准。该项目采用全地下式结构,构筑物共壁合建,配套建筑在地下结构内分层布置,结构紧凑,厂区占地仅 37.5 亩,如图 6-2 所示。建筑出水全部回用,其中 1 万吨/天成为高品质再生水,经综合管廊输送到科学城用于公建清洗、道路冲洗、绿化浇洒等;其余作为普通再生水,为鹿溪河生态湿地提供景观及生态补水。污水厂内,有近 1/3 的能耗来自鼓风曝气,该项目采用世界领先的磁悬浮式鼓风机,可降低能耗约 15%。

图 6-2 天府新区第一污水处理厂

Figure 6-2 Chengdu Tianfu New District No. 1 Wastewater Treatment Plant

In order to apply the green and low-carbon concept to all aspects of urban planning, construction and management, Chengdu actively promotes the construction of sponge city and underground utility tunnel, strengthens the use of green energy and harmless treatment of waste, increases the popularization and application of environmental protection technology, and improves the ability of sustainable operation and development of the city. The first sewage treatment plant in Tianfu New Area is constructed according to the concept of "friendly environment, intensive land and resource utilization". The main indexes of the effluent quality reach the class IV water standard of surface water, superior to the relevant national standards for reclaimed water. In terms of construction form, the sewage treatment of the project is completed in the underground plant area, and on the ground is a landscape water park integrating environmental protection, science popularization, leisure and recreation, which effectively improves the environmental quality of surrounding communities. In terms of construction standards, first of all, the main indexes of the designed effluent reach the class IV water standard for surface water, superior to the current most stringent national standard; second, the construction is fully under the ground, with mechanical noise isolation and no noise pollution to the surrounding; third, the exhaust gas is fully collected and treated, which meets the national first-class discharge standard and the most stringent standard for exhaust gas of domestic sewage treatment plants, based on the construction of sewage treatment in scenic spots. The project has the underground structures with the structure built on the same wall. In the underground structure, the supporting buildings are arranged in layers with compact structure. The plant area is only 6.18 acres, as shown in Figure 6-2. All the building effluent is reused, of which 10,000 tons per day becomes high-quality reclaimed water, which is transported to the science city through the comprehensive utility tunnel for public building cleaning, road washing, greening and sprinkling; the rest is used as ordinary reclaimed water to provide landscape and ecological water supplement for Luxi River Ecological Wetland. Nearly 1/3 of the energy consumption in the sewage treatment plant comes from blast aeration. The world-leading magnetic levitation blower is adopted in the project, which can reduce the energy consumption by about 15%.

▷▷▷ 第四节　创意经济
Section Four　Creative Economy

一、创意经济的内涵
1. Connotation of Creative Economy

创意经济是数字技术、人工智能技术等在文化创意产业领域的广泛应用，促使文化生产由批量化、标准化向定制化、个性化方向转变，以更高效的多样化产品/服务满足人民对美好生活的需要。

Creative economy is the wide application of digital technology and artificial intelligence technology in the field of cultural and creative industries, which promotes the transformation of cultural production from batch and standardization to customization and personalization, and satisfying people's needs for a better life with more efficient and diversified products and services.

二、创意经济的特征
2. Feature of Creative Economy

（一）依附性

（1）Dependence

创意经济的价值实现以物质产品的使用价值为基本承载。表现在：一是创意向其他产业部门的渗透。主要集中在消费性创意产业，如游戏动漫产业巨大的经济收益，有70%都来自玩具、服装、文具、音像出版物等衍生产品。二是传统产业部门对创意的投入。主要集中于生产性创意产业。由于产业竞争更加关注创意带来的价值增值，创意活动部门逐渐分离出来成为独立盈利部门，为传统产业提供创意性的中间投入品。如工业设计中的产品设计、包装设计、工艺设计等，都是依托产品的使用价值实现创意价值的倍增。

The value realization of creative economy is based on the use-value of material products. The first is the penetration of creativity into other industries, mainly in consumer creative industries. For example, 70% of the substantial economic benefits in the game animation industry come from toys, clothing, stationery, audio-visual publications and other derivative products. The second is the creativity input of traditional industries, mainly in productive creative industries. As the industry competition pays more attention to the added value brought by creativity, the creative activity department is gradually separated to become an independent profit department, providing creative intermediate inputs for traditional industries. For example, product design, packaging design and process design in industrial design all rely on the use value of products to realize the multiplication of creative value.

（二）跨界性

2. Cross-border

创意的辐射、渗透、融合作用，决定了创意经济跨行业、跨领域衍生的特征。创意经济衍生路径有两个：一是产业链衍生。创意、创意活动、创意产业都位于产业链的高端，以先进技术和持续创新为依托，延长创意产业链条。二是跨边界衍生。创意、创意活动、创意产业都位于价值链的高端，且创意产业具有边界模糊化的特征，即不以固定的传统行业和产业边界为限。从价值链的高端出发，一方面通过知识产权转化实现创意产业化，另一方面通过向三次产业延伸强化生产过程的创意化，实现产业创意化。

The radiation, penetration and integration of creativity determine the cross-industry and cross-field derivative characteristics of creative economy. There are two ways of creative economy derivation: one is industry-chain derivation.

Creative thinking, creative activities and creative industries are all located at the high end of the industrial chain, which is based on advanced technology and continuous innovation to extend the creative industry chain; second, cross-border derivation, in which creativity, creative activities and creative industries are all located at the high end of the value chain, and creative industries have the characteristics of fuzzy boundaries, that is, they are not limited to fixed traditional industries and industrial boundaries. Starting from the high end of the value chain, on the one hand, Chengdu achieve creative industrialization through the transformation of intellectual property rights; on the other hand, Chengdu achieve industrial creativity through the extension to the three industries to strengthen the creative production process.

（三）文化性

3. Culture

创意经济极大地体现了文化艺术对经济的推动作用。创意集知识、技术和文化于一体，使其区别于其他生产要素。创意要素的投入，带动了新兴的经济活动和产业部门发展，拓展了传统产品附加值提升的空间，提高了单位产品的利润价值。产品创意、服务创意、营销创意等市场表现，更多地体现为一种精神价值的消费体验，正如星巴克总裁霍华德·舒尔茨所说，"星巴克出售的不是咖啡，而是对于咖啡的体验"。

Creative economy greatly reflects the role of culture and art in promoting the economy. Creativity integrates knowledge, technology and culture, different from other production factors. The input of creative factors has led to the development of emerging economic activities and industrial sectors, expanded the space for enhancing the added value of traditional products, and improved the profit value of unit products. Product creativity, service creativity, marketing creativity and other market performances are more embodied in a consumption experience of spiritual value. As Howard Schultz, President of Starbucks, said, "what Starbucks sells is not coffee, but the experience of coffee."

（四）传承性

4. Inheritability

创意经济的知识经济特征决定了它也是一种可持续经济。与工业经济的土地、劳动力、资本等常规资源不同，知识、技术、创造力等战略资源成为知识经济的核心要素。创意经济的第一要素是创意，与其他客体资源不同，创意是一种主体资源，具有知识性、独特性、可传承性、非磨损性、流动性、共享性、可再生性和永续利用的特征，是一种无形的、取之不尽、用之不竭的资源。

The knowledge economy characteristic of creative economy determines that it is also a sustainable economy. Unlike conventional resources such as land, labor and capital in industrial economy, strategic resources such as knowledge, technology and creativity become the core factors of knowledge economy. The first factor of creative economy is creativity. Unlike other object resources, creativity is a kind of subject resource, characteristic of knowledge, uniqueness, inheritability, non-abrasion, mobility, shared, renewability and sustainable utilization. It is an intangible and inexhaustible resource.

（五）集聚性

5. Agglomeration

创意经济兴起于现代城市，这种现象并非偶然。一种经济形态对地域空间的选择，是为了获得要素配置效率提高所产生的经济效益。创意人群、人文环境、社会氛围、城市文化、技术基础等，既是创意经济的城市特征，也是创意经济发展所需要的城市要素。

The rise of creative economy in modern cities is not accidental. The choice of an economic form for regional space is to obtain the economic benefits produced by improving the efficiency of factor allocation. Creative people, cultural environment, social atmosphere, urban culture and technological foundation are not only the urban characteristics of creative economy, but also the urban factors needed for the development of a creative economy.

二、创意经济的产业特征
2. Industrial Characteristics of Creative Economy

（一）兼具产业与意识形态属性
（1）Industrial and Ideological Attributes

创意产业最为特殊之处，是具有双重属性和双重功能，既有产业属性又有意识形态属性，既有经济效益功能又有社会效益功能，能够实现两者的有机统一。创意产业在本质上具有文化属性，是文化与经济互动的结果，也是技术与文化融合的结果。文化艺术成为产品生产的重要资源，产品具有象征、体验等特定的文化内涵。创意产业与文化生产力有着不可分割的内在联系，通过文化与科技的结合，利用高新技术创新文化生产方式，成为城市文化软实力的重要载体。文化生产力的提出是生产性领域对文化附加值的追求提升到一定高度的必然产物，也是文化提升核心竞争力的产物①。

The most special feature of creative industry is its dual attributes of industry and ideology and its dual functions of economic and social benefits, with the organic unity of the two aspects. In essence, creative industry has cultural attributes, resulted from the interaction between culture and economy, and from the integration of technology and culture. Culture and art have become an important resource for the production of products with specific cultural connotations such as symbol and experience. Creative industry and cultural productivity are inseparable from each other. The combination of culture and science and technology, it has become an important carrier of urban cultural soft power to use high-tech for the innovation of cultural production mode. Cultural productivity is the inevitable product by pursuing cultural added value in the productive field to a certain height, and it is also the product of promoting cultural core competitiveness.

① 朱宁嘉. 创意产业：理论管窥与中国经验［M］//上海交通大学国家文化产业创新与发展研究基地. 中国文化产业评论. 上海：上海人民出版社，2007：52.

（二）裂变式成长

2. Multiplied Growth

创意产业集中了智力、知识、科技、信息等高质要素，与常规要素相比，在相同的投入下，具有更高的产出和增长率，产业成长的潜力巨大。物质生产和精神生产的高度融合，改变了文化艺术的生产方式。科学技术的创新使得这一要求成为可能。创意为文化生产力提供不竭的动力源泉，文化艺术的生产方式、生产规模，文化生产、文化消费、文化贸易、文化服务等，都发生了巨大的变化。创意作为文化艺术和文化竞争力的核心，逐渐走上了产业化的道路。创意活动在经济活动和物质产品中注入了文化内涵，使经济发展不仅实现了量的持续扩张，而且实现了质的飞跃提升，增强了文化对其他产业乃至全社会的辐射力和影响力。

Creative industry gathers intelligence, knowledge, science and technology, information and other high-quality factors. Compared with conventional factors, with the same input, it has higher output and growth rate with great potential for industrial growth. The high integration of material production and spiritual production has changed the production mode of culture and art. The innovation of science and technology makes it possible. Creativity provides an inexhaustible source of power for cultural productivity, of which great changes have taken place in the mode of production, scale of production, cultural production, cultural consumption, cultural trade and cultural services. As the core of culture and art and the core of cultural competitiveness, creativity has gradually embarked on the road of industrialization. Creative activities inject cultural connotation into economic activities and material products, so that economic development not only realizes the continuous expansion of quantity, but also realizes the leap of quality and enhances the radiation and influence of culture on other industries and even the whole society.

（三）覆盖式嵌入
3. Embed by Overlaying

创意产业以知识产权为核心，占据价值链的高端，向产业链的各个环节渗透，广泛覆盖三次产业，产生极强的产业关联效应。在全球化、国际化和信息化的大背景下，经济的发展已经与整个社会的发展紧密联系在一起，产业的发展也呈现出了新的格局，产业融合已经使产业间的界限趋于模糊，产业的发展模式也突破了传统的思维，形成了新的范式。创意产业通过特有的机制作用于国民经济系统中的其他产业部门，以创意对生产消费过程进行重组、改造和创新，在实现其自身价值的过程中，提升和改造传统产业、催生新兴产业、丰富产业内涵，带动第三产业发展。

With intellectual property rights as the core, creative industries occupy the high end of the value chain, penetrate into all links of the industrial chain, widely overlay the three industries, and produce a strong industrial correlation effect. Under the background of globalization, internationalization and information, the development of economy has been closely linked with the development of the whole society, and the development of industry also presents a new pattern. Industrial integration has blurred the boundaries between industries, and the development mode of industry has also broken through the traditional thought and formed a new paradigm. Creative industries act on other industrial sectors in the national economic system through a unique mechanism and restructure, transform and innovate the production and consumption process with creativity. In the process of realizing its own value, it promotes and transforms traditional industries, spawns new industries, enriches industrial connotation, and drives the development of the tertiary industry.

三、创意经济的成都实践
3. Chengdu Practice of Creative Economy

为贯彻落实成都市新经济发展战略部署，结合创意经济发展实际，成都市文化广电新闻出版局等 7 部门共同发布了《成都市关于推进创意经济发展的实施方案》，提出到 2022 年，培育创意独角兽企业 2 家，创意瞪羚企业 15 家以上，以文创为核心的创意产业增加值超过 2 600 亿元，GDP 占比约 12%，将成都建设成为具有国际竞争力和区域带动力的西部文创中心，如图 6-3 所示。今日头条大数据平台显示，成都文创关注度仅次于北京、上海，增势位居全国第一，成为"中国文创第三城"。

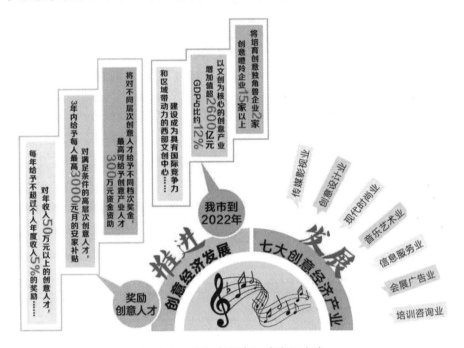

图 6-3　成都市创意经济发展方案

Figure 6-3　Chengdu Creative Economy Development Plan

To implement the Chengdu's new economic development strategy, combined with the actual development of creative economy, seven departments including Chengdu Culture, Radio, Television, Press and Publication Bureau jointly issued "Implementation Plan of Chengdu to promote the Development of Creative Economy". It proposed that by 2022 there would be two creative Unicorn enterprises and more than 15 creative gazelle enterprises. The added value of creative industries with cultural innovation as the core will exceed 260 billion Yuan, accounting for about 12% of GDP. Chengdu will be built into a

Western cultural and creative center with international competitiveness and regional driving force, as shown in Figure 6 – 3. According to the big data platform of Tou Tiao, Chengdu's attention to cultural and creative industries is only second to Beijing and Shanghai, ranking first in the country in terms of growth and ranking "the third city of cultural and creative industries in China".

构建创意产业核心区。成都围绕二环路以内的天府锦城区域，大力发展都市休闲、时尚创意、音乐娱乐等业态。沿天府大道布局人南文创集聚区，重点发展动漫游戏、创意设计、文化会展、文化贸易、信息服务、音乐演艺，培育功能性总部和区域性营运中心。

Build the core area of creative industry. Around the Tianfu-Jincheng area within the Second Ring Road, Chengdu vigorously develops urban leisure, fashion creativity, music and entertainment. Along Tianfu Avenue, Rennan cultural and creative cluster will be arranged, focusing on the development of animation games, creative design, cultural exhibition, cultural trade, information services, music performance, and cultivating functional headquarters and regional operation centers.

布局创意产业集聚区，在天府锦城、天府新区、龙泉山和龙门山创意经济产业带等区域重点布局统筹推进26个创意产业功能集聚区。推进创意产业全面发展，推动创意产业链垂直整合和横向融合，构建文创、科技、金融、旅游、商业、体育、康养融合发展的产业生态，促进全域创意产业发展。

Creative industry cluster areas will be laid out by promoting 26 functional cluster areas of creative industry in the creative economic industrial belts of Tianfu Jincheng, Tianfu New Area, Longquan Mountain and Longmen Mountain, etc. Promote the all-round development of creative industries and the vertical and horizontal integration of creative industry chain, build the industrial ecology of cultural and creative industries, science and technology, finance, tourism, commerce, sports and health care, and enhance the development of creative industries in the whole region.

发展七大创意经济产业形态。重点发展传媒影视业，大力推动现代传媒业、数字出版业和影视娱乐业的发展，打造国家级网络视听产业园区和传媒文化产业园。发展创意设计业，重点发展工业设计、建筑设计和景观设计，聚集创意设计机构，孵化创意设计空间，打造创意设计品牌。发展现代时尚业，重点发展时尚消费品工业、时尚用品业和时尚服务业，创建时尚产业园区，引进时尚设计大师，培育知名时尚品牌。发展音乐艺术业，重点发展音乐演艺业、艺术品业和非遗生产性保护，实施文创名家驻留创作行动，打造具有全国影响力的音乐产业基地、特色音乐小镇。发展信息服务业，重点发展软件服务业、动漫游戏业，培育中国软件和动漫游戏百强企业。发展会展广告业，重点发展会展服务业、广告服务业，培育国际认证的专业化会展品牌。发展培训咨询业，重点发展教育培训业和咨询服务业，培育具有全国影响力的艺术院校、知名教育培训机构和咨询服务机构。

Develop seven major forms of creative economic industries. The first is to develop media, film and television industry, vigorously promote the modern media industry, digital publishing industry and film and television entertainment industry, and build a national network audio-visual industrial park and media culture industrial park. The second is to develop creative design industry, especially in industrial design, architectural design and landscape design, gather creative design institutions, incubate creative design space and create creative design brand. The third is to develop modern fashion industry, especially in fashion consumer goods industry, fashion products industry and fashion service industry, create fashion industrial park, introduce fashion design masters, and cultivate well-known fashion brands. The fourth is to develop the music and art industry, especially in music performing industry, art industry and intangible cultural heritage protection in production, implement the resident creation of cultural and creative celebrities, and build a music industry base and characteristic music town with national influence. The fifth is to develop information service industry, especially in software service industry and animation game industry, and cultivate top 100 software and animation game enterprises in China. The sixth is to develop exhibition advertising industry, especially in exhibition service industry and advertising service industry, and cultivate international certified professional exhibition brand. The seventh is to develop the training and consulting industry, especially in education and training industry and consulting service industry, and cultivate art colleges, well-known education and training institutions and consulting service institutions with national influence.

构建三大创意经济应用场景。针对创意经济的发展特点,培育 IP 经济应用场景、跨界融合应用场景、创意体验应用场景三大应用场景。培育 IP 经济应用场景:激发原创活力,沉淀 IP 资源;延伸产业链条,培育品牌 IP;培育授权产业,放大 IP 效应等途径,培育创意经济产业链和最具竞争力的价值量核心资源。培育跨界融合应用场景:促进创意与科技、产业、城市的跨界融合。培育创意体验应用场景:围绕扩大世界文创名城、世界赛事名城、世界旅游名城的影响力,培育 5A 级旅游景区和国家级旅游度假区,大力发展特色商业街区、创意小镇和创意空间,丰富创意体验场景。

Build three application scenescapes of creative economy. According to the development characteristics of creative economy, three application scenescapes are constructed, including IP economy, cross-border integration and creative experience. The first is to stimulate the creative vitality, accumulate the IP resources, extend the industrial chain, cultivate the IP brand, cultivate the creative economy industrial chain and the most competitive core resources of value by cultivating the authorized industry and enlarge the IP effect, etc. The second is to promote cross-border integration of creativity with technology, industry and city. The third is to focus on expanding the global influence of the city in culture and creation, events-holding and tourism, cultivate 5A tourist attractions and national tourist resorts, vigorously develop characteristic commercial blocks, creative towns and creative space, and enrich creative experience scenescapes.

典型案例：提升消费层次应用场景
之成都崇州市道明镇竹艺村"竹里建筑"

Typical Case：Improving Application Scenescapes for Consumption

— "Buildings in Bamboos" in Zhuyi Village, Daoming Town, Chongzhou City, Chengdu

道明镇巧借老旧院落融入林盘景致设计的"竹里建筑"，如图 6-4 所示，衍生了住宿、旅游、文化手工体验等相关业态，众多新村民也纷纷被招募加入竹艺村，为这座川西平坝村落增添了丰富的体验感和文化魅力。"竹里建筑"还获得了国际空间设计艾特奖，并受邀参加威尼斯"双年展"。

As shown in Figure 6-4, Daoming Town skillfully designs the old courtyard into the "Buildings in Bamboos" by integrating the bamboo landscape around the buildings, from which some related business forms have derived such as accommodation, tourism, cultural and manual experience. Many new villagers have also been recruited to join Zhuyi Village, adding a rich sense of experience and cultural charm to this village in Western Sichuan flatland. "Buildings in Bamboos" also won the International Space Design Award and was invited to participate in the Venice Biennale.

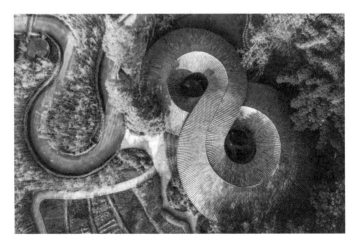

图 6-4 崇州市道明镇竹艺村"竹里建筑"

Figure 6-4　"Zhuli Building"（Building Surrounded by Bamboos），

Zhuyi Village, DaomingTown, Chongzhou City

▷▷▷ 第五节　流量经济

Section Five　Flow Economy

一、流量经济的内涵

1. Connotation of Flow Economy

存量和流量是国民经济核算体系中记录经济信息的两种基本形式。存量是指在某一时点上测算的量，如某一时点的资产和负债的状况，具有时点的基本特征。流量是按某一时段测算的量，反映一定时期内经济价值的产生、转换、交换、转移或消失。当经济运行模式从以实体经济为主的工业化时代进入以实体经济和虚拟经济共同组成的信息化时代，对于存量与流量的需求也同时发生了变化。在工业化时代追求投资，以增加存量；信息化时代则追求资源要素的流动，增加流量，减少存量。而新经济的流量包含物资流、商品流、技术流、信息流、人才流等。

Stock and flow are two basic forms to record economic information in the system of national accounts. Stock refers to the quantity measured at a certain time, such as the status of assets and liabilities at a certain time. Flow is the amount measured during a certain period of time, reflecting the generation, conversion, exchange, transfer or disappearance of economic value during a certain period of time. When the economic operation mode changes from the industrialization era dominated by the real economy to the information age composed of the real economy and the virtual economy, the demand for stock and flow also changes at the same time. In the era of industrialization, Chengdu pursues investment to increase stock; in the era of information, Chengdu pursues the flow of resource factors to increase flow and reduce stock. The new economy flow includes material flow, commodity flow, technology flow, information flow and talents flow.

流量经济主要是指一个区域以相应的平台和条件，吸引区外的物资、资金、人才、技术、信息等资源要素向区内集聚，通过各种资源要素的重组、整合来促进和带动相关产业的发展，并将形成和扩大的经济能量、能极向周边地区乃至更远的地区辐射。在集聚辐射过程中，各资源要素通过高效、有序、规范的流动实现价值，再通过循环不断的流量规模，从而达到促进地区经济规模扩大、经济持续发展的目的。

Flow economy mainly means that a region with the corresponding platform and conditions attracts resources such as materials, funds, talents, technology and information outside the region to gather in the region, promote and drive the development of related industries through the reorganization and integration of various resources, and radiate the formed and expanded economic energy and energy pole to the surrounding areas and even further regions. In the process of agglomeration and radiation, each resource factor realizes its value through efficient, orderly and standardized flow, and then through the circulation of continuous flow scale, to achieve the purpose of promoting the expansion of regional economic scale and sustainable economic development.

二、流量经济的特征
2. Characteristics of Flow Economy

全面数字化。流量经济作为信息时代的产物，依托通信技术的快速发展，信息的快速流通和广泛传播是流量经济发展的重要支撑。数字化信息在流量经济的发展历程中扮演着十分重要的角色，同时数字通信技术也打破了空间的限制，运用于全球经济的行业和领域中，实现在网络空间中资源配置的跨时空流动。

All-round digitization. As a product of the information age, flow economy relies on the rapid development of communication technology. And the rapid circulation and wide spread of information is the important support for the development of flow economy. Digital information plays a very important role in the development of flow economy. At the same time, digital communication technology has also broken the space limit and applied to the industries and fields of global economy to realize the cross-space-time flow of resource allocation in cyberspace.

信息共享化。在信息化时代的大背景下，由于信息流的作用，处于高效率生产状况下的供给已处于过剩的状态，而流量经济共享化的出现成为解决这一困境的核心。共享经济作为流量经济的一种表现形式，改变了单一的经济运作模式和发展方式，其产生是对生产力进步导致产能过剩问题的改善，打破并重构了原有的经济"存量"理论，以全新的"流量共享"理念实现了资源配置方式的转换。

Information shared. Under the background of information age, due to the role of information flow, the supply under the condition of high-efficiency production has been in a state of surplus, and the emergence of flow economy shared has become the core to solve this dilemma. As a form of flow economy, shared economy has changed the single mode of economic operation and development, whose emergence is to improve the problem of overcapacity caused by the progress of productivity, break and reconstruct the original economic "stock" theory, and realize the transformation of resource allocation mode with a new "flow shared" concept.

流动平台化。指的是在一定"流动空间"内要素的流量化，且该"流动空间"是满足经济要素在不同层次的充分便利流动。1996年，曼纽尔·卡斯特尔提出，世界城市是一个"流动空间"，在信息技术演进和全球化的进程中，流动空间将存在于电子通信网络、物质网络和精英网络三个层面，三个层面的流动空间汇集在城市之中，再通过将各种经济要素流量在城市加工整合最后流向世界各地。

Flow platform. It refers to the flow of factors in a particular "flow space", and the "flow space" is to meet the entirely convenient flow of economic factors at different levels. In 1996, Manuel Castells proposed that the world city is a "flow space". In the process of information technology evolution and globalization, the flow space will exist in the three levels of electronic communication network, material network and elite network. The three levels' flow space will gather in the city, and then flow to all parts of the world through processing and integrating various economic factors in the city.

限制减弱化。各流量要素向区域内集聚和向区域外辐射，均根据区域内外经济发展需求自由实现，要素流动的时间、地点不受限制和干扰。

Weakened restriction. The flow factors gather in the region and radiate out of the region freely according to demand for the economic development inside and outside the region, and the flow time and place of factors are not limited and disturbed.

三、流量经济的成都实践
3. Practice of Flow Economy in Chengdu

流量经济具有平台化特征，通过强集聚性和辐射性吸引全球范围内的资本、信息等要素，实现重塑供应链、整合产业链、融合价值链，推动产业体系跃升和高级化。2018 年 2 月，成都市商务局、成都市新经济发展委员会共同印发《关于推进流量经济发展的实施方案》，明确重点发展总部经济、新兴金融、现代物流、现代商贸、高新技术服务、信息服务、人力资源七大细分领域及 17 个行业，加快流量经济在消费提档升级、枢纽门户建设、对外互联互通及平台打造 4 个方面 14 个场景的深度应用。到 2022 年，基本建成国家流量经济发展高地，形成与国家中心城市相适应的流量经济深度应用格局。财新数联发布的《2017 年中国流量经济指数发展报告》显示，成都流量经济指数位列新一线城市榜首。

The flow economy has the characteristics of a platform. It can attract capital and information from all over the world through strong agglomeration and radiation, reshape the supply chain, integrate the industrial chain and the value chain, and promote the leap and upgrading of the industrial system. In February 2018, Chengdu Municipal Bureau of Commerce and Chengdu New Economic Development Committee jointly issued the "Implementation Plan on

Promoting the Development of Flow Economy", which clearly focused on the development of seven sub sectors of headquarters economy, emerging finance, modern logistics, modern commerce and trade, high-tech services, information services and human resources, and 17 industries, accelerated the depth application of flow economy in 14 scenescapes of consumption upgrading, hub portal construction, external interconnection and platform building. By 2022, the national highland for the development of flow economy will be basically built, and a deep application pattern of flow economy corresponding to the national central city will be formed. According to Development Report of China's Flow Economy Index in 2017 released by Caixin Business Big Data, Chengdu's flow economy index ranks first in the new first-tier cities.

在促进消费升级、提升流量经济吸附力方面，成都着力打造现代商圈，打造特色商业街区，打造国际消费体验中心。建设一批绿色商场，提升以"春盐商圈"为代表的城市商圈知名度，大力推动国际名店街等国际活动落地，将"春盐商圈"等商业中心建设成为具有全国乃至全球影响力的国际名品展示发布中心。突出各特色商业街的文化特色、产业特色和人文特色，打造锦江区水井街、青羊区宽窄巷子、龙泉驿区洛带古镇、青白江区弥牟历史文化街区等62条主题鲜明、功能齐备的特色商业街区。

To promote consumption upgrading and enhance flow economic adsorption, Chengdu is striving to build modern business districts, characteristic commercial districts and international consumption experience centers. It will build a number of green shopping malls, enhance the popularity of urban business districts represented by Chunxi Road-Yanshikou Business District, vigorously promote the implementation of international activities such as famous international store street, and build Chun-Yan Business District and other business centers into international famous product exhibition and release centers with national and even global influence. Highlight the cultural, industrial and cultural characteristics of each characteristic commercial street, and build 62 characteristic commercial blocks with distinctive themes and complete functions, including Shuijing Street in Jinjiang District, Kuanzhai Alley in Qingyang District, Luodai Ancient Town in Longquanyi District, and Mimu Historical and Cultural Block in Qingbaijiang District.

在强化枢纽作用、提升流量经济运作力方面，成都加快建设国际航空港、国际铁路港和国际信息港。加快构建"一市两场"航空枢纽格局，实现双流国际机场和天府国际机场优势互补、"两翼"协同发展。依托青白江国际铁路港，加快布局支撑成都向西向南开放格局的战略性铁路物流通道。高水平打造全国重要的信息通信节点、数据中心，建设国际交通信息枢纽和国家门户城市。

To strengthen the hub role and improve the flow economic operation, Chengdu is accelerating the construction of international airport, railway port and information port. Accelerate the construction of aviation hub pattern "one city, two airports", and realize the complementary advantages of Shuangliu International Airport and Tianfu International Airport and the coordinated development of "the two wings". Relying on Qingbaijiang international railway port, Chengdu are accelerating strategic railway logistics channel's layout supporting Chengdu's opening pattern from west to south. It will build an important national information and communication node and data center at a high level and build an international transportation information hub and a national gateway city.

在深化互联互通、提升流量经济承载力方面，成都重点从加快自贸试验区建设、做实国别合作园区、塑造国际品牌展会三方面入手。完善现有及在建口岸配套设施，鼓励企业利用指定口岸政策进行货物贸易，加快复制推广国内先进自贸试验区通关监管模式改革经验，完善自贸试验区成都片区口岸服务能力。充分利用中德（蒲江）中小企业合作园、中法（成都）生态园等国际合作示范园区，实施国际品牌展会打造工程，加强与国际知名会展企业的合作，打造一批国际领先、国内一流的展会赛事。

To deepen the interconnection and improve the carrying capacity of flow economy, Chengdu focuses on accelerating the construction of pilot Free Trade Zone, strengthening the national cooperation park, and shaping the international brand exhibition. First improve the existing port supporting facilities and those under construction, encourage enterprises to use the designated port policy for trade in goods, accelerate the replication and promotion of domestic advanced experience of customs clearance supervision mode reform in the pilot Free Trade Zone, and improve the port service capacity of Chengdu area in the pilot free trade zone. Make full use of international cooperation demonstration parks such as Sino-German (in Pujiang County) Small and Medium Enterprises Cooperation Park and Sino-French (in Chengdu) Ecological Park, implement international brand exhibition building project, strengthen cooperation with international well-known exhibition enterprises, and create a number of internationally-leading and domestic first-class exhibition events.

在打造流量平台、提升流量经济控制力方面，成都重点搭建供应链协同平台、生活性服务平台、商品交易和服务贸易平台、跨境电商平台、专业服务平台。支持建设"互联网+"物流公共服务平台、物流公共信息服务平台，加快培育一批协同研发、众包设计、解决方案、智慧仓储、融资租赁及金融服务等供应链协同平台，增强经济辐射能级，构建具有全球竞争力和区域带动力的流量经济产业体系。

To build flow platform and improve flow economic control, Chengdu focuses on building supply chain collaboration platform, life service platform, commodity trading and service trade platform, cross-border e-commerce platform and professional service platform. It supports the construction of the "Internet plus" logistics public service platform and logistics public information service platform, accelerates the cultivation of supply chain collaboration platforms such as collaborative R&D, public sourcing design, solutions, smart warehousing, financial leasing and financial services, and enhances the economic radiation level, to build a flow economic industrial system with global competitiveness and regional impetus.

典型案例：推进现代供应链创新应用场景之天虎云商平台

Typical Case：Promote Modern Supply Chain Innovation
Application Scenescapes（Tianhu Cloud Business Platform）

天虎云商是成都本土综合性电子商务信息化平台。天虎云商通过成千上万个线上线下合作网点互动产生的数据，依托中国电信先进的大数据、云计算技术，为合作客户提供从产品展示、营销、订购到支付、物流配送和售后服务的全程电商应用服务，为其量身定制电子商务及信息化的全套解决方案，用信息化提升企业竞争力，推动产业结构转型升级，并有力助推农村电商发展提速，如图6-5所示。

Tianhu Cloud Business is a comprehensive e-commerce information platform in Chengdu. Based on the data generated by the interaction of thousands of online and offline cooperation points, and relying on China Telecom's advanced big data and cloud computing technology, Tianhu Cloud Business provides cooperative customers with the whole-process e-commerce application services from product display, marketing, ordering to payment, logistics, distribution and after-sales service, and customizes a complete set of e-commerce and informatization solutions for them, so as to enhance its competitiveness with informatization, promote the transformation and upgrading of industrial structure, and promote the development of rural e-commerce, as shown in Figure 6-5.

图 6-5　天府云商网站首页

Figure 6-5　www.tyfo.com Website Homepage

▷▷▷ 第六节　共享经济
Section Six　Sharing Economy

一、共享经济的内涵
1. Connotation of Sharing Economy

一般认为，共享经济是以信息化技术为支撑，以互联网平台为依托，以信任为纽带，以所有者生活不受影响为前提，所形成的个人闲置物品或资源使用权共享的开放性交换系统。从产权的角度讲，共享经济本质上是共享使用权，使用者不享有所有权。因此，共享经济亦可称为"使用权经济"。使用者在共享经济的消费过程中，由以往的"购入所有权"转变为"租赁使用权"；在契约与制度方面，由租赁合同取代了买卖合同①。

It is generally believed that sharing economy is an open shared exchange system of personal idle goods or resource use right, on the basis of information technology, Internet platform, trust and the premise that the owner's life is not affected. From the perspective of property rights, sharing economy is essentially sharing the right of use, and users do not enjoy ownership. Therefore, sharing economy can also be called "use right economy". In the consumption process of sharing economy, the user changes from the former "purchase ownership" to "lease right"; in terms of contract and system, the lease contract replaces the sales contract.

二、共享经济的特征
2. Characteristics of Sharing Economy

（1）核心是资源共享。共享经济提倡"人们需要的是产品的使用价值，而非产品本身"，用户可以绕过取得所有权所必须支付的成本而只

---

① 李东. 以共享居住空间诠释共享经济 [J]. 经济研究导刊，2017（26）：71-72.

付出使用的成本，其本质是资源使用权的转移，是一种社会化的分享，这也符合当下人们对于物品和资产的态度，人们不追求如何拥有它，而是考虑如何使用它。同时，共享经济又远不同于一般的分享，它要求有更大的数字化平台以实现更低的成本和更多的选择，最终使得个人或团体借助平台提供的共享资源获取利益。比如，众创空间鼻祖 WeWork 倡导的共享工作空间、共享配套资源，在此基础上实现社交圈的共享扩充，最终一切工作资源的共享又带动了公司的发展。企业在 WeWork 注册为会员进入创业者社区后，可以付费享受其提供的个性化办公空间、会议室和各种线上资源商业服务等。注册的企业对 WeWork 提供的各种办公资源的使用，就是一种对资源的共享。

The core is resource sharing. Sharing economy advocates that "what people need is the use value of the product, not the product itself". Users can only pay the cost of use instead of the cost of ownership. Its essence is the transfer of the right to use resources and a kind of socialized shared, which is also in line with people's attitude towards goods and assets. People do not pursue how to own it, but how to use it. At the same time, the sharing economy is far different from the general sharing, which requires a larger digital platform to achieve lower cost and more choices, and ultimately makes individuals or groups gain benefits through the sharing resources provided by the platform. For example, WeWork, the originator of maker space, advocates the sharing of workspace and supporting resources to realize the sharing and expansion of social circle and drive the development of the company. After registering as a member in WeWork, enterprises can pay to enjoy the personalized office space, conference room and various online resources and business services provided by WeWork. The use of various office resources provided by WeWork for registered enterprises is a kind of resource shared.

（2）分享是重要理念。随着社会生产力的发展，人们拥有了更多的闲置资源。随着互联网技术兴盛，越来越多的个体开始自发地在网上与陌生人进行分享，对手头闲置资源的交换热情被点燃。如早期各大论坛上经常会出现寻求二手物品交换的帖子，但由于当时未出现专业的第三方共享平台，这样的共享行为规模有限，人们的交换信息只是被放在偌大网络论坛里一个或几个小小的帖子后面，不仅交换的选择面窄，而且操作流程不规范，风险较大。

Sharing is an important idea. With the development of social productivity, people have more idle resources. With the prosperity of Internet technology, more and more individuals begin to share with strangers on the Internet spontaneously, and their enthusiasm for exchanging idle resources is ignited. For example, in the early major forums, there were often posts seeking to exchange second-hand goods, but because there was no professional third-party sharing platform at that time, the scale of such sharing behavior was limited, and people's exchange information was only put in one or several small posts in the large network forum. Moreover, not only the choice of exchange was narrow, but also the operation process was not standardized, and the risk was high.

（3）平台是共享基础。随着互联网、智能设备等现代信息技术的发展，第三方支付、基于位置定位服务（LBS）技术、云计算、大数据等创新技术的进步，为共享经济发展提供技术支撑，以这些技术为支撑的第三方平台发挥了信息集中的作用，是共享经济发展的最重要基础。

Platform is the basis of sharing. With the development of Internet, intelligent devices and other modern information technology, the progress of third-party payment, location-based services （LBS） technology, cloud computing, big data and other innovative technologies provide technical support for the development of shared economy. The third-party platform supported by these technologies plays the role of information centralization and is the most important foundation for the development of shared economy.

（4）共享是信任延伸。在商业活动中，很多环节都会出现交易双方彼此缺乏信任而影响活动的问题。互动式平台的大量出现，就能促使共享经济拥有广泛的信任基础。通过互动式平台，用户可以看到以前使用过相同产品或服务的个体留下的评价。同时，能支撑起这样大规模平台运作的往往也是在市场中有一定地位且具有公信力的企业，相比直接与个人进行交易，消费者觉得更加可靠，也会更加信任。

Sharing is an extension of trust. In business activities, it is common in many links that little trust between the two sides of the transaction may affect the activities. The emergence of a large number of interactive platforms can promote the sharing economy to have a broad foundation of trust. Through the interactive platform, users can see the comments left by individuals who have used the same products or services before. At the same time, the enterprises that can support the operation of such a large-scale platform often have a certain position in the market and have credibility. Compared with directly trading with individuals, consumers feel these sharing plats more reliable and trustable.

（5）技术是依赖路径。共享经济之所以发展得那么快，一个原因是其商业模式易被模仿复制。早期的各大共享经济项目百花齐放，成功的企业多是依赖雄厚的资本，用其高额的补贴回馈用户吸收大批流量，使得其他资本薄弱的企业市场份额急剧缩减，从而占领市场。目前，共享经济市场上留存的是少数财力雄厚的寡头企业，必须突破以往"烧钱"的圈地发展模式，需要利用信息技术加强平台建设，稳定平台客户量。为了维护庞大的系统和海量的用户数据，共享经济平台积极运用大数据、云计算以及人工智能等前沿技术，实现网状点对点分享，平台的价值随着分享者的加入和分享的增多呈指数级增长。

Technology is the dependent path. One of the reasons why the sharing economy develops so fast is that its business model is easy to be copied. In the early years, all kinds of sharing economic projects were in full bloom, and most of successful enterprises relied on abundant capital to repay users with their high subsidies and absorb a large number of flows, which made the market sharing of other enterprises with little capital rapidly reduced to occupy the market. At present, there are a few oligarchic enterprises with strong financial resources in the sharing economy market. They must break through the previous "money burning" enclosure development mode and strengthen the platform construction by using information technology to stabilize the number of platform customers. In order to maintain the huge system and massive user data, the sharing economy platform actively uses cutting-edge technologies such as big data, cloud computing and artificial intelligence to realize network point-to-point shared. The value of the platform increases exponentially with the addition and increase of sharers.

（6）灵活是劳资特点。共享经济中的劳动者不再受制于公司与员工间的传统雇佣关系，他们无须固定的办公场所，也不需要接受人格化"老板"的直接监督，组织及管理更为松散，劳动呈现出很大的灵活性。个体可以根据自身的实际情况选择感兴趣和擅长的任务，自主选择工作时间。在传统的劳动关系中，主体之间存在着组织依赖性、经济从属性和人格上的从属性，劳动者需要听从指挥，存在着一定的隶属关系。滴滴平台上的司机可以灵活地选择工作时间、工作地点，自愿选择是否承接某一订单任务，滴滴公司也不需要为司机提供工作场地、工作条件等一系列要素，只是作为一个信息中介起到了平台整合作用。

Flexibility is the characteristic of labor and capital. In sharing economy, workers are no longer subject to the traditional employment relationship between the company and employees. They do not need fixed office space, nor do they need to accept the direct supervision of the personified "boss". The organization and management are looser, and the labor presents great flexibility. Individuals can choose the tasks they are interested in and good at according to their own actual situation and choose their own working hours. In the traditional labor relations, there are organizational dependence, economic subordination and personality subordination between the subjects. Workers need to obey the command, subordinate to their employers. While drivers on DiDi platform can flexibly choose their working time and place, and voluntarily choose whether to undertake a certain order task. DiDi company does not need to provide a series of factors such as working site and working conditions for drivers, but just acts as an information intermediary on the whole platform.

三、共享经济的成都实践
3. Practice of Sharing Economy in Chengdu

自 2016 年 3 月"分享经济"首次写入国务院《政府工作报告》以来，成都市涌现和入驻了一大批共享企业，充分利用互联网等现代信息技术整合、共享海量分散化闲置资源，推进供需资源连接、配置最优化，使共享经济快速发展。面对共享经济迅猛发展的势头，成都市积极转变组织经济工作方式，坚持按照"鼓励创新、包容审慎"的原则，针对共享经济新业态新模式，积极探索推进分类指导、创新监管等工作，研究出台相应配套政策，促进共享经济健康有序发展。目前，成都市共享经济模式已渗透于交通、物流、住宿、医疗、教育、旅游、生产等诸多领域，初步聚集共享经济企业超过 100 家。独角兽企业"医联"成功入选国家发改委首批"共享经济典型案例"。

Since the "sharing economy" was first written into the government work report of the State Council in March 2016, a large number of shared enterprises have sprung up and settled in Chengdu, making full use of the Internet and other modern information technology to integrate and share massive decentralized idle resources, promoting the optimal connection and allocation of supply and demand resources, and making the sharing economy develop rapidly. In the face of the rapid development of shared economy, Chengdu actively changes the operating mode to organize economy, adheres to the principle of "encouraging innovation, inclusiveness and prudence", actively explores and promotes classified guidance, innovative supervision and other work, studies and introduces corresponding supporting policies, and promotes the healthy and orderly development of shared economy. At present, the mode of sharing economy in Chengdu has penetrated into many fields, such as transportation, logistics, accommodation, medical treatment, education, tourism, production and so on. More than 100 enterprises of sharing economy have initially gathered in Chengdu. Unicorn enterprise medical association was selected into the first batch of "typical cases of shared economy" by National Development and Reform Commission.

成都在共享经济打造中，主要采取了以下做法：

一是明确共享经济发展思路。基于成都资源禀赋、产业基础以及对未来发展方向的判断，将共享经济列为聚焦发展的新经济六大形态之一，并梳理明晰了发展思路。

大力发展生产性服务共享经济，通过众创、众包、众扶、众筹等多种方式，推动办公空间、生产线、研发中心等创新资源，专利技术成果、知识技能服务、人力资本服务等创新能力和供应链管理、智慧仓储、现代交通运输等流通资源共享，提高资源有效利用率和生产服务供给能力。

大力发展生活性服务共享经济，精准把握分众化需求，垂直细分衣食住行生活服务领域，开发面向商贸流通、教育、医疗等领域的新型共享应用软件和平台，推动传统服务业再造升级，努力建设成为共享经济发展的策源地和领先城市。

大力发展公共性服务共享经济，进一步打破信息壁垒、制度障碍，重点推动政府闲置资源和能源、交通、通信等领域公共设施资源共享，实现社会价值和经济价值最大化。

In the process of building the sharing economy, Chengdu has mainly adopted the following measures:

First, clarify the development ideas of the sharing economy. Based on Chengdu's resource advantages, industrial foundation and our judgment of future development direction, the sharing economy is listed as one of the six major forms of new economy focusing on development. The development ideas are sorted out and clarified as follows:

Vigorously develop the sharing economy of productive service, promote the sharing of innovation resources such as office space, production line, R&D center, of innovation ability such as patent technology achievements, knowledge and skill services, human capital services, and of circulation resources such as supply chain management, smart storage, modern transportation, etc., through various ways such as crowd-making, crowd-sourcing, crowd-supporting, crowd-funding, etc., to improve effective utilization of resources and supply capacity of production services.

Vigorously develop the sharing economy of life service, accurately grasp the demand of differentiation, vertically subdivide the life service field of clothing, food, housing and transportation, develop new sharing application software and platform for business circulation, education, medical and other fields, promote the upgrading and reconstruction of traditional service industry, and strive to build the source place and leading city for the development of shared economy.

Vigorously develop the shared economy of public service, further break the information barriers and institutional barriers, and focus on promoting the sharing of government idle resources and public facilities in energy, transportation and communication, to maximize the social and economic value.

二是出台专项支持政策。按照"变'事前设限'为'事中划线''事后监管',多出'指导意见'、慎出'管理办法'"的思路,针对经济社会发展中出现的新业态、新模式,在推进普适性政策落地的基础上,及时跟进研究促进和规范行业发展的专项政策。落实国务院、省政府部署,拟订了《成都市创新管理优化服务培育壮大经济发展新动能加快新旧动能接续转换工作实施方案》;在全国率先出台了《关于鼓励共享单车发展的试行意见》,并配套实施《关于进一步加强共享单车管理的工作方案》;同时,为统筹推进共享经济等新经济形态发展,正在研究拟订《关于营造新生态发展新经济培育新动能的意见》;为推动互联网平台企业重塑供应链、整合产业链、融合价值链,构筑平台经济优势,正在研究拟订《关于加快平台经济发展的意见》;为提升城市停车服务水平,引导各类停车资源开放共享、集约利用,缓解城市停车设施资源供需矛盾,在实施《关于加强全市停车设施建设管理的实施意见》的基础上,正在研究拟订《关于推进停车资源共享利用工作的实施意见》。

Second, introduce special support policies. In accordance with the idea of changing "setting limits in advance" to "drawing lines in the process" and "supervising afterwards", and of putting forward more "guiding opinions" and less "management measures", Chengdu will timely follow up and study the special policies to promote and standardize the development of the industry, in view of the new forms of business and new models emerging in the economic and social development, based on promoting the implementation of universal policies. To implement the deployment of the State Council and the provincial government, Chengdu has formulated "Implementation Plan for Innovating Management, Optimizing Services, Cultivating and Strengthening New Growth Driver for Economic Development and Accelerating the Continuous Transformation of New and Old Driver"; it has taken the lead nationwide in issuing "Trial for Encouraging the Development of Bike Sharing", and implemented the work plan on "Further Strengthening the Management of Bike Sharing". At the same time, in order to promote the development of new economic forms such as sharing economy as a whole, Chengdu are studying and drafting "Creating New Ecology, Developing New Economy and Cultivating New Growth Driver"; in order to promote Internet platform enterprises to reshape supply chain, integrate industrial chain and integrate value chain, and build platform economic advantages, Chengdu are studying and drafting "Accelerating Platform Economic Development"; in order to improve the level of urban parking service, guide the open shared and intensive utilization of all kinds of parking resources, and alleviate the contradiction between supply and demand of urban parking facilities resources, we are studying and drafting "Implementation on Promoting the Sharing and Utilization of Parking Resources" on the basis of "Implementation on Strengthening the Construction and Management of Urban Parking Facilities".

三是持续转变监管服务方式。全面深化商事制度改革。持续推进注册资本登记、"多证合一"、"先照后证"、企业简易注销登记、"局所联动、全域通办"、企业登记全程电子化和电子营业执照等商事制度改革,不断降低市场准入门槛，优化营商环境，鼓励共享经济主体快速进入市场。

强化企业信用监管。建立以信用监管为核心的事中事后监管体系，对失信企业实施联合惩戒。将未按照《企业信息公示暂行条例》履行公示义务或涉及《企业信息公示暂行条例》所规定的严重违法行为的企业，依法纳入"经营异常名录"或"严重违法失信企业名单"管理。通过国家企业信用信息公示系统向社会公示，并对失信企业实施联合惩戒，促进市场公平竞争、维护市场正常秩序。

积极拓展消费维权。按照"谁提供服务谁负责"的原则，建立健全商品质量和服务规范承诺、不合格商品退市、消费纠纷和解、消费侵权赔偿等制度，完善涉及共享经济的消费维权部门协同共治机制，实现消费投诉快速联动应急处置，有效处理疑难消费投诉，切实增强群众获得感。

Third, continuously change the mode of supervision services. Comprehensively deepen the reform of commercial system. Chengdu will continue to promote the reform of commercial systems, such as the registration of registered capital, the integration of multiple certificates, business license first, the simple registration cancellation of enterprises, the linkage between bureaus and institutes, electronic registration of enterprises through the whole process, and the electronic business license. Chengdu will continue to reduce the market access threshold, optimize the business environment, and encourage the shared economic entities to enter the market quickly.

Strengthen enterprise credit supervision. Chengdu will establish the supervision system during and after the process with credit supervision as the core and implement joint punishment on dishonest enterprises. Enterprises that fail to perform the obligation of publicity in accordance with " Interim Regulations on Enterprise Information Publicity" or that involve serious illegal acts specified in " Interim Regulations on Enterprise Information Publicity" shall be included in the management of "abnormal operation list" or "list of serious illegal and dishonest enterprises" according to law, and publicized to the public through the national enterprise credit information publicity system, and joint punishment shall be implemented for dishonest enterprises to promote the market fair competition and normal market order.

Actively expand consumption rights protection. Following the principle of "One that provides the service takes responsibility", Chengdu will establish and improve the systems of commitment to commodity quality and service specification, delisting of unqualified commodities, settlement of consumers' dispute, compensation for consumer tort, etc., so as to improve the collaborative governance mechanism of consumer rights protection departments involved in the shared economy, realize the rapid linkage emergency disposal of consumers' complaints, effectively deal with difficult consumers' complaints, and effectively enhance the people's sense of access.

在共享经济科学分类指导下，共享经济各业态在成都展现良好发展态势，如图6-6所示。

Under the guidance of scientific classification of sharing economy, various formats of sharing economy show a good development trend in Chengdu, as shown in Figure 6-6.

图6-6　共享经济两大维度八大领域

Figure 6-6　Two Dimensions and Eight Areas of the Sharing Economy

生产共享领域。成都洪泰智造工场通过建立智能制造创业服务平台，为人工智能及智能制造创业者提供小批量试产及投资服务。目前，已成功孵化高科技创业公司 24 家，为超过 60 个创业团队提供小批量试产及测试服务，智造投资总额达 1 900 万元，公共技术服务平台累计生产点数达 760 万点，生产高科技产品 11 000 余件。

Sharing manufacturing. Chengdu Aplus Labs provides a small batch of trial production and investment services for artificial intelligence and intelligent manufacturing entrepreneurs through the establishment of intelligent manufacturing entrepreneurship service platform. At present, it has successfully incubated 24 high-tech start-up companies, providing a small batch of trial production and testing services for more than 60 start-up teams, with the total investment of intelligent manufacturing reaching 19 million Yuan, the cumulative production points of public technology service platform reaching 7. 6 million points, and the number of high-tech production reaching 11, 000.

共享单车领域。至今，成都市共享单车总量超过 120 万辆，累计注册用户数超过千万，日均骑行约 400 万人次，"共享单车+公共交通"出行新模式有力支撑全市科学治堵工作推进。

Sharing bikes. So far, the total number of sharing bicycles in Chengdu has exceeded 1. 2 million, with the total number of more than 10 million registered users, and the average of about 4 million riders per day. The new mode of "sharing bicycles plus public transport" strongly supports the promotion of scientific congestion control work in the city.

共享汽车领域。当前多家共享汽车企业抢滩成都市场，投入运营车辆约 3 000 辆，服务网点约 1 700 个，日均车辆使用频率约为 3 次，累计注册用户数约 60 万人次，主要在车站、机场、景区等出行需求热点区域布设站点，打造新能源汽车绿色出行全网通道。

Sharing cars. At present, a number of shared automobile enterprises have entered the market in Chengdu, with about 3, 000 vehicles in operation and 1, 700 service networks. The average daily use frequency of vehicles is about three times, and the total number of registered users is about 600, 000, mainly setting up branches in hot spots such as stations, airports and scenic spots, to create a green travel network for new energy vehicles.

共享医疗领域。多家本地共享医疗企业有效整合医疗资源，有序推进家庭医生在线签约服务，推动国家分级诊疗制度落地。2016 年 10 月，四川微医互联网医院在线诊疗平台在成都上线，开启了成都医疗服务共享新模式，目前共上线 4 565 名医生，通过图文问诊、视话问诊等方式服务患者 11 万余人次。

Sharing Health care. A number of medical-resources-shared local enterprises effectively integrate medical resources, orderly promote family physician online contract service, and promote the implementation of national graded diagnosis and treatment system. In October 2016, the online diagnosis and treatment platform of Sichuan Wedoctor Internet hospital was launched in Chengdu, opening a new mode of medical service sharing in Chengdu. At present, there are 4, 565 doctors online, having served more than 110, 000 patients ustilizing consultation in forms of pictures, messages and videos.

房屋短租行业。成都本地的优客逸家已在成都、武汉、北京、杭州四地开展运营服务，累计管理房屋近 3 万间，为 1 万名以上业主、5 万名优质租客提供了租房服务①。

In short-term housing rent industry. The local UOKO has carried out operation services in Chengdu, Wuhan, Beijing and Hangzhou. It has managed nearly 30, 000 houses and provided services to more than 10, 000 owners and 50, 000 high-quality tenants.

---

① 国家发改委高技术司. 中国共享经济发展报告：成都市分类指导推动共享经济多业态蓬勃发展［EB/OL］.（2020 - 04 - 22）［2021 - 01 - 08］. https://www.ndrc.gov.cn/xwdt/ztzl/zgzxjjbg/202004/t20200422_1226349.html.

典型案例：提升新技术、新模式服务实体经济能力

应用场景之"医联"慢病管理平台

Typical Case：Application Scenescapes of Improving the Ability

of New Technology and New Mode to Serve the Real Economy —

"Medical Union" Chronic Disease Management Platform

医联成立于 2014 年，致力于为广大慢病患者提供长期规范的专科慢病管理服务，用科技让慢病患者过上有品质的生活，如图 6-7 所示。目前，医联平台上汇聚了全国超过 80 万实名认证医生和 5 万余名签约医生，覆盖了肝病、糖尿病、HIV、肿瘤、肾病、心脑血管、儿科、精神心理、呼吸哮喘等多个慢病领域，为患者提供治疗建议、治疗效果评价、电子处方、用药指导、心理辅导、生活方式干预等一系列有效、低价、可及的院外慢病管理服务，从而使患者的疾病得到有效控制。2018 年 12 月，医联成功入选成为国家发改委首批"共享经济典型案例"，成为四川省唯一一家受邀来到现场分享的企业。

数百种患者慢病管理工具更好地服务患者
——

图 6-7　医联 APP 功能简介

Figure 6-7　Brief Introduction to Medical Union App

Founded in 2014, it is committed to providing long-term standardized specialist chronic disease management services for the majority of patients with chronic diseases and using science and technology to enable those patients to live a quality life, as shown in Figure 6-7. At present, more than 800,000 real name certified doctors and more than 50,000 contracted doctors are gathered on the platform, covering many chronic diseases such as liver disease, diabetes, HIV, tumor, kidney disease, cardio cerebrovascular disease, pediatrics, psycho psychology, respiratory asthma, providing patients with effective, low-cost and accessible out-of-hospital chronic disease management services such as treatment suggestions, treatment effect evaluation, electronic prescription, medication guidance, psychological counseling, lifestyle intervention etc., so as to effectively control patients' diseases. In December 2018, the platform was selected as one of the first batch of "typical cases of shared economy" by National Development and Reform Commission and became the only enterprise in Sichuan Province invited to share their experience on the spot.

CiNED

第七章

新经济"成长密码"——场景营城

Chapter Seven

"Growth Code" of New Economy —

City Growth by Scenescapes

2017 年，成都在全国首创提出应用场景理论。2020 年，成都召开新经济新场景新产品首场发布会，以"场景营城 产品赋能 新经济为人民创造美好生活"为主题，展现出成都场景营城、机会营城和新经济营城的良好城市生态，展示了成都将场景营城理念加速落地的决心。场景营城的意义和作用突出体现在四个方面：一是培育城市发展的内生动力，通过不同的生活与消费场景营造吸引有相同兴趣的人才集聚和交流，从而促进创新源泉充分涌流，驱动城市发展。二是激发潜在的消费行为，针对不同人群的消费偏好设计特殊场景，激发人们消费欲望和潜能。三是标识城市的个性特征，区分不同城市的最重要因素就是空间载体，而这种空间载体在城市中往往容易趋同，因而可通过与众不同的场景和功能植入吸引消费偏好和需求的人群集聚。四是引导人们的行为方式，场景营造有利于避免传统商业对现代中心城区商业业态同质化带来的负面影响，从而构建一个超越传统消费模式、引领消费时尚的消费空间。

In 2017, Chengdu initiated the "application scenescapes" theory in China. In 2020, the first press conference of new economy, new scenescapes and new products was held in Chengdu, with the theme of "new economy for a better life empowered by products and constructed by scenescapes". It shows the good urban ecology of city management by scenescapes, opportunity and new economy, and shows Chengdu's determination to accelerate the implementation of the concept of city growth by scenescapes. The significance and role of the concept are highlighted in four aspects: first, to cultivate the endogenous power of urban development, to attract talents with the same interest to gather and exchange through different life and consumption scenescapes, to promote the full flow of innovation sources and drive urban development. The second is to stimulate the potential consumption behavior, design special scenescapes according to the consumption preferences of different groups and stimulate the desire and potential of consumption. The third is to identify the personality of the city. The most important factor to distinguish different cities is the space carrier, which often tends to converge in cities to attract people with consumption preference and demand through different scenescapes and functions. The fourth is to guide people's behavior. The creation of scenescapes is conducive to avoiding the negative impact of traditional commerce on the homogenization of commercial formats in modern central urban areas to build a consumption space that goes beyond the traditional consumption mode and leads the consumption fashion.

▷▷▷ 第一节　场景营城理论

Section One　Theory of City Growth by Scenescapes

一、场景营城的概念

1. Concept of City Growth by Scenescapes

场景可理解为未来城市的基本构建单元，也可认为是都市的微型生态圈，不同的资源要素组合形成了不同的场景，不同的场景组合又形成了不同的城市形态。场景是城市中不同舒适物设施与活动的有机组合，是在特定的时空范围内，将新技术、新产品、新业态、新模式等创新要素融入经济社会发展过程，重构人、事、物之间的相互关系，促进供需方对接的过程和结果，是承载城市生产、生活、治理功能的集成系统，也是具有价值导向、文化风格、美学特征、行为符号的城市空间。从根本上看，场景是科技要素、人文美学、商业价值、空间结构的统一，其核心理念是为人民创造美好生活。

The scenescapes can be understood as the basic building unit of the future city and can also be regarded as the micro ecosystem of the city. Different resource factors form different scenescapes, and combination of different scenescapes form different urban forms. Scenescape is an organic combination of different amenities and activities in a city. It is a process and result of integrating innovative factors such as new technologies, new products, new forms of business and new models into economic and social development, reconstructing the relationship among people, things and promoting the docking of supply and demand. It is an integrated system with the functions of urban production, life and governance, and also an urban space with value orientation, cultural style, aesthetic characteristics and behavioral symbols. Fundamentally, the scenescape is the unity of scientific and technological factors, humanistic aesthetics, commercial value and spatial structure, and its core idea is to create a better life for the people.

场景思维是一种运用场景将新技术、新业态、新模式等创新要素与文化要素融入经济社会活动中的思考方式，场景思维的本质是"以场景链接万物"，重塑人、事、物之间的相互关系与作用机理，特别是在丰富的空间维系中密切串联人与人之间的经济联系和社会联系，最终迸发形成具有蓬勃生机的城市创造力。场景营城是运用场景化思维对原有生产、流通、消费与社会生活等城市生态系统进行重构，在生活导向下以场景营造为基底进行城市形态重塑，创新城市资源配置与公共产品供给，创造人文价值鲜明、商业功能融合的美学体验空间，吸引与聚集创新创意等高端人力资本，从而由内而外地创新城市运营组织方式、激发城市内生活力、培育城市发展新动能的一系列活动。

Using scenescapes is a way of thinking that integrates innovative and cultural factors such as new technology, new form of business and new mode into economic and social activities by using scenescapes. The essence of the thinking is to "link everything with scenescapes", reshape the relationship and mechanism between people, things and objects, especially closely connecting the economic and social ties between people in the maintenance of rich space, and finally shape the city's creativity with vigorous vitality. The concept is to reconstruct the original urban ecosystem of production, circulation, consumption and social life using scenescapes. Under the guidance of life, it remolds the urban form based on scenescape construction, innovates the allocation of urban resources and the supply of public products, creates aesthetic experience space with distinct humanistic value and integration of commercial functions, and attracts and gathers high-end human resources with innovation and creativity, to innovate the urban operation and organization mode from the inside to the outside, stimulate the vitality in the city, and cultivate a series of activities of new growth driver of urban development.

二、场景营城理论的发展梳理
2. Development of the Theory "City Growth by Scenescapes"

芝加哥学派的特里·克拉克认为都市娱乐休闲设施与市民生活的组合都可看作都市"场景",并认为这些不同的场景蕴含着不同的文化价值取向,这些文化价值进而吸引着不同的人群来进行文化实践消费,最终为区域创造经济价值。城市经营理论认为,城市经营是城市政府运用市场经济手段,对城市各种可以经营的包括土地、基础设施等有形资产以及城市形象、城市品牌等无形资产进行资本化的市场运作,以实现城市资产在容量、结构、秩序和功能上的最大化和最优化,从而提升城市的综合竞争能力,促进城市可持续发展。空间结构理论认为城市空间结构包括形式和过程两个方面,分别指城市结构要素的空间分布和空间作用的模式。城市空间结构的形式是指城市各个要素如物质设施、公共机构的空间分布模式,过程则是指城市要素之间的相互作用,它们将个体土地利用、群体活动的形式和行为,整合成为一个个功能各异的实体,也称为子系统。流程再造理论认为应该重新设计和安排企业的整个生产、服务和经营过程,使之合理化,通过对企业原来生产经营过程的各个方面、每个环节进行全面的调查研究和细致分析,彻底变革不合理、不必要的环节。城市美学理论将审美活动领域从单一的艺术哲学拓展为城市日常生活,将审美活动方式由传统的审美观赏拓展为多方面的审美体验,从而使传统的对象式审美转变为栖居式审美。

Terry Clark of Chicago School thinks that the combination of urban entertainment and leisure facilities and people's life can be regarded as urban "scenescapes", and that these different scenescapes contain different cultural values, which in turn attract different people to carry out cultural practice consumption, and ultimately create economic value for the region. According to the theory, city management is a market operation in which the city government use means of market economy to capitalize all kinds of tangible assets such as land and infrastructure, and intangible assets such as city image and city brand, to realize the maximization and optimization of city assets in capacity, structure, order and function, enhance the city's comprehensive competitiveness, promote the city's sustainable development. According to the theory of spatial structure, urban spatial structure includes two aspects: form and process, which respectively refer to the spatial distribution of urban structural factors and the mode of spatial function. The form of urban spatial structure refers to the spatial distribution pattern of urban factors such as physical facilities and public institutions, while the process refers to the interaction between urban factors, which integrate individual land use and group activities into entities with different functions, also known as subsystems. According to the theory of process reengineering, the whole process of production, service and operation should be redesigned and arranged for rationalization. Through the comprehensive investigation and detailed analysis of all aspects and links of the original production and operation process, the unreasonable and unnecessary links should be completely changed. The theory of urban aesthetics expands the field of aesthetic activities from a single art philosophy to daily urban life and expands the mode of aesthetic activities from traditional aesthetic appreciation to various aesthetic experiences, thus transforming the traditional object-oriented aesthetics into dwelling aesthetics.

我们认为，相关经济学理论的产生总是与城市发展趋势或阶段需求有内在关联，场景营城的核心理念与时代背景及成都发展历史阶段充分契合，可以说场景营城理论来源于城市经营理论、流程再造理论等相关经济学论述，同时也与城市规划、城市建设、城市经营、城市治理息息相关，它将在成都新经济发展实践中不断被论证、丰富。

It is believed that the emergence of relevant economic theories is always intrinsically related to the trend or stage demand of urban development, and the core concept of urban development by scenescapes is fully consistent with the background of the times and the historical stage of Chengdu's development. It can be said that the theory comes from urban development theory, process restructuring theory and other relevant economic theories, as well as related to urban planning, urban construction, urban development, and urban governance, which will be demonstrated and enriched in the practice of Chengdu's new economic development.

三、场景营城的经济学思考
3. Analysis from Economics

（一）场景营城的作用机理
（1）Mechanism of City Growth by Scenescapes

场景营城通过流程再造实现系统增值。场景营城即场景在城市经营中的运用，通俗地讲就是城市主体通过使用新经济应用场景、创造新经济应用场景来经营城市的一系列活动。场景营城包括运营主体、运营工具和方法、运营客体、运营效能等要素，是一个从城市场景向场景城市迭代演化的过程，或者说是一个场景识别、场景收集、场景分析和聚类、场景应用和场景创造并推动城市功能优化升级，促进新经济快速发展的循环迭代的过程①。其机理如图7-1所示。

City growth by scenescapes realizes value-added of system through process restructuring. It is the application of scenescapes in urban development. Generally speaking, it is series of activities that the city's main body manages the city by using and creating the new economy scenescapes application. It includes subjects, tools and methods, objects, efficiency of management, etc. It is a process of iterative evolution from urban scenescapes to scenescapes city,

---

① 张宇，张梦雅，于惠洋，李艳春. 场景营城的经济学思考及路径研究 [J]. 先锋，2020（8）：39-41.

or a process with iterative cycle of scenscapes recognition, collection, analysis and clustering, application and creation to promotes the optimization and upgrading of urban functions and promotes the rapid development of new economy. The mechanism is shown in Figure 7−1.

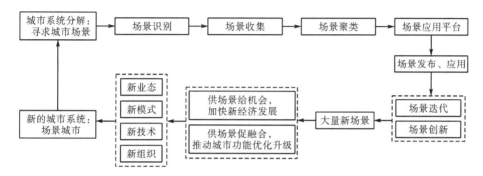

图 7−1　场景营城机理

Figure 7−1　Mechanism of New Economy — City Growth by Scenescapes

1. 识别与收集

1）Identification and Collection

实现场景营城，使场景与城市的生产生活有效融合，首先需要拥有足够数量的场景。比如，2020 年 3 月 31 日成都首次发布的 100 个新场景，大多数可归为产业级细分场景。

To realize city growth by scenescapes and effectively integrate the scene with the production and life of the city, Chengdu need to have enough scenescapes at first. For example, on March 31, 2020, most of the 100 new scenescapes first released in Chengdu can be classified as industry-level segmented scenescapes.

城市运营的主体包括民众、企业、产业（行业）和政府，因此可以从不同的主体活动空间对新经济应用场景及其核心功能进行识别并收集，也可以从技术应用等视角进行场景及其核心功能的识别和收集。

The main body of urban operation includes the public, enterprises, industries (professions) and governments. Therefore, Chengdu can identify and collect the new economy application scenescapes and their core functions from different main activity spaces and from the perspective of technology application.

2. 分析与分类

由于收集到的场景功能不同、特征不同、类型不同，需要将收集的场景进行规范化，突出其核心功能，用统一的格式进行数据描述，并对这些场景进行聚合分类，形成场景库。在此基础上，根据创新性、商业性、社会效益、可复制和示范价值等不同评价标准开展场景分析，并支持新技术、新业态、新模式融合创新的市场验证，验证商业模型，评估市场前景，高效利用场景存量，大大降低场景应用与推广风险，加速新场景在市场中的成熟，帮助企业创新产品（服务）寻找更适合的市场。

2）Analysis and Classification

Due to the different functions, characteristics and types of the collected scenescapes, it is necessary to standardize the collected scenes, highlight their core functions, describe the data in a unified format, and aggregate and classify these scenescapes to form a scenescapes database, and then carry out scenescapes analysis according to different evaluation criteria of innovation, commerciality, social benefit, replicability and demonstration value, and support the market verifying of integration and innovation of new technology, new form of business and new mode, to verify the business model, evaluate the market prospect, efficiently utilize scenescapes stock, significantly reduce the risk of scenescapes application and promotion, accelerate the maturity of new scenescapes in the market and help enterprises innovate products (services) to find a more suitable market.

3. 发布和应用

编制应用场景规划和年度供给计划，将筛选后的场景定期通过平台统一发布，建立常态化的应用场景发布机制，并对已发布的场景清单进行动态调整和适时更新，为有相应需求的城市运营主体提供供需对接平台，各类主体根据自身需求获取场景资源或提供场景服务，将应用场景转化为市场机会，并和城市生产生活相结合打造应用场景示范。

3）Release and Application

Prepare the scenescapes application planning and annual supply plan, release the selected scenescapes through the platform regularly, establish a normalized application scenescapes release mechanism, and dynamically adjust and timely update the released scenescapes list, to provide a supply-demand docking platform for urban operators with corresponding needs. Various subjects can obtain scenescapes resources or provide scenescapes services according to their own needs to turn application scenescapes into market opportunities and combine with urban production and life to create application scenescapes demonstration.

4. 迭代和创造

在场景应用过程中通过各城市运营主体与新经济场景的深度互动产生"1+N"的场景裂变效应，即由若干个已成熟的新场景带动产生跨行业、跨领域、跨层级的多个创新应用场景。这些新产生的场景又将被征集、发现、应用，同时又丰富已有的应用场景，实现场景再生，形成场景营城的全流程闭环。具体如图7-2所示。

4）Iteration and Creation

In the process of scenescapes application, the "1 + N" scenescapes multiplied effect is generated through the deep interaction between the city operators and the new economic scenescapes, that is, a number of mature new scenescapes drive the generation of multiple innovative scenescapes application across industries, fields and levels. They will afterwards be collected, discovered and applied and meanwhile enrich the existing application scenescapes to realize scenescapes regeneration and form the closed loop of the whole process. As shown in Figure 7-2.

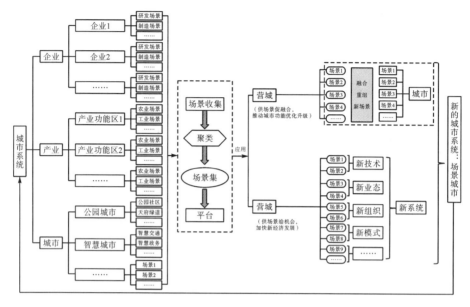

图 7-2 场景营城全流程

Figure 7-2 Whole Process of New Economy — City Growth by Scenescapes

（二）从经济到文化：场景营城的再思考

2. From Economy to Culture：Rethinking of City Growth by Scenescapes

经济与文化总是相互交融又息息相关，随着后知识经济时代的来临，文化力量正崛起成为城市发展的新兴动力源。场景营城的文化内涵是将不同的文化要素融入特定时空实现特殊功能，功能的不断迭代促进城市组织方式的不断创新。场景营城的文化机理是通过打造具有不同文化属性的区域，吸引特定阶层的人群汇聚，如传统社区空间正在向地域、生活、情感价值于一体的场景延伸，不同社区场景拼接成生活的全貌和图景，承载着市民的梦想和美好向往。场景营城已成为现代城市发展的必然趋势和满足美好生活需要的物化空间。

Economy and culture are always blended and closely related. With the coming of the post-knowledge economy era, cultural power is rising and becoming a new power source of urban development. The cultural connotation of "City Growth by Scenescapes" integrate different cultural factors into specific time and space to achieve special functions. The continuous iteration of functions promotes the continuous innovation of urban organization. The cultural mechanism of "City Growth by Scenescapes" attracts people of specific classes to gather by creating regions with different cultural attributes. For example, the traditional community space is extending to the scenescapes of integrating region, life and emotional value. Different scenescapes community are spliced into the panorama and picture of life, carrying the dream and beautiful yearning of citizens. Scenescapes construction has become an inevitable trend of modern urban development and a materialized space to meet the needs of a better life.

　　文化是吸引高级人力资本个体的重要因素，场景营城的核心要素是人，人才资源是推动国家与地区高效发展的动力引擎，是实现经济结构转型、提升城市功能的关键要素。场景营城具有供需两端的不同特性，从城市供给角度来看，蕴含不同文化的场景营城吸引了特定阶层的人才涌向成都，这些高端人才将成为推动城市高质量发展的基本战略资源；从人才需求角度来看，不同人才需要的要素各不相同，各要素间不断迭代促进场景不断优化升级，不同场景的营造及融合又将倒逼城市功能不断提升，供需两端共同塑造了未来城市形态。

　　Culture is an important factor to attract high-level human capital individuals. The core factor of "City Growth by Scenescapes" is people. Human resources are the power engine to promote the efficient development of the country and region, and the key factor to realize the transformation of economic structure and enhance the city's function. It has different characteristics at the two ends of supply and demand. From the perspective of urban supply, scenescapes with different cultures attract talents from specific strata to Chengdu. These high-end talents will become the basic strategic resources to promote the high-quality development of the city. From the perspective of talents demand, different talents need different factors, and the continuous iteration of each factor promotes the continuous upgrading and optimization of scenescapes. The construction and integration of different scenescapes will force the continuous improvement of urban functions, and both supply and demand will jointly shape the future urban form.

▷▷▷第二节 场景是发展新经济培育新动能的动力源

Section Two Scenescapes — Source Power to Develop New Economy and Cultivate New Growth Drivers

一、场景是新技术的实验室

1. Scenescapes — Laboratory of New Technology

在新经济时代，大量的新技术被发明出来，在这个时候应用场景就扮演了新技术的实验室的角色。新技术被实施在真实场景中，场景给新技术带来更为准确的行业状况和真实的客户需求实验数据，使企业找准了方向，让新技术能更加快速地发展起来。场景成为新技术的实验室主要表现为这三方面：一是场景创造新需求，提供了数据收集的环境；二是场景提供市场，完善算法、迭代产品；三是场景提供数据，迭代商业模式。另外场景也是新技术出现与发展的强大驱动力，任何一个公司或企业只有不断地创新才能长期存活，如阿里巴巴在数十年的发展中都在不断地创造出新技术新模式，因为当今世界瞬息万变，不断有新场景被创造出来。要适应当今世界发展，在新的场景之下不被淘汰，就必须不断地创新，不断地探索出新技术新模式，所以说场景是新技术的强大驱动力量。

In the new economic era, a large number of new technologies have been invented. At this time, scenescapes application plays the role of laboratory of new technologies. New technologies are implemented in real scenescapes, which bringing more accurate industry conditions and real customer demand experimental data to new technologies. Therefore enterprises can find the right direction and make new technologies develop more rapidly. Scenescapes becomes the laboratory of new technology mainly in the following three aspects: first, scenescapes create new requirements and provide an environment for data collection; second, scenescapes provide the market, improve algorithms and iterates products; third, scenescapes provide data and iterates business model. In addition, scenescapes are the powerful driving force for the emergence and development of new technologies. Only by constant innovation can any company survive for a long time. For example, Alibaba has been constantly creating new technologies and new models in decades of development; because today's world is changing rapidly and new scenescapes are constantly created. If a company want to adapt to the development of today's world, it requires constant innovation. Therefore, scenescapes are the powerful driving force of new technology.

二、场景是新技术产业的聚合器
2. Scenescapes — Aggregator of New Technology Industry

场景将成为新技术的聚合器主要表现在三个方面：其一，新技术产业的发展离不开场景，场景能够给产业带来巨大的新需求，创造更多的新机会和新市场，带动企业快速发展。其二，场景是技术创新的中心，场景能够激活新理论新技术的研发及产业化应用，间接带动跨界研究合作及上下游产业链相关企业的衍生与汇聚，场景驱动最核心的企业壮大发展，发展后的核心企业又可以带动其他企业的发展，进而场景将所有的相关企业聚合成为一个整体。其三，场景是新技术的价值网络。城市是人群集聚区域，对于细分领域的多元长尾需求在人群的数量足够多的时候就会带动新场景的集体爆发，能够为"科技+生活网络"的创新型公司的商业模式创新、发展提供足够多的用户和商家数量。

Scenescapes will become the aggregator of new technology, mainly in three aspects: first, the development of new technology industry is inseparable from the scenescapes, which can bring huge new demand to the industry, create more new opportunities and new markets, and drive the rapid development of enterprises. Secondly, scenescapes are the center of technological innovation, which can activate the R&D and industrial application of new theories and technologies, indirectly drive the cross-border research cooperation and the derivation and aggregation of related enterprises in the upstream and downstream industrial chain. Scenescapes drive the growth and development of the most core enterprises, which can drive other enterprises's development, and then scenescapes will bind all related enterprises together. Third, scenescapes are the value network of new technology. The city is a crowd gathering area. When the number of people is enough, the multi-demand in the segmentation field will lead to the collective outbreak of new scenescapes, which can provide enough users and businessmen for the innovation and development of business model of "technology plus life network" innovative companies.

三、场景是高科技独角兽企业的孵化器
3. Scenescapes — Incubator of High Tech Unicorn Enterprises

企业利用高科技探索出更加适合和方便人类生活的新环境，利用新手段打造出更符合人类需求的产品和服务，就可能爆发式地成长，成为同行业中的独角兽企业。独角兽企业在探索成为独角兽的过程中不仅需要有场景为其提供市场，也需要场景为其提供新技术新产品试验的场所。例如短租应用 Airbnb，据统计，2014 年 6 月 Airbnb 在巴黎和西雅图推出餐饮共享服务后，估值迅速攀升，Airbnb 估值快速升高的主要原因在于它既有房屋短租场景又创新地开拓了餐饮场景。中国已经涌现了大量独角兽企业，成为借助场景创新实现高速成长的标杆。长城战略咨询发布的《2018 年中国独角兽企业研究报告》中显示，我国独角兽企业共有 202 家，总估值 7 441 亿美元。这些独角兽企业都是依托特定的场景才取得了巨大成功。

Enterprises, which use high technology to explore a new environment more suitable for and convenient for human life and use new means to create products and services more in line with human needs, may grow explosively and become Unicorn enterprises in the same industry. In their exploration to become unicorns, these enterprises not only need to have scenescapes to provide the market for them, but also need scenescapes to provide the place for them to test new technologies and products. For example, according to statistics, short-term rent APP Airbnb's valuation rose rapidly after launching the catering shared service in Paris and Seattle in June 2014. The reason for the rapid rise is that it not only has scenescapes of short-term housing rent, but also innovates the catering scenescapes. A large number of unicorn enterprises have emerged in China, becoming a benchmark for achieving high-speed growth with the help of scenescapes innovation. According to the "Research Report on Chinese Unicorn enterprises in 2018" released by Great Wall Strategy Consulting, there are 202 Unicorn enterprises in China, with a total valuation of 744.1 billion US dollars. These Unicorn enterprises can achieve great success by relying on specific scenescapes.

四、场景供给是城市发展的新竞争点
4. Scenescapes Supply—New Competitive Point of Urban Development

在新经济时代，越来越多的城市将场景作为自己经济发展的基础，越来越多的城市开始注意到应用场景的经济力量，越来越多的城市开始发展应用场景。在新经济时代，拥有"全景化"应用场景的城市将会变得越来越有吸引力和有价值。城市发展新的竞争点在于场景的供给能力，一个城市想要发展出自己较强的场景供给可以从以下三个方面考虑：一是规划新场景，前瞻性思考全球科技、产业变革方向，尽可能考虑科技对城市交通、教育、医疗、环境、行政等各方面的渗透和改变，在城市规划编制中充分留白，超前谋划、前瞻布局如充电桩、无人驾驶道路等应用场景空间，建设人工智能测试场、游戏测试实验区、科技街区等测试应用场所。二是创造新场景，鼓励企业围绕高质量发展、高品质生活提供解决方案，定期发布主体功能区建设、创新生态培养、十五分钟生活圈构建、公园城市规划等领域的"城市机会清单"，为新经济发展提供应用端口。三是包容新场景，对于已经在积极推进市场化的新技术和模式，给予包容，推进当下管理流程、规制与其相融合。成都在智慧城市规划编制中设计应用场景，构建成都市"政务云"，超前规划200平方千米智慧交通生态圈，启动建设5平方千米无人驾驶汽车测试场，建远洋太古里全国首个 5G 示范街区，建全国第一个 5G 地铁站，通过共享停车试点为全市 460 个小区提供车位共享服务，加快盒马鲜生、缤果盒子等新零售场景布局，支持无人工厂和无人快递等新场景落地。只有大力构建发展与新经济发展高度融合的多元应用场景，有了更强大的供给力，城市才能在新经济时代谋求最好的发展。

In the new economic era, more and more cities take the scenescape as the foundation of their own economic development and begin to pay attention to the economic power of application scenescapes and develop application scenescapes. In the new economic era, cities with "panoramic" application scenescapes will become more and more attractive and valuable. The new competitive point of urban development lies in the supply capacity of scenescapes. To develop its own strong scenescapes supply, the city has to consider the following three aspects: first, planning new scenescapes, thinking forward the direction of global science and technology and industrial change, and considering the penetration and change of science and technology in urban transportation, education, health care, environment, administration, etc. as far as possible, make full use of the space for scenescapes application in the process of urban planning, plan and lay out in advance the scenescape space such as charging piles, driverless roads, and build such test application site as artificial intelligence test fields, game test experimental areas, science and technology blocks, etc. The second is to create new scenescapes, encourage enterprises to provide solutions around high-quality development and high-quality life, and regularly release "urban opportunity list" in the fields of main functional area construction, innovative ecological cultivation, 15-minute-life circle construction, park city planning, etc., to provide application ports for new economic development. The third is to accommodate new scenescapes. For the new technologies and models under marketization, Chengdu should actively and boldly accommodate them, and promote their integration with current management processes and regulations. And design scenescapes application in smart city planning, build

Chengdu's "Government Cloud", plan ahead 200 square kilometers of smart transportation ecosystem, start the construction of 5 square kilometers of driverless car test field, build the first 5G demonstration block in Yuanyangtaiguli, the first 5G subway station in China, and pilot plan to provide parking space shared service for 460 residential areas in the city, and speed up the construction of new retail scenescapes such as Hema, Bingguo, and support new scenescapes such as unmanned factory and unmanned express delivery. Only by constructing diversified application scenescapes highly integrated with the development of new economy can the city have more powerful supply and achieve better development in the new economic era.

▷▷▷第三节　运用场景营城理念 加快新旧动能转换的路径

Section Three　Paths to Speed Up Transformation from Old to New Drivers by Scenescapes

一、以包容审慎的营商环境催生新场景

1. Creating New Scenescapes with an Inclusive and Prudent Business Environment

培育新动能，促进经济发展方式的转变，需要市场和政府"双手"合力。政府的职责是通过创新体制机制，为企业创造一个良好的、舒适的、通畅的营商环境。用审慎包容的监管方式应对新技术、新模式、新组织及新产业，破解制约新经济场景构建的制度障碍，柔性发展新场景，为企业发展提供更多市场机会。具体来看：

To cultivate new growth drivers and promote the transformation of the mode of economic development needs the joint efforts of the market and the government. The responsibility of the government is to create a good, comfortable and smooth business environment for enterprises by innovating the system and mechanism. Chengdu should deal with new technologies, models, organizations and industries in a prudent and inclusive way, break the institutional barriers restricting the construction of new economic scenescapes, and develop new scenesacapes flexibly, to provide more market opportunities for the development of enterprises.

（1）建立场景供给统筹推进机制。由成都新经济发展工作小组办公室领导、统筹协调场景供给工作，制定场景供给、实施、反馈调整等相关政策措施，指定行业主管部门牵头协调，指派专人负责落实。设立新经济委，负责新经济推进工作，协调解决重大问题，形成政策体系并统筹推进；建立新经济发展研究院，提供趋势预测、政策设计、决策判断、平台运营、对外合合作等方面的服务和支撑。

（1）Establish the overall promotion mechanism of scenescape supply. The office of the Chengdu new economic development working group shall lead and coordinate the scenescapes supply work, formulate the scenescapes supply, implementation, feedback, adjustment and other relevant policies and measures, assign the competent department of the industry to lead the coordination, and assign special personnel to be responsible for the implementation. The new economic committee is set up to be responsible for promoting of the new economy, coordinating and solving major problems, forming a policy system and promoting it as a whole. The new economic development research institute is set up to provide services and support for trend prediction, policy design, decision-making, platform operation, foreign cooperation, etc.

（2）制定出台工作方案。围绕场景构建、清单收集发布、清单应用、组织保障等方面，出台《关于建立城市机会清单发布机制推进应用场景供给工作方案》，有效指导场景工作顺利推进，完善城市机会清单发布体系机制。

（2）Formulate and issue work plans. Around the scenescapes construction, list collection and release, list application, organization guarantee and other aspects, Chengdu issued "Work Plan on Establishing the City Opportunity List Release Mechanism to Promote the Supply of Application Scenescapes", effectively guiding the smooth progress of the scenescapes work, and improving the city opportunity list release system and mechanism.

（3）建立场景需求清单征集和发布机制。以市场需求为导向，面向全社会发布场景需求清单，并报送成都市新经发展工作小组办公室，由工作小组办公室对场景需求清单进行筛选，择优确定一批场景，以城市机会清单的形式发布，并根据需求变化、企业反馈等情况对已发布的清单进行动态调整和适时更新，如图7-3所示。截至2019年年底，成都已发布三批次12大类1 400条供需信息，引进新经济500强企业45家，实现融资85.8亿元。面对新冠疫情，成都新经济企业俱乐部遴选了一批适用于各类抗疫场景的产品和服务，编制出《成都新经济企业疫情防控能力清单》。这份清单包含成都市新经济企业疫情防控、居家生活产品（服务）、新经济企业能力渠道三张子清单，发布各类清单信息111条，为打赢疫情防控阻击战贡献成都新经济力量。2020年3月，成都市印发《供场景给机会加快新经济发展若干政策措施》，旨在以场景组织新经济工作，进一步夯实场景突破的基础，创新场景供给的方式，深耕场景培育的土壤，持续巩固成都新经济先发优势，提升最适宜新经济发展的城市品牌。

（3）Establish the mechanism of scenescapes requirement list collection and release. Guided by market demand, Chengdu publishes scenescapes demand list publicly and submits it to the working group office, who screens the list and issues the best scenescapes in the form of city opportunity list, and dynamically adjusts and timely updates the released list according to demand changes and enterprises' feedback, as shown in Figure 7-3. By the end of 2019, Chengdu has released 1,400 pieces of supply and demand information of 12 categories in three batches, introduced 45 new economy top 500 enterprises, and achieved financing of 8.58 billion Yuan. In the face of novel coronavirus pneumonia, Chengdu's new economic enterprise club has selected a number of products and services suitable for all kinds of pandemic situations, and compiled "List of Pandemic Prevention and Control Capabilities of Chengdu's New Economic Enterprises". This list includes three sub lists: pandemic prevention and control of Chengdu's new economy enterprises, products (services) for home life and capability channels of new economy enterprises, releasing 111 items of list information to win the battle of pandemic prevention and control with Chengdu's new economic strength. In March 2020, Chengdu printed and issued "Policies and Measures to Provide Scenescapes and Opportunities to Accelerate the Development of New Economy", aiming at organizing new economy work with scenescapes, further consolidating the foundation of scenescapes breakthrough, innovating the way of scenescapes supply, enriching the soil of scenescapes cultivation, continuously consolidating the early development advantages of Chengdu's new economy, and enhancing the city brand most suitable for the development of new economy.

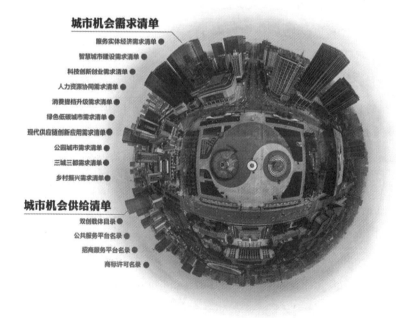

图 7-3　成都城市机会清单

Figure 7-3　Chengdu City Opportunity List

（4）建立场景供需对接推进机制。基于场景需求清单，行业主管部门对已对接的场景需求项目做好跟踪协调工作，工作小组办公室做好跟踪问效工作，对取得显著成效的需求单位纳入应用场景示范单位。

（4）Establish promotion mechanism of scenescapes supply and demand docking. Based on the scenescapes demand list, the industry authorities track for coordinating the docked projects of scenescapes demand. The working group offices tracks for efficiency and brings the demand units that have achieved remarkable results into the scenescapes application demonstration units.

（5）建立场景供给动态评价机制。将城市机会清单发布、供需对接落地等工作纳入负责场景供给对应部门的工作绩效考核体系，建立动态评价机制，及时跟踪处理城市机会落地落实相关问题①。

（5）Establish dynamic evaluation mechanism of scenescapes supply. The released list of urban opportunities and the implementation of supply and demand docking will be included in the performance appraisal system of the corresponding departments responsible for scenescapes supply, and a dynamic evaluation mechanism will be established to track and deal with the implementation of urban opportunities in time.

二、搭建链接市场需求各方的细分场景
2. Building Segmentation Scenescapes for all Parties in the Link Market

政府通过城市机会信息收集发布机制，全面挖掘整合企业、消费者的需求，解构需求，细分产业链，搭建细分场景，提供市场机会，最终形成城市机会清单并对外发布。发布城市机会清单，以新思维和新应用场景，有利于引导市场上优秀的要素聚集到新经济领域，或者运用创新模式改造存量产业，最终实现产业结构调整，推动经济高质量发展。具体到制造业、现代服务业和现代农业，主要聚焦在以下场景中：

---

① 人民网. 3问新经济"机会之城"［EB/OL］. （2019-04-02）［2021-01-10］. http://sc.people.com.cn/n2/2019/0402/c379471-32803910.html.

Through the collection and release mechanism of urban opportunity information, the government comprehensively excavates and integrates the needs of enterprises and consumers, deconstructs the needs, subdivides the industrial chain, builds segmentation scenescapes, provides market opportunities, and finally forms and publishes the list of urban opportunities. The list release of urban opportunities, with new thinking and new application scenescapes, is conducive to guiding the outstanding factors in the market to gather in the new economic field, or transforming the stock industry by using innovative mode, finally realizing the adjustment of industrial structure and promoting high-quality economic development. Specifically, manufacturing industry, modern service industry and modern agriculture mainly focus on the following scenescapes:

（1）在制造业中，围绕加快融入全球智能制造创新体系，推进智能制造试点示范和智能化改造，鼓励企业利用物联网、云计算、大数据等新技术、新产品（服务）在智能生产、大规模个性化定制、网络化协同制造等企业生产过程中的应用，打造示范试点技术应用场景。

（1）In the manufacturing industry, around speeding up the integration into the global intelligent manufacturing innovation system, promoting the pilot demonstration and intelligent transformation of intelligent manufacturing, enterprises are encouraged to make use of the application of new technologies and new products（services）such as Internet of things, cloud computing and big data in the production process of intelligent production, mass customization, networked collaborative manufacturing and other enterprises, to create the application scenescapes of demonstration pilot technologies.

（2）在现代服务业中，围绕推进现代服务业发展，实现服务业数字化网络化智能化，鼓励物流、旅游、新零售、供应链等重点领域的企业挖掘物联网、人工智能、VR 等新技术、新产品（服务）在本行业中的应用场景，打造示范应用场景，提升消费层级，推动行业发展。

（2）In the modern service industry, around promoting the development of modern service industry, realizing the digitalization, networking and intellectualization of service industry, enterprises in crucial fields such as logistics, tourism, new retail and supply chain are encouraged to explore the application scenescapes of new technologies and new products (services) such as Internet of things, artificial intelligence and VR in this industry, to create demonstration application scenescapes, enhance consumption level and promote the development of the industry.

（3）在现代农业中，围绕国家都市现代农业示范城市建设，推进智慧农业发展，鼓励企业运用互联网、物联网、大数据等新经济、新产品（服务）、新模式在农业生产、销售、农业信息服务等领域的应用，打造试点示范应用场景。

（3）In modern agriculture, around constructing national urban modern agriculture demonstration city, promoting the development of smart agriculture, enterprises are encouraged to apply new economy, new products (services), new models such as the Internet, Internet of things, big data to agricultural production, sales, information services and other fields, to create pilot demonstration application scenescapes.

三、以关键核心技术孵化培育新场景
3. Incubating New Scenescapes with Core Technologies

关键核心技术作为一种新技术，其市场是未知的，为解决新技术及新技术衍生的产品（服务）落地的市场问题，要围绕关键核心技术，孵化培育新技术、新产品（服务）应用"试验场"新场景，主动释放资源要素，为企业提供入口机会，激发企业创新创造的活力和信心，从而将技术优势转化为生产力，用生产力去推动市场经济的发展，最终实现以技术引领领市发展。具体来看：

As a new technology, the market of core technology is unknown. In order to solve the market problem of new technology and its derived products (services), Chengdu will focus on the core technology, incubate and cultivate the new scenescapes of new technology and new product（service）application "testing ground", actively release resource factors, provide entry opportunities for enterprises, and stimulate enterprises' vitality and confidence of innovation to transform technological advantages into productivity, use productivity to promote the development of market economy, and finally realize the urban development led by technology.

（1）强化科技基础设施群和研发平台。以提升原始创新力和支持关键核心技术发展为目标，瞄准市场需求，借助高等院校、科研院所等现有设施和平台的优势，加强基础投入，连"点"成"群"。为新技术的诞生、改进、应用及市场化提供基础支持。

（1）Strengthen science and technology infrastructure group and R&D platform. With the goal of enhancing the original innovation ability and supporting the development of core technologies, Chengdu will aim at the market demand, take the advantages of existing facilities and platforms such as colleges and universities, scientific research institutes, etc., strengthen the basic investment, and connect "points" into "groups", to provide basic support for the birth, improvement, application and marketization of new technology.

（2）增加场景新供给，深化场景供给产品。研究不同主体的新变化、新模式，掌握行业痛点、难点，推动传统场景转型升级。围绕城市重大战略，根据政策导向，融合需求，引导需求，重点打造创新型场景。围绕场景供给产品，政府上游重点规划新场景、创造新场景、包容新场景，企业下游重点选择新场景、适用新场景、建设新场景。

（2）Increase the new supply of scenescapes and deepen the product supply of scenescapes. Chengdu will study the new changes and new models of different subjects, grasp the pain points and difficulties of the industry, and promote the transformation and upgrading of traditional scenes. Around the city's major strategy, according to the policy guidance, Chengdu integrates and guides demand, and mainly builds innovative scenescapes. Centering on scenescape supply products, the government focuses on planning, creating and accomadating new scenescapes, while the enterprises focus on selecting, applying and constructing new scenescapes.

（3）要谋划形成场景库，构建"未来场景实验室"。围绕5G关键技术、人工智能、大数据、云计算等关键核心技术，编制形成场景库。聚焦关键共性技术和前沿引领技术转化应用，实施城市"未来场景实验室"培育计划。通过开展应用场景创新项目申报，以产业功能区为载体，搭建新场景试验场，为新经济企业提供开放式线上线下测试空间，集聚优质人才和创新要素，完善以企业为主体、市场为导向深度融合的创新体系。

（3）Chengdu plans to form scenescapes database and build "future scenescapes laboratory". Around 5G key technologies, artificial intelligence, big data, cloud computing and other core technologies, the scenescapes database will be compiled and formed. Focus on transformation and application of key common technologies and leading technology and implement the cultivation plan of urban "future scenescapes laboratory". By applying for the application scenescapes innovation project and taking the industrial function zone as the carrier, Chengdu will build a new scenescape testing field, provide open online and offline testing space for new economy enterprises, gather high-quality talents and innovation factors, and improve the innovation system with enterprise as the main body and market as the guidance.

（4）构建创新型应用场景。发挥政府规划引导作用，围绕生产生活、社会治理等领域，超前谋划场景，在城市发展规划、产业发展规划、民生规划等编制中植入前沿技术、创新产品、新兴业态，预设应用场景，为新场景构建充分留白。围绕生产、生活、生态与文化等领域，举办场景沉浸式沙龙。综合行业规模、商业化、发展前景、创新能力等因素，邀请国内外专家学者、行业领军人物、企业代表等就具有增长潜力的主题场景进行深度研讨，为构建城市未来新场景提供智力支持。

（4）Build innovative application scenescapes. Give play to the guiding role of governments' planning, Chengdu will plan scenescapes ahead of time in the fields of production and life, social governance and so on, implant cutting-edge technologies, innovative products and emerging formats in the planning of urban development, industrial development and people's livelihood, preset application scenescapes, and leave enough space for the construction of new scenescapes. Around the fields of production, life, ecology and culture, the scenescapes immersion salon will be held. Considering the industry scale, commercialization, development prospects, innovation ability and other factors, domestic and foreign experts and scholars, industry leaders and enterprise representatives will be invited to conduct in-depth discussions on the theme scenescapes with growth potential, so as to provide intellectual support for the construction of new urban scenescapes in the future.

（5）推进应用场景示范。聚焦宏观城市战略、中观行业规划、微观企业创造三大维度，协调行业主管部门、区市县结合城市战略和区域特色推进应用场景试点示范，推动前沿技术、创新产品、新兴业态在城市生产生活和治理领域延伸渗透。

（5）Promote application scenescape demonstration. Focus on the three dimensions of macro city strategy, medium industry planning and micro enterprise creation, coordinate the industry authorities and districts/cities/counties to promote the pilot demonstration of application scenescapes in combination with urban strategy and regional characteristics, and promote the extension and penetration of cutting-edge technology, innovative products and emerging business forms in the field of urban production, life and governance.

▷▷▷ 第四节 场景营城的实施路径

Section Four Implementation Paths of City Growth by Scenescapes

场景营城是成都发展新经济 2.0 的"先手棋"。在城市层面，场景是新时代城市转型与社区治理的实践空间；在产业层面，场景是推动新经济活动爆发的生态载体；在企业层面，场景是推动新产品新技术新模式规模化的应用平台①。

City growth by scenescapes is the "first move" for Chengdu developing new economy 2.0. At the city level, the scenescape is the practice space of urban transformation and community governance in the new era; at the industry level, the scenescape is the ecological carrier to promote the outbreak of new economic activities; at the enterprise level, the scenescape is the application platform to promote the scale of new products, new technologies and new models.

（一）通过城市级场景释放新经济发展的战略机遇

1. Releasing Strategic Opportunities for New Economic Development through City-level Scenescapes

围绕西部国际门户枢纽、中国（四川）自由贸易试验区、国家数字经济创新发展试验区、国家新一代人工智能发展试验区、公园城市示范区等国家战略，以及国际消费中心城市、三城三都、成都东部新区、成德眉资同城化、中日（成都）城市建设等省市建设目标和机遇，持续开放城市级场景，编制发布机会清单，以市场为主导，将城市发展需求明确为可感知、可视化、可参与的机会，构筑社区发展治理新优势，并形成城市发展的新竞争点与内生动力。

Around the national strategies such as Western International Gateway Hub, China (Sichuan) Free Trade Pilot Zone, National Digital Economy Innovation and Development Pilot Zone, National New Generation Artificial Intelligence Development Pilot Zone, Park City Demonstration Zone, as well as provincial and municipal construction goals and opportunities of International Consumption Center City, International City of Culture, Tourism, Sports, Gourmet, Music and Exhibition, Chengdu Eastern New Area, Urban Integration of Chengdu-Deyang-Meishan-Ziyang, China-Japan (Chengdu) urban construction, continue to open the city-level scenescape, compile and release the list of

---

① 常晓鸣. 以场景营城和产品赋能推动新经济实践 ［N］成都日报，2020-04-28（07）.

opportunities, take the market as the leading, make the urban development needs clear as perceptible, visual and participatory opportunities, build new advantages of community development governance, and form new competitive points and endogenous driving forces of urban development.

公园城市是成都最大的城市级场景之一，也是成都打造城市级场景的重要体现。由绿道串联生态区、公园、微绿地形成城乡一体、全域覆盖的绿化体系，以天府绿道、龙泉山城市森林公园、兴隆湖水生态治理、"三治一增"等作为重要支撑和抓手已成为建设公园城市的"成都模板"。社区场景是城市场景的基本子系统，成都坚定把社区场景营造作为深化城乡社区发展治理的着力点。着力营造以智慧智能为基础的社区场景地图，打造集合多种信息的社区基底数据库；着力营造以科创空间为形态的社区生产场景，以科创空间和微创智能工厂的形式实现以社区为单元的生产生活平衡；着力营造以多元体验为特征的社区生活场景，打造具有复合功能的社区舒适物设施体系；着力营造以创业平台为载体的社会机会场景，推动个体创业需求与社区服务供给零距离对接。

Park City is one of the largest city-level scenescapes in Chengdu, and it is also an important embodiment of creating city-level scenescapes in Chengdu. The greenway connects ecological areas, parks and micro green space to form the green system of urban-rural integration and full-area coverage. It has become the "Chengdu Model" for the construction of Park City to take Tianfu Greenway, Longquanshan Urban Forest Park, Xinglong Lake water ecological management and "three governance and one increase" etc. as important support. Scenescapes community is the basic subsystem of urban scenescapes. Chengdu firmly regards scenescapes community construction as the focus of deepening the governance of urban and rural community development. Chengdu is focusing on creating scenescapes community maps based on wisdom and intelligence and create community based database with a variety of information; it is focusing on creating community production scenescapes in the form of scientific and technological innovation space and realize the balance of production and life in the form of scientific and technological innovation space and micro-innovative intelligent factory; it is focusing on creating community life scenescapes characterized by multiple experiences, and create community amenity system with complex functions; it is focusing on building social opportunity scenescapes with the entrepreneurial platform as the carrier and promote the zero distance connection between individual entrepreneurial demand and community service supply.

（二）通过产业级场景创造产业裂变的市场机会

2. Creating Market Opportunities for Industry Fission through Industry-level Scenescapes

以产业生态圈和产业功能区建设为载体，规划高品质科创空间，推动新经济与实体经济深度融合，构建高技术含量、高附加值的新经济产业体系。一方面加速传统产业转型升级，延长产业价值链使之重焕生机；另一方面加快战略性新兴产业发展，打造城市未来场景实验室，持续挖掘新技术、新产业、新模式与新业态落地，以此将产业裂变增长作为厚植新经济发展优势的原动力，激发市场活力同时营造全新的城市经济形态。

With the construction of industrial ecosphere and industrial function zone as the carrier, it'll plan high-quality science and innovation space, promote the deep integration of new economy and real economy, and build the new economic and industrial system with high technology content and high added value. On the one hand, it'll accelerate the transformation and upgrading of traditional industries, extend the industrial value chain and revitalize them. On the other hand, it'll accelerate the development of strategic emerging industries, build the future scenescapes laboratory of the city, and continue to explore new technologies, new industries, new models and new forms of business, to take the fission growth of industries as the source power to promote the advantages of new economic development, stimulate the market vitality and create a new urban economic form.

在产业级场景实践中，成都整合优势资源，探索 5G 在文创、大健康、消费、智慧城市等各垂直领域的融合应用，打造"5G+"生态体系，促进新经济发展。在五大融合发展方向细分领域，重点实施 5G 网络视听、5G 大健康、5G 智慧旅游、5G 智慧消费等"八大工程"，以此构建产业、生活、消费等特色 5G 应用场景，从而促进新技术推广应用、新业态衍生发展、新模式融合创新、新产业裂变催生，形成具有比较优势的多元化 5G 产业融合发展体系。

In the practice of industrial scenescapes, Chengdu integrates advantageous resources, explores the integrated application of 5G in various vertical fields such as cultural innovation, big health, consumption and smart city, and creates "5G Plus" ecosystem to promote the development of new economy. In the five major areas of integration development, it'll focus on the implementation of 5G audio-visual network, 5G health care, 5G smart tourism, 5G smart consumption and other "eight projects", to build industry, life, consumption and other characteristic 5G application scenescapes, which will enhance the promotion and application of new technologies, the derivative development of new form of business, the integration and innovation of new modes, the fission and birth of new industries, and form a diversified 5G industrial integration development system with comparative advantages.

（三）通过企业级场景加速产品创新的成果变现

3. Accelerating the Achievement Realization of Product Innovation through Enterprise-level Scenescapes

搭建具有鲜明新经济特色的产业生态圈与创新生态链，以企业创新产品为基本单元和核心内容，嵌入全产业链，以产品创新助推企业加快数字化转型，以企业转型推动整个产业提档升级，加快形成种子企业、准独角兽企业、独角兽企业梯队，支持新经济企业抱团发展，推动企业创新成果加速变现，提升市场核心竞争力。

Build the industry ecosystem and innovation ecological chain with distinctive new economic characteristics. Take enterprises' innovation of products as the basic unit and core content, which should be embedded in the whole industry chain, so that products innovation can accelerate the digital transformation of enterprises which can promote the upgrading of the whole industry and accelerate the echelons' formation of seed enterprises, quasi unicorn enterprises and unicorn enterprise. Chengdu will support the development of new economy enterprises and accelerate the realization of enterprise innovation achievements to enhance their core competitiveness in the market.

在搭建企业级场景方面，成都为创新型企业提供了机会，鼓励企业研发新产品，提升人民群众生活品质。以中国天府农业博览园为例，农博园立足数字化建设，以农业为核心促进多领域跨界融合，通过搭建科技农业、休闲农业、文创农业和农业总部等多领域融合应用场景展厅，以及新型农业产品交易平台和现代农耕文化体验基地体验区等，打造现代农业场景，为农业和新技术、新业态和新模式之间的结合搭建桥梁，通过促进现代农业新产品的推广应用助力企业转型升级①。

In terms of setting up enterprise scenescapes, Chengdu provides opportunities for innovative enterprises, encourages enterprises to develop new products for improving people's quality of life. Take China Tianfu Agricultural Expo Park as an example. Based on the digital construction, the Park takes agriculture as the core to promote the cross-border integration of multiple fields. Through the construction of multi-field integration application scenario exhibition hall such as science and technology agriculture, leisure agriculture, cultural and creative agriculture and agricultural headquarters, as well as the new agricultural product trading platform and modern farming culture experience base, the Agricultural Expo park creates a modern agricultural scene, which builds a bridge for the combination of agricultural with new technology, new forms of business and new modes to help enterprises' transformation and upgrading through enhancing the promotion and application of modern agricultural new products.

---

① 张宇，张梦雅，于惠洋，李艳春. 场景营城的经济学思考及成都路径研究 [J]. 先锋，2020 (8)：39-41.

CiNED

结语

Conclusion

当前，中国经济发展前景向好。国际机构施罗德近期在评价中国经济发展前景时称："经济复苏有力，中国这艘巨轮正破浪前行。"但与此同时，我国也面临着周期性、结构性等错综复杂因素带来的巨大挑战。在新冠疫情持续影响下，外部环境进一步恶化，经济保护主义、单边主义频频抬头，全球产业链、供应链遭受巨大冲击。2020年7月，中央提出了加快形成以国内大循环为主体、国内国际双循环相互促进的新发展格局。在此背景下，寻求新的经济增长点和新动能是当务之急，也是发展的关键。

At present, China's economic development prospects are good. Schroeders Group, an international organization, recently commented on the prospects of China's economic development China's economic development prospects that China's economic recovery is strong and it is riding the waves like a cruise. Nevertheless, at the same time, China is also faced with great challenges because of cyclical, structural and other complex factors. Under the influence of COVID-19, the external environment has deteriorated, and economic protectionism and unilateralism have been rising frequently. The global industrial supply chain has been dramatically affected. In July 2020, the central government proposed to speed up the formation of a new development pattern with domestic circulation as the main body and domestic and international double circulation promoting each other. In this context, it is imperative to seek new economic growth points and new growth driver, which is also the key to development.

新冠疫情期间，以数字经济为代表的新经济展现出强大的活力与韧性。得益于互联网等数字技术的快速发展，各类线下活动加速向线上迁移。如在线教育、在线会议、在线娱乐、在线医疗等业务量猛增。同时，电子商务等更是迎来了新一轮的经济增长机遇，实现了进一步突破。不难预见，新经济发展必将在后疫情时代继续引领新旧动能深度转化，以新基建为新兴动力，推动我国大步迈入全面数字经济时代，催生出更多的新产业、新业态和新商业模式。据国家统计局核算数据，2019年我国"三新"经济增加值为 161 927 亿元，相当于 GDP 的比重为 16.3%，比上年提高 0.2 个百分点；按现价计算的增速为 9.3%，比同期 GDP 现价增速高 1.5 个百分点。分三次产业来看，"三新"经济第一产业增加值为 6 685 亿元，相当于 GDP 的比重为 0.7%；第二产业增加值为 70 443 亿元，相当于 GDP 的比重为 7.1%；第三产业增加值为 84 799 亿元，相当于 GDP 的比重 8.6%。

During the pandemic, the new economy represented by digital economy shows strong vitality and resilience. Due to the rapid development of digital technologies such as the Internet, all kinds of offline activities have accelerated to move online, such as online education, online conference, online entertainment, online medical. At the same time, e-commerce met a new round of economic growth opportunities and achieved further breakthroughs. Obviously, the development of new economy will continue to lead the profound transformation of new and old drivers in the post-pandemic era. With the new infrastructure as the new driving force, China will stride into the era of comprehensive digital economy and spawn more new industries, new form of business and new business modes. According to the accounting data of the National Bureau of Statistics, in 2019, the added value of China's "Three New Economy" is 16,192.7 billion Yuan, equivalent to 16.3% of GDP, 0.2 percentage point higher than that of the previous year; the growth rate at current price is 9.3%, 1.5 percentage points higher than that of GDP at current price in the same period. In terms of three industries in the" Three New Economy", the added value of the primary industry is 668.5 billion Yuan, equivalent to 0.7% of GDP; the added value of the secondary industry is 7,044.3 billion Yuan, equivalent to 7.1% of GDP; the added value of the tertiary industry is 8,479.9 billion Yuan, equivalent to 8.6% of GDP.

毋庸置疑，科技创新在我国经济社会发展中的战略地位已可见一斑。2021 年是中国"十四五"规划的开局之年。"十四五"规划期内，中国也必将在全面建成小康社会的基础上，乘势而上开启全面建设社会主义现代化国家新征程，进入高质量发展的"新阶段"，而其中高质量发展的重要动力就是科技创新驱动。加快发展以数字经济、智能经济等为代表的新经济，必须继续为新经济发展增添活力，增强新经济发展的韧性，才能为进入新发展阶段的中国经济提供足够的新旧动能转换动力，引领长期低迷的世界经济走出困境。

Undoubtedly, scientific and technological innovation occupies the strategic position in China's economic and social development. The year of 2021 is the beginning of China's 14th five year plan. During the period of the plan, China will also embark on a new journey of building a modern socialist country on the basis of a moderately prosperous society in an all-round way and enter a "new stage" of high-quality development, of which the important driving force is scientific and technological innovation. Only by speeding up the development of new economy by digital economy and intelligent economy, continuing to increase the vitality of new economic development, and enhancing the toughness of new economic development, can China's economy in the new development stage be provided with enough driving force for the transformation of old and new growth drivers, and lead the long-depressed world economy out of difficulties.

成都作为最适宜新经济发展的城市，三年探索期间，历经认知革新、应用实践和理论升华三个阶段，在城市新经济发展中探索出了一条切实可行的"成都道路"，形成了一套未来城市营造的"场景理论"。接下来成都将应时而谋、顺势而为，深刻把握成渝地区双城经济圈建设战略机遇和新冠疫情催生新经济新场景的市场机遇，主动迎接疫情后数字经济和智能经济时代加速到来的新变革，以新经济构筑城市发展新优势，为推动践行新发展理念的公园城市示范区建设贡献新经济力量。

Being the most suitable city for the development of new economy, Chengdu has explored a feasible "Chengdu Road" in the development of new economy and formed its theory of "scenescapes" about the future urban construction through three stages of cognitive innovation, application practice and theoretical sublimation during three years. Chengdu will take the strategic opportunity brought by the Chengdu-Chongqing Twin Cities Economic Circle construction and the market opportunities of new economy and new scenescapes due to the novel coronavirus pneumonia. It will take the initiative to meet the new changes of accelerated arrival of the digital economy and intelligent economy after the pandemic, build new advantages of the city in the form of the new economy and contribute new economic strength to promote the construction of Park City demonstration area with the new development concept.

参考文献
References

［1］赵建. 美国经济复苏之谜: 新周期、新能源还是新技术［J］. 国际金融, 2018（11）: 26-33.

［2］刘平. 日本经济社会发展新模式: 社会 5.0［J］. 上海经济, 2017（5）: 82-89.

［3］黄培. 揭秘工业互联网的内涵、热点与难点［EB/OL］.（2018-03-18）. http://blog.e-works.net.cn/6399/articles/1363615.html.

［4］李东. 以共享居住空间诠释共享经济［J］. 经济研究导刊, 2017（26）: 71-72.

［5］王如忠, 徐清泉. 创意产业的特质及其在中国的实践［M］//厉无畏, 王如忠. 创意产业: 城市发展的新引擎. 上海: 上海社会科学院出版社, 2005: 104.

［6］周振华. 现代服务业发展研究［M］. 上海: 上海社会科学院出版社, 2005: 53.

［7］张京成. 中国创意产业发展报告（2006）［M］. 北京: 中国经济出版社, 2006: 26-27.

［8］朱宁嘉. 创意产业: 理论管窥与中国经验［M］//上海交通大学国家文化产业创新与发展研究基地. 中国文化产业评论. 上海: 上海人民出版社, 2007: 52.

［9］孙智英. 创意经济的形态和业态研究［J］. 东南学术, 2008（6）:

56-59.

　　[10] 张彦华. 文化创意产业与信息传播科技结合新形态探析：基于经济学视角的思考 [J]. 内蒙古社会科学（汉文版），2013, 34（5）：128-134.

　　[11] 厉春雷, 顾学勤. 创意经济背景下文化企业的品牌营销：浙江海利集团"网娃"模式的案例研究 [J]. 文化产业研究，2012：147-153.

　　[12] 人民网. 3 问新经济"机会之城" [EB/OL]. （2019-04-02）[2021-01-10]. http://sc. people. com. cn/n2/2019/0402/c379471-32803910.html.

　　[13] 张宇, 张梦雅, 于惠洋, 李艳春. 场景营城的经济学思考及成都路径研究 [J]. 先锋，2020（8）.

　　[14] 孙安会. 释放人才创新潜能 [J]. 国企管理，2017（11）.

　　[15] 刘理晖. 关注产业人力资本新需求 [N]. 经济日报，2017-06-17（007）.

　　[16] 刘建成. 我国新经济人才供求失衡的成因及对策分析 [J]. 经济师，2002（3）：124-125

　　[17] 周孟奎, 董立平. 从应对金融危机看高等教育改革创新 [J]. 中国高等教育，2009（21）：51-52.

　　[18] 王靖华. "外国专家"和"海外高层次人才"来华（回国工作）配偶、子女、住房方面的优惠政策 [J]. 国际人才交流，2009（12）：54-55.

　　[19] 成都市政协课题组. 保持新经济发展领先地位策略研究 [R]. 2019.

　　[20] 张宇, 李艳春. 从新动能看中国经济中长期问题：案例与对策 [J]. 新经济导刊，2020（3）：42-44.

　　[21] 邓玲, 等. 新经济新动能 [M]. 北京：中国科学出版社，2020.

　　[22] 周跃辉. 经济新动能重塑发展新优势 [N]. 成都日报，2019-05-29（007）.

　　[23] 张红凤, 吕杰. 新旧动能转换及实现路径 [N]. 光明日报，

2018−09−06（007）.

[24] 任保平. 何苗. 我国新经济高质量发展的困境及路径选择 [J]. 西北大学学报（哲学社会科学版），2020（1）：40−48.

[25] 国务院发展研究中心，世界银行. 创新中国：培育中国经济增长新动能 [M]. 北京：中国发展出版社，2019.

[26] 季正松. 论新经济的特点及其与传统经济的联系 [J]. 镇江高专学报，2003（1）：13−16.

[27] ZHAO JIAN. The mystery of American economic recovery：New cycle，new energy or new technology [J]. International Finance，2018（11）：26−33.

[28] LIU PING. The new pattern of economic and social development of Japan：Society 5.0 [J]. Shanghai Economy，2017（5）：82−89.

[29] HUANG PEI. Uncover the connotation，issues and difficulties of industrial internet [EB/OL].（2018−03−18）. http://blog.e−works.net.cn/6399/articles/1363615.html.

[30] LI DONG. Interpretation of shared economy with shared living space [J]. Economic Research Guide，2017（26）：71−72.

[31] WANG RUZHONG，XU QINGQUAN. Characteristics of creative industry and its practice in China. In creative industry：The new engine of urban development，Wang Ruzhong，Ed. [M]. Shanghai：Shanghai Academy of Social Sciences Press，2005：104.

[32] ZHOU ZHENHUA. Research on the development of modern service industry [M]. Shanghai：Shanghai Academy of Social Sciences Press，2005：53.

[33] ZHANG JINGCHENG. China creative industry development report（2006）[M]. Beijing：China Economic Publishing House，2006：26−27.

[34] ZHU NINGJIA. Creative industry：Theory and Chinese experience. In China's Cultural Industry Review [M]. Shanghai：Shanghai People's Publishing House，2007：52.

［35］ SUN ZHIYING. Research on the form and format of creative economy ［J］. Southeast Academic Research, 2008 （6）: 56-59.

［36］ ZHANG YANHUA. New form of combination of cultural creative industry and information communication technology—from the perspective of Economics ［J］. Inner Mongolia Social Sciences, 2013, 34 （5）: 128-134.

［37］ LI CHUNLEI, GU XUEQIN. Brand marketing of cultural enterprises under the background of creative economy: A case study of "Wangwa" mode of Zhejiang Haili group ［J］. Cultural Industry Research, 2012: 147-153.

［38］ Three Auestions about "City with Opportunity" of the New Economy, http://sc.people.com.cn/n2/2019/0402/c379471-32803910.html.

［39］ ZHANG YU, ZHANG MENGYA, YU HUIYANG, LI CHUNYAN. City construction by scenesapes in perspectives of economics and its patterns in Chengdu ［J］. Xian Feng, 2020 （8）.

［40］ SUN ANHUI. Release the innovative potential of talents ［J］. China State-owned Enterprise Management, 2017 （11）.

［41］ LIU LIHUI. Paying attention to the new demand of industrial human capital ［N］. Economic Daily, 2017-06-17 （007）.

［42］ LIU JIANCHENG. Causes and countermeasures of the imbalance between supply and demand of talents in China's new economy ［J］. China Economist, 2002 （3）: 124-125

［43］ ZHOU MENGKUI, DONG LIPING. On the reform and innovation of higher education in response to the financial crisis ［J］. China Higher Education, 2009 （21）: 51-52.

［44］ WANG JINGHUA. Preferential policies for spouses, children and housing of "foreign experts" and "overseas high-level talents" working in China ［J］. International Talents, 2009 （12）: 54-55.

［45］ Research group of Chengdu CPPCC. Research on the strategy of maintaining the leading position of new economic development, 2019.

［46］ ZHANG YU, LI CHUNYAN. On the medium and long term

problems of China's economy from perspective of new growth driver: Cases and countermeasures [J]. New Economy Leader, 2020 (3): 42-44.

[47] DENG LING, etc. New economy and new growth drivers [M]. Bei Jing: China Science Press, 2020.

[48] ZHOU YUEHUI. New economic drivers reshapes new development advantages [N]. Chengdu Daily, 2019-05-29 (007).

[49] ZHANG HONGFENG, LV JIE. Transformation and realization of new and old drivers [N]. Guangming Daily, 2018-9-6 (007).

[50] REN BAOPING, HE MIAO. The dilemma of High-quality development of China's new economy and its path selection [J]. Journal of Northwest University (Philosophy and Social Sciences Edition), 2020 (1): 40-48.

[51] Development Research Centre of the State Council. World Bank. Innovating China: Fostering new growth driver of China's economic growth [M]. Beijing: China Development Press, 2019.

[52] JI ZHENGSONG. On the characteristics of new economy and its relation with traditional economy [J]. Journal of Zhenjiang College, 2003 (1): 13-16.